IMAGES
of America

FITCHBURG

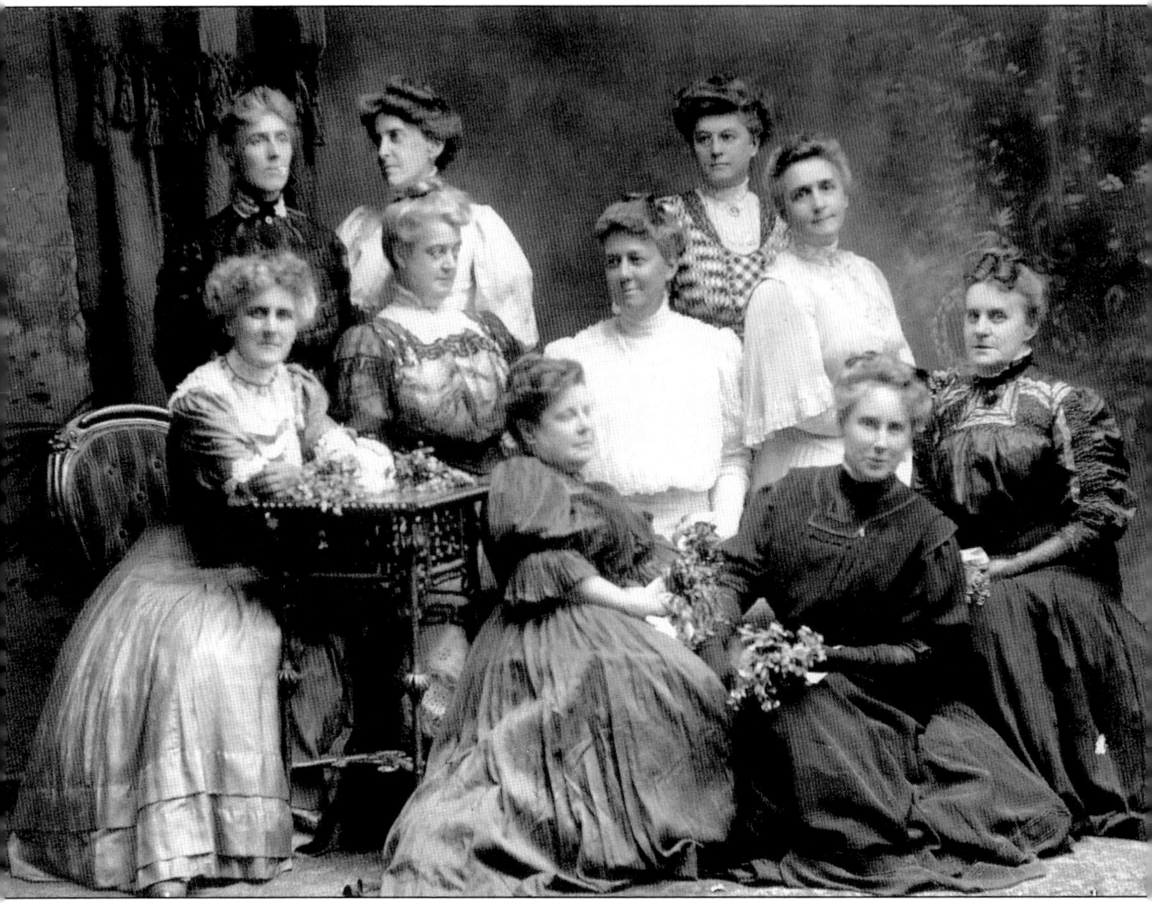

GIRLS OF 1876. This photograph, entitled "Girls of 1876," was taken at a 1907 reunion at the home of Amy Wallace. From left to right are (first row) Frances Sprague, Cora Blood, Carrie Fessenden, and Mary Aldrich; (second row) Jane Colony, Josie Harrington, and Louise Crocker Smith; (third row) Anna Bailey, Hattie Delahanty, and Amy L. Wallace.

IMAGES
of America
FITCHBURG

Fitchburg Historical Society

ARCADIA
PUBLISHING

ISBN 978-0-7385-3757-3

Published by Arcadia Publishing
Charleston, South Carolina

Printed in the United States of America

Library of Congress Catalog Card Number: 2004115877

For all general information contact Arcadia Publishing at:
Telephone 843-853-2070
Fax 843-853-0044
E-mail sales@arcadiapublishing.com
For customer service and orders:
Toll-Free 1-888-313-2665

Visit us on the Internet at www.arcadiapublishing.com

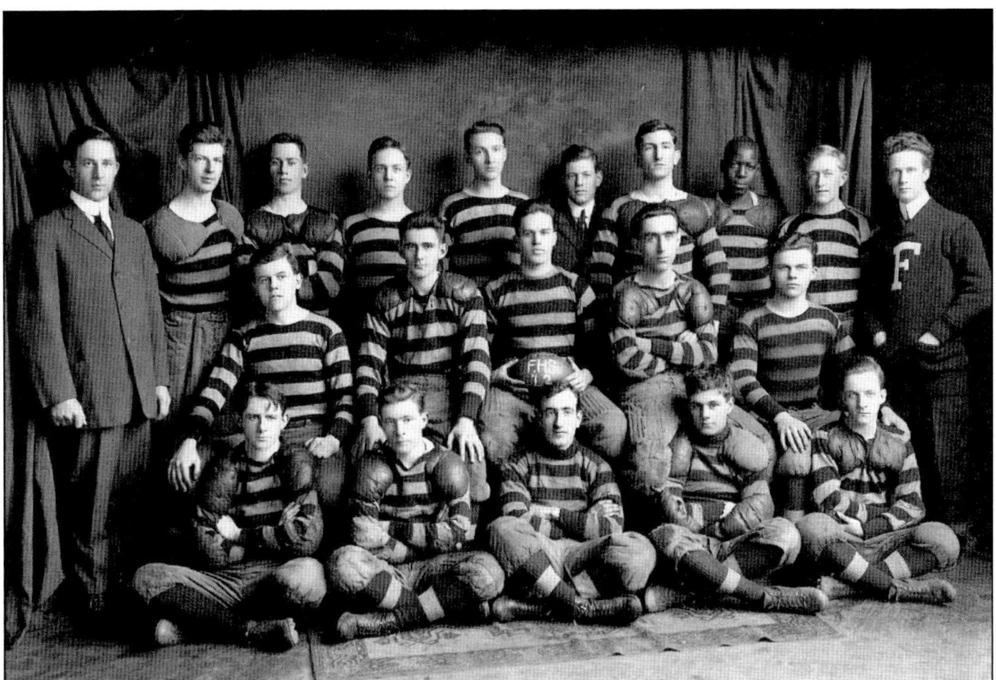

FITCHBURG FOOTBALL. Pictured are the members of the Fitchburg High School football team of 1913.

Contents

ACKNOWLEDGMENTS

A project of this size could not have been possible without the help of many people. Our research and writing staff were Barbara Edsall, Joy Contois, Betty Gardner, Anne Beauchemin, and Helen Obermeyer Simmons. Eleanor Gilmartin, Stuart McDermott, George Mirijanian, Sally Cragin, and Cathy Little provided additional assistance and expertise. The staff extends a special thanks to attorney Kysa Crusco for editing the completed manuscript. Barbara Edsall and Helen Obermeyer Simmons completed the layout of the book.

We owe a special debt of gratitude to Phil Jordan for his knowledge of fire department history. We also thank Betsy Hannula, director of the Fitchburg Historical Society, for her advice and guidance.

Although the majority of the images in the book are from the collection of the Fitchburg Historical Society, several photographs were loaned to us by Barbara Edsall, Anne Beauchemin, Stuart McDermott, Theresa Longsjo, Hillary Keating, Nancy Chrostowski, and Betty Pagnotta.

INTRODUCTION

The history of Fitchburg begins thousands of years ago. During the ice age, the glaciers that covered North America deposited a large boulder on Rollstone Hill. The famous landmark, which became known as the Rollstone Boulder, was a popular destination for hikers and picnickers during Fitchburg's heyday. In 1929, residents had the boulder blown apart and brought down to the common, where it remains today.

David Page was the first to settle in the westerly part of Lunenburg, which would later become Fitchburg. He built a garrison home in the area of Pearl Street, well away from the Nashua River, which was known to flood in the spring. In 1756, settlers in Lunenburg filed a petition with the town to secede and form a new community. Their petition was granted in 1764, and they named the new town Fitchburg.

The new town grew along the banks of the Nashua River, which provided power for gristmills and sawmills in the 18th century. Other businesses came to Fitchburg, and the town soon had its first general store, shoe shop, and scythe shop. Thomas Cowdin's tavern became the heart of the town. People gathered there to discuss town business and to listen to visiting preachers' sermons. The tavern also functioned as a place for town meetings, a court of law, and a school.

Fitchburg experienced a golden age in the second half of the 19th century. The city's population grew sixfold, from 5,120 in 1850 to over 31,000 in 1900. At the end of the 19th century, 97 passenger trains were pulling into the Union Depot on Main Street every day.

As Fitchburg's population grew, so did the need for churches, schools, and a hospital. Residents founded a variety of churches, from St. Bernard's Roman Catholic parish to the Calvinistic Congregational Church. The churches often reflected the ethnic makeup of their surrounding neighborhoods. Fitchburg built schools around the city, from the one-room Dean Hill School in 1798 to the magnificent 1895 Fitchburg High School. In 1901, Burbank Hospital opened its doors, thanks to a $500,000 gift from Gardner S. Burbank and his wife, Sarah.

As the city's industry grew along the Nashua River, the city center buzzed with development. Hotels, photography studios, department stores, and even a candy shop added to the downtown hustle and bustle. Wealthy philanthropist Rodney Wallace commissioned Fitchburg architect Henry M. Francis to design and build the city's first library in 1884. Other wealthy residents were also eager to beautify Fitchburg, leading to the construction of large architect-designed buildings along Main Street, such as the Dickinson Block, the YMCA, the Safety Fund Bank, the Johnsonia, the Wallace Building, and the Phoenix Building. Rows of Victorian-style homes decorated with stained-glass windows and ornate woodwork graced the hills of Fitchburg.

During the 19th century, Fitchburg was widely recognized for its industry. Across the country, Americans considered "Made in Fitchburg" a mark of excellence. The city mills produced a wide assortment of goods, from cotton and wool to machinery and tools. The Putnam Machine Company's steam engines, the Simonds Saw and Steel company's circular, crosscut, band, and hand saws, Parkhill Manufacturing's "toile du norde," chambray, and gingham textiles, and Iver Johnson's bicycles and guns all helped to secure Fitchburg as a leading industrial city. By 1890, Fitchburg claimed a total of 59 different industries. Such inventions as the Burleigh rock drill, the Brown bag filling machine, and the Brown cut-off engine helped put Fitchburg on the industrial map.

Fitchburg's growth and expansion was due in large part to the unique vision of residents who recognized the city's potential. Alvah Crocker (1801–1874) was one of Fitchburg's most notable citizens. Crocker began working in a Leominster paper mill at the age of eight. By the time he was 25, Crocker had opened his own paper mill in West Fitchburg. By 1874, the Crocker Burbank Paper Company was producing 17 tons of paper a day in its seven mills across the city. Alvah Crocker also aided Fitchburg's development by initiating and advocating for the extension of the railroad to Fitchburg and then to the west through the drilling of the Hoosac Tunnel.

Other distinguished citizens of Fitchburg included Iver Johnson, a gun and bicycle manufacturer; Abel Simonds, a scythe maker; Rodney Wallace, a bookseller and papermaker; Walter Heywood, a chair maker; and Elijah Dickinson, a shoe manufacturer. Fitchburg women also contributed to the city's affluence. Caroline Mason was a poet, Eleanor Norcross was an artist and founder of the Fitchburg Art Museum, and Martha Goodrich was a Civil War nurse.

Fitchburg's population included a large class of immigrants, who came to the city to seek work in the paper, textile, and machine mills. Neighborhoods such as the Irish "Patch," the French Canadian "Cleghorn," and the Greek "Greektown" flourished in the city. By 1910, French Canadians made up the largest immigrant population, numbering 4,000. Fitchburg's Finnish community numbered 3,000. These two ethnic groups were followed in size by the Irish, English, Scottish, Welsh, Italian, Norwegian, Swedish, Dutch, German, and Greek populations.

Today, Fitchburg is a diverse city with a population of 39,000. Although the face of Fitchburg has changed throughout the years, many of the old mills still line the Nashua River, and Victorian houses still dot the surrounding hills. The city's commerce, once dependent on the paper industry, has developed into diverse pursuits in pharmaceuticals, tool and die making, machine production, and plastic molding. Fitchburg continues to gain national prominence through the Arthur Longsjo Memorial Race, named after the Fitchburg native who was the first person ever to compete in both the Summer Olympics (cycling) and Winter Olympics (speed skating) in the same year. The race has been held annually since 1960.

Join us now in a journey through the city's rich history as Fitchburg looks toward a bright future.

One

DOWNTOWN

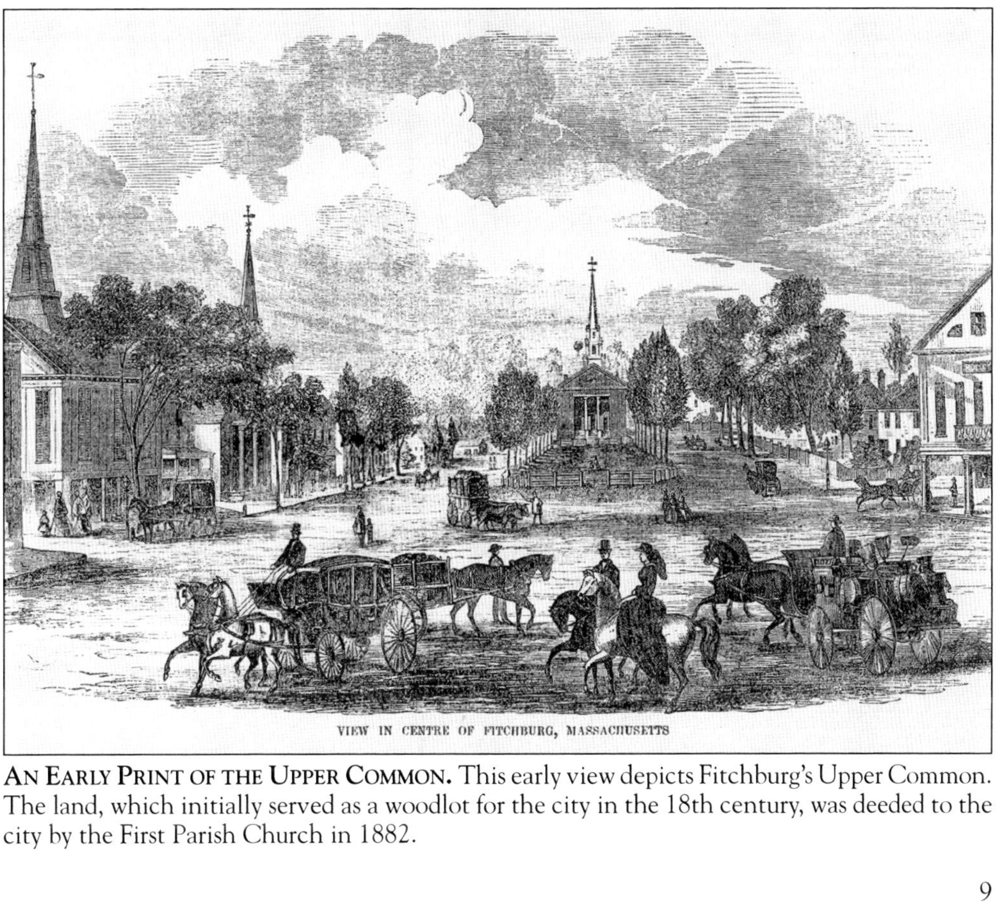

AN EARLY PRINT OF THE UPPER COMMON. This early view depicts Fitchburg's Upper Common. The land, which initially served as a woodlot for the city in the 18th century, was deeded to the city by the First Parish Church in 1882.

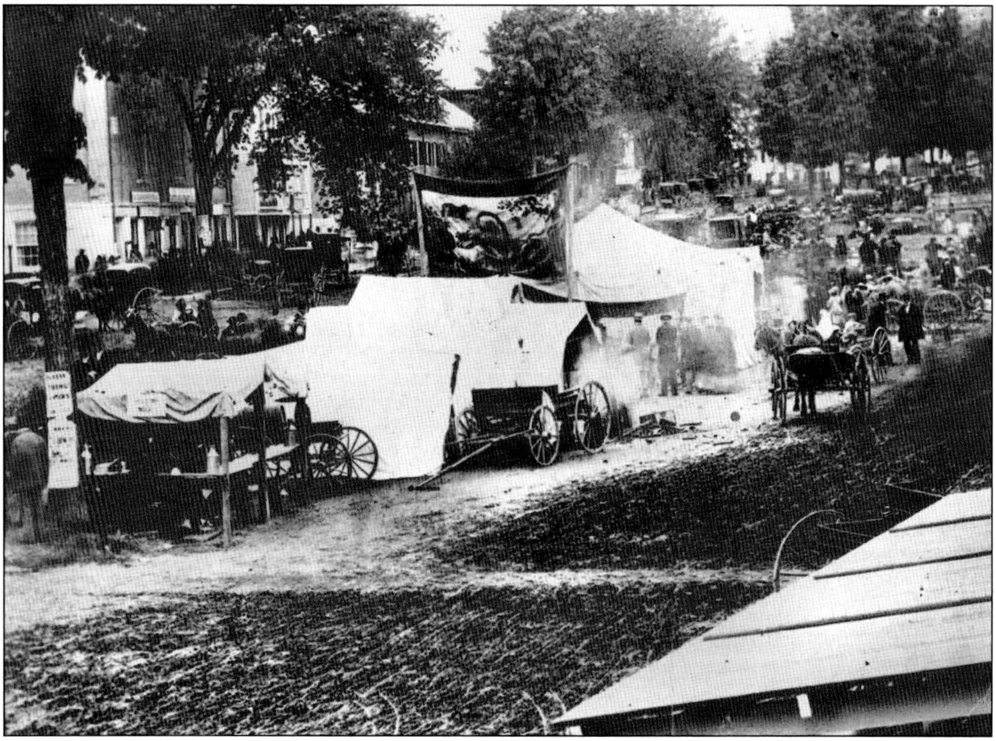

A Cattle Show, 1870s. A cattle show on the common was a typical sight in the 1870s. Men came from miles around to buy, sell, and trade stock.

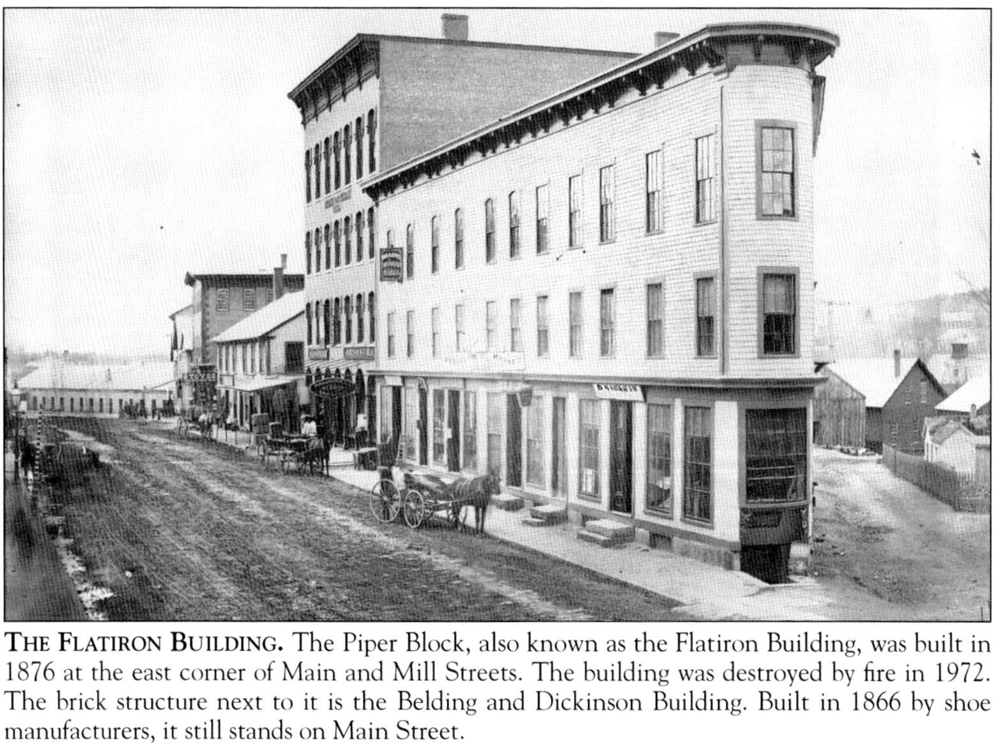

The Flatiron Building. The Piper Block, also known as the Flatiron Building, was built in 1876 at the east corner of Main and Mill Streets. The building was destroyed by fire in 1972. The brick structure next to it is the Belding and Dickinson Building. Built in 1866 by shoe manufacturers, it still stands on Main Street.

LOOKING WEST UP MAIN STREET. In this *c.* 1870 photograph, sleighs carry residents on their winter errands. The three churches visible here are, from left to right, the Baptist church, Christ Church, and the Trinitarian church. City hall is in the center.

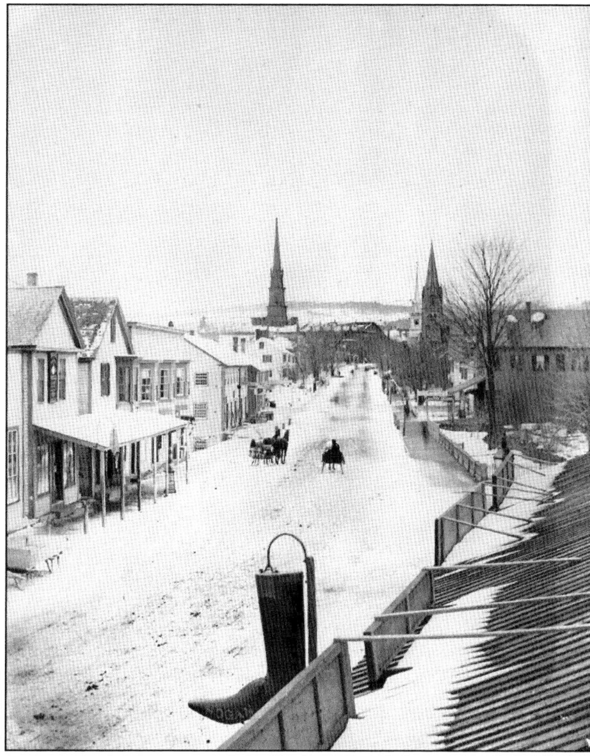

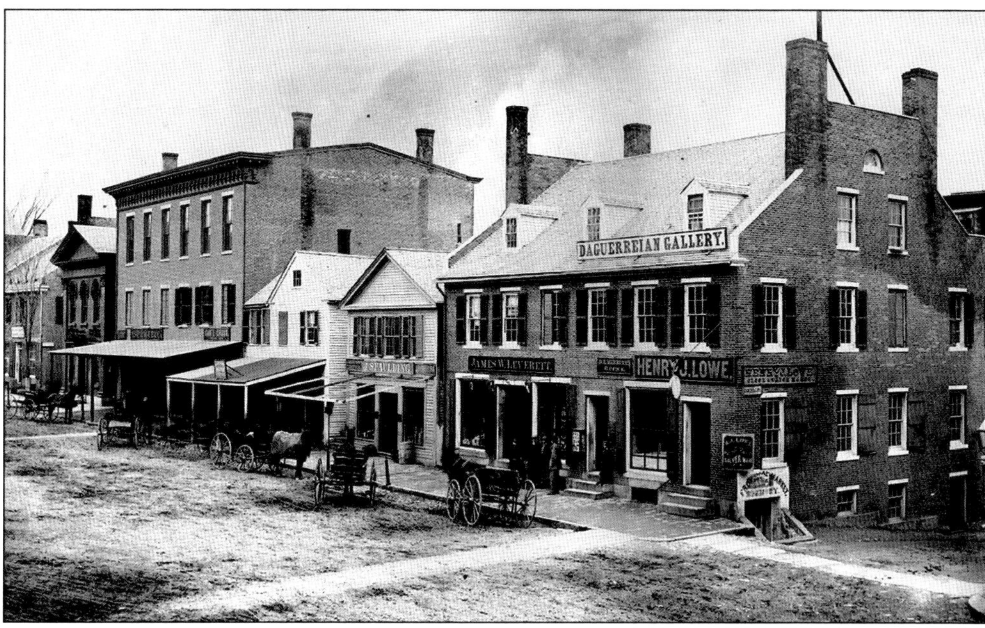

HENRY LOWE'S WATCH REPAIR SHOP. The brick building at Central and Main Streets is the present site of Fitchburg Mutual Life Insurance. The daguerreotype gallery was a photographer's studio. Daguerreotypes, popular from 1839 until the early 1860s, were photographs printed on a silver plate. This *c.* 1865 paper print shows Henry Lowe's sign, in the form of a watch, hanging outside his door. The watch is now in the historical society's collection.

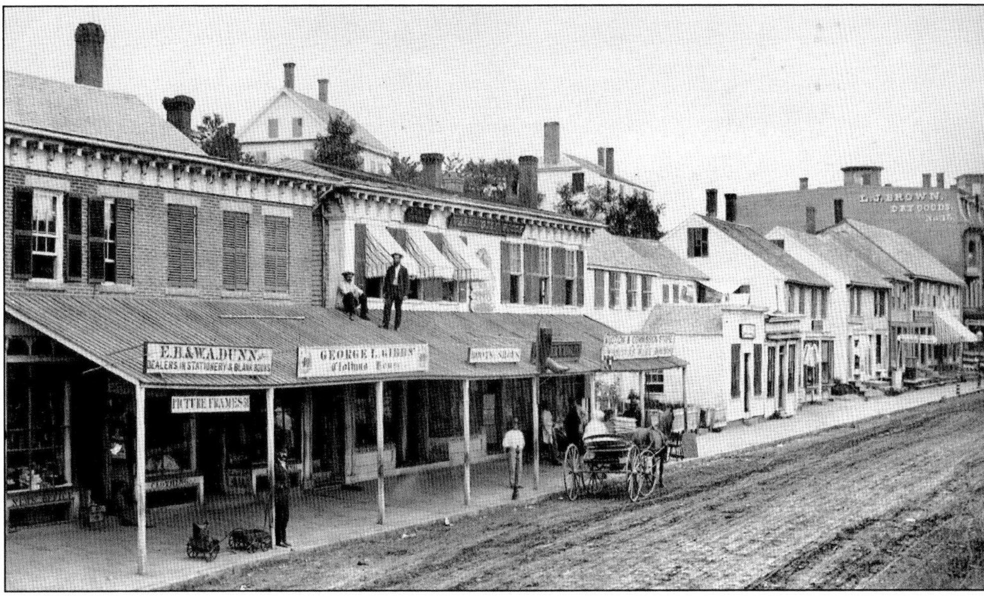

MAIN STREET FROM PRICHARD STREET TO OLIVER STREET. Main Street between Prichard and Oliver Streets had over a dozen businesses around 1870. Just above the horse and buggy is the familiar boot of the Hogan boot and shoe store. The Dunn store carried birds, cages, and seed supplies, as well as picture frames and stationery.

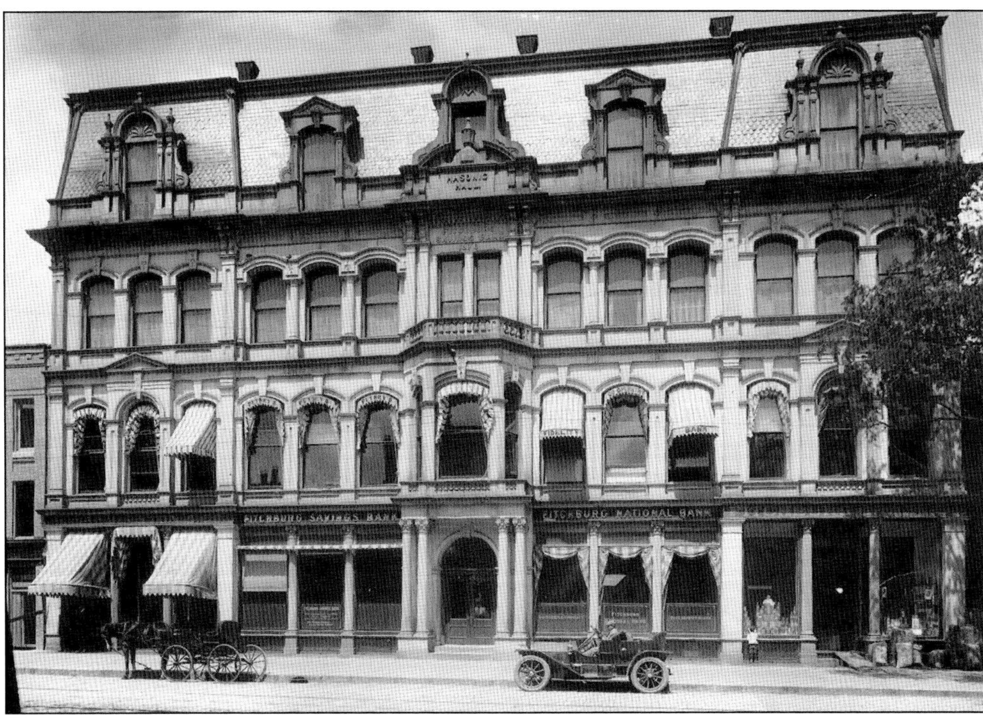

THE FITCHBURG SAVINGS BANK. The Fitchburg Savings Bank, established in 1846, erected this building on upper Main Street in 1871. Besides the savings bank, the building housed the Fitchburg National Bank and the Masonic hall.

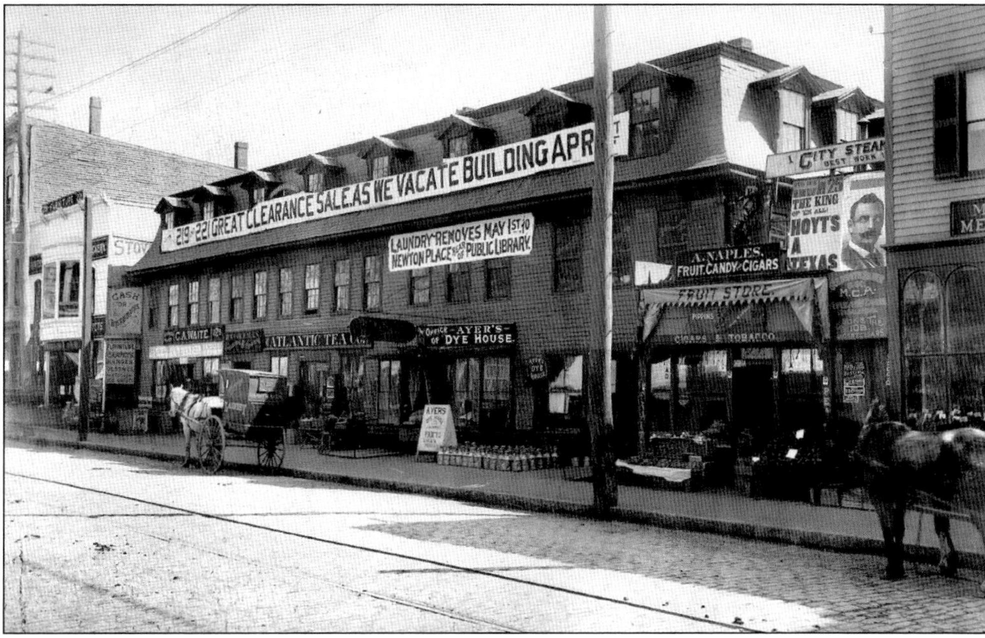

THE CANAL BLOCK. A few wealthy Fitchburg citizens were eager to beautify Main Street in the last decade of the 19th century. This block was demolished to make way for the Safety Fund Bank building.

THE SAFETY FUND BANK, 470 MAIN STREET. The Safety Fund Bank was granted a charter in June 1874 and opened shop at the Belding and Dickinson Block on lower Main Street. The bank commissioned H. M. Francis in 1894 to design a new bank building in the Renaissance Revival style. The building was completed in 1895, and the lower façade was modernized in the early 1960s.

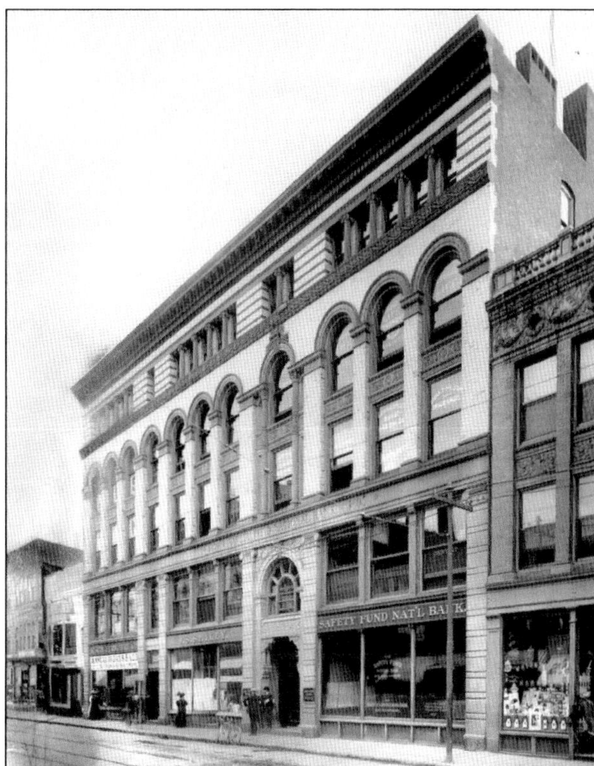

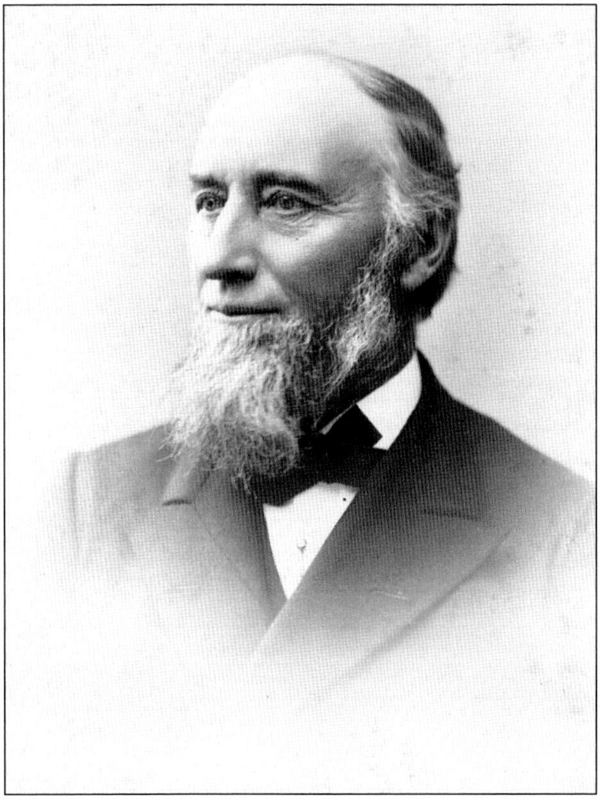

RODNEY WALLACE. Rodney Wallace (1823–1902) was a leading industrialist of 19th-century Fitchburg and one of the city's most noted benefactors. He was already an owner of several businesses when he founded one of the city's leading industries, the Fitchburg Paper Company. Between 1885 and his death, he was responsible for the construction of a public library and of the Wallace Walkway, stairs that connected the high school with Prichard Street. He also commissioned a fountain that graced the Upper Common.

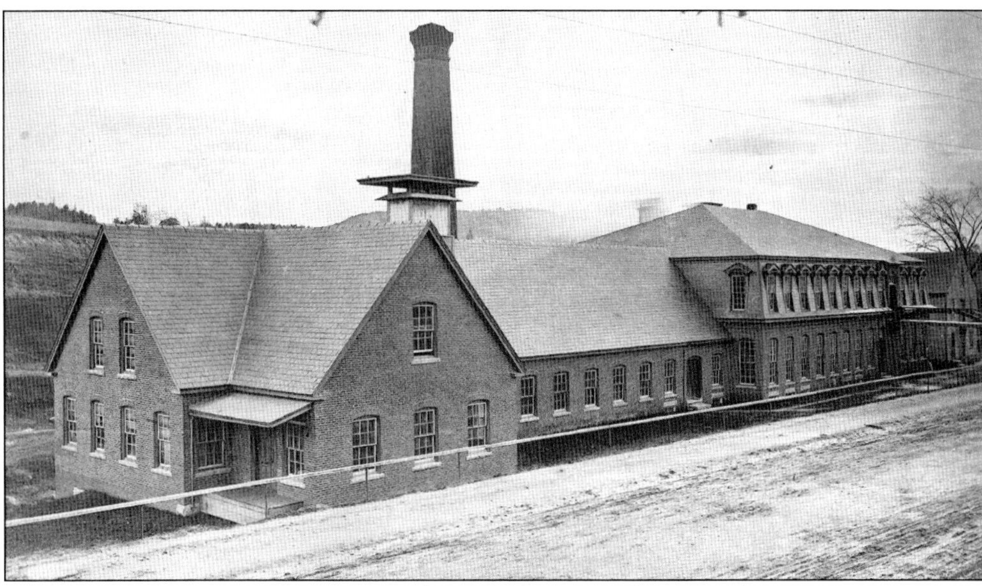

THE FITCHBURG PAPER COMPANY. Rodney Wallace started the Fitchburg Paper Company in 1864. After a fire in one of his mills, he contracted with H. M. Francis to design a new mill in 1878. A fashionable mansard roof capped part of Mill No. 2. The mill and all the machinery, except one very large papermaking machine, were products of Fitchburg companies.

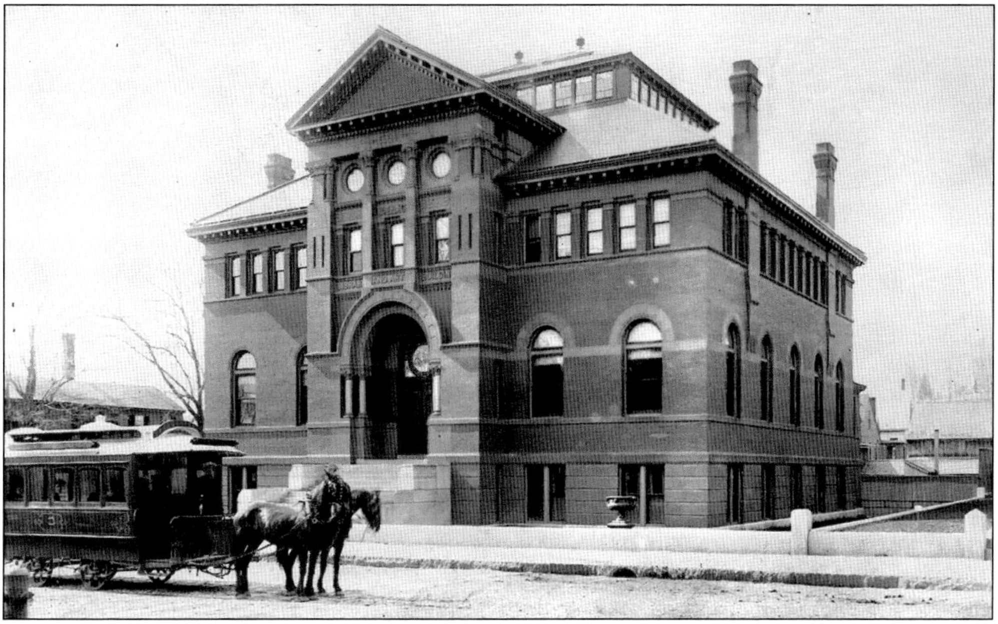

THE WALLACE LIBRARY AND ART BUILDING. Between 1875 and 1917, there was a national movement among philanthropists to provide public library buildings for their local communities. When library construction was still in its infancy, Rodney Wallace commissioned H. M. Francis to design a library for Fitchburg in 1884. The second floor housed an art gallery illuminated by a skylight. The building was razed in 1965 to make way for a modern library.

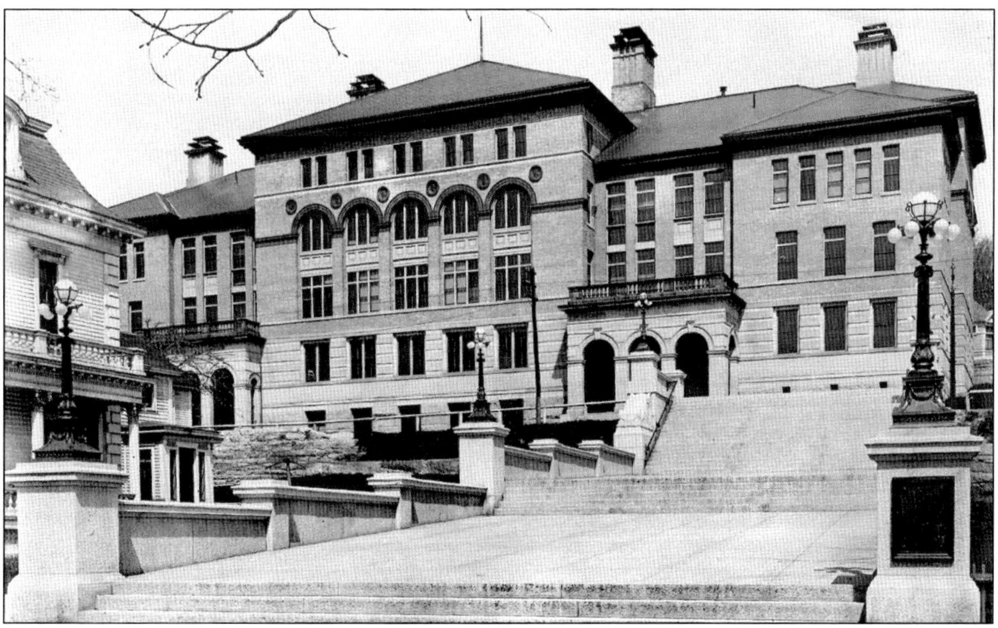

THE WALLACE WALKWAY. Rodney Wallace's last gift to the city was the Wallace Walkway. It was dedicated on December 31, 1902, just two months before his death. The project was prompted by citizens and the local government in an effort to beautify the city. Wallace hired H. M. Francis to design the steps, which were made from Rollstone granite and graced by six lampposts.

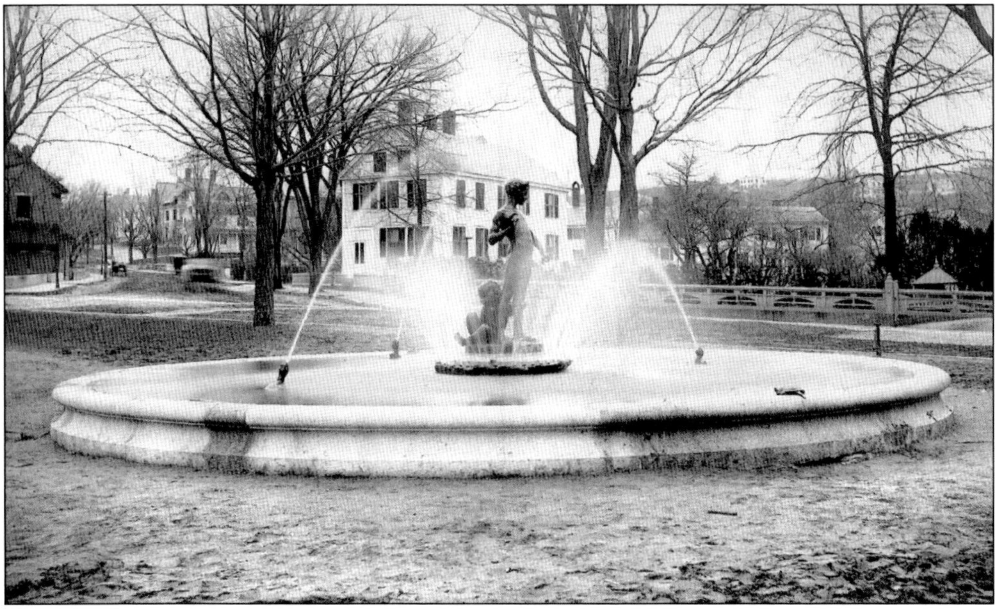

THE BOYS AND TURTLES FOUNTAIN. Herbert Adams, a renowned American sculptor, spent his childhood in Fitchburg on Chestnut Street. He left the city to study in Paris in the 1880s. Three Fitchburg businessmen presented him with his first commission in 1889, the Boys and Turtles fountain for the Upper Common. It was cast in bronze in Brussels. The stonework for the fountain's base was executed by Fitchburg stonemason Daniel O'Connor.

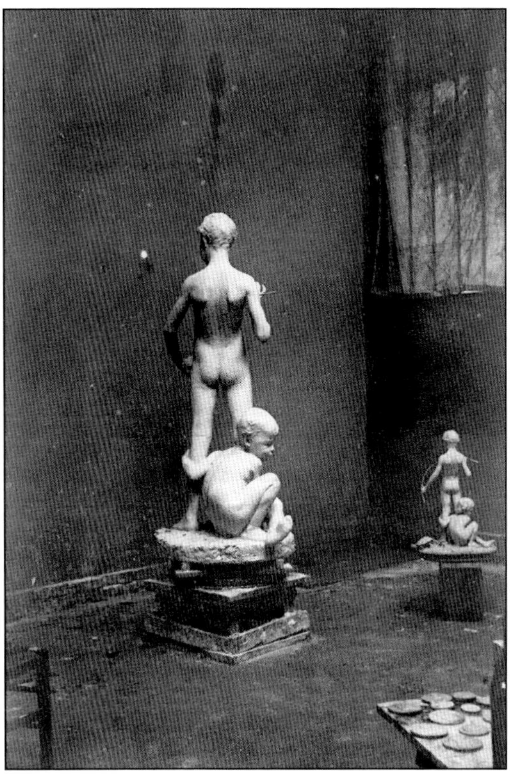

HERBERT ADAMS'S PARIS STUDIO, 1888. In 1888, Rodney Wallace traveled to Paris to view a model of the sculpture at the artist's studio. It was the first sculpture to be brought to the United States that had been cast in the lost wax method. The process was not used in this country until 1900.

THE WORLD WAR I MEMORIAL. In 1928, Adams completed his last public monument, a World War I memorial that was placed near the Boys and Turtles fountain on the Upper Common. Engraved on the monument are the names of 65 Fitchburg men and women who perished in the war. The sculptor's wife, Adeline, posed as the model for Victory. Both Herbert and Adeline Adams are buried in Forest Hill Cemetery.

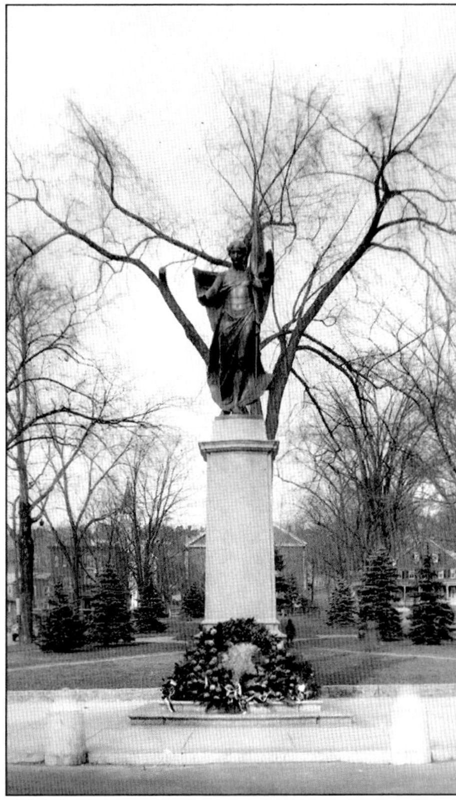

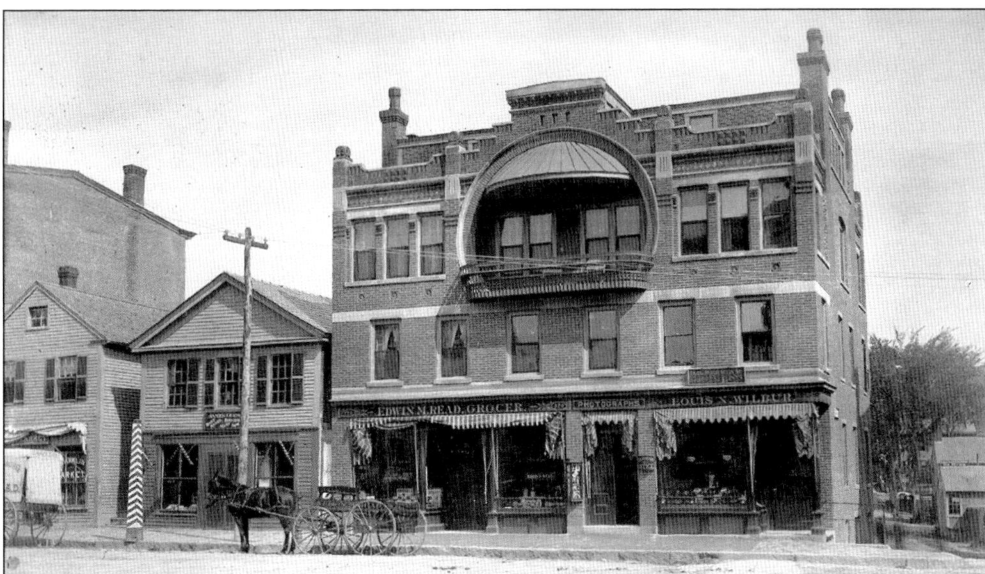

A FITCHBURG PHOTOGRAPHER. Photography studios flourished in the city in the 19th century and into the early 20th century. Joseph C. Moulton arrived in Fitchburg in 1848. His early studio was at 159 Main Street. This Queen Anne–style building housed his studio from 1876 to 1900. There were a number of addresses along Main Street that turned over from one photographer to the next to take advantage of natural light requirements.

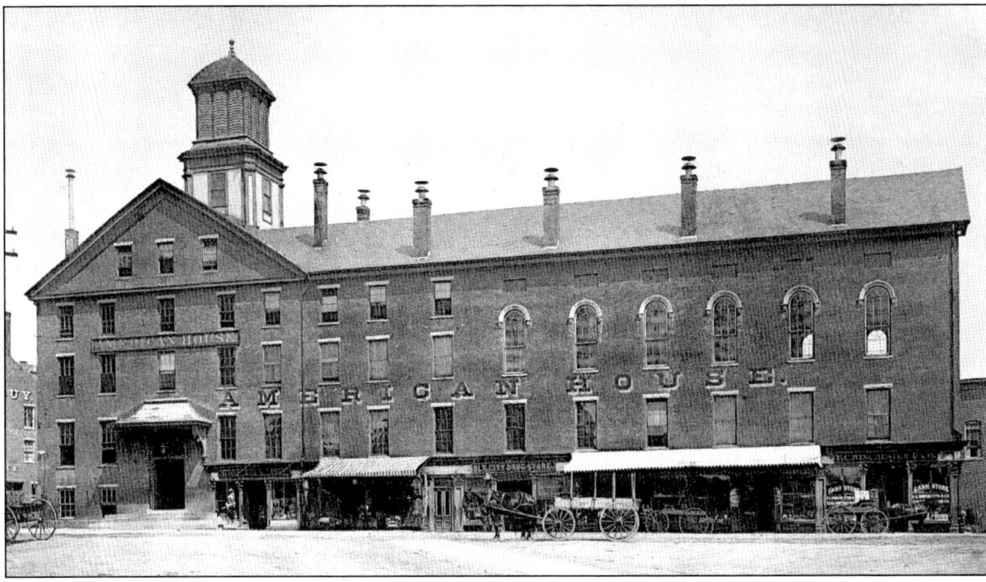

THE AMERICAN HOUSE. The railroad came to Fitchburg in 1845. The next year, David Boutelle built a large hotel on his property across from the station. The American House catered to the railroad traffic and provided a place for local functions, such as sleighing parties. The owner of Hotel Raymond purchased the property in 1933, but its time had passed. It was closed in 1952 and was demolished several years later.

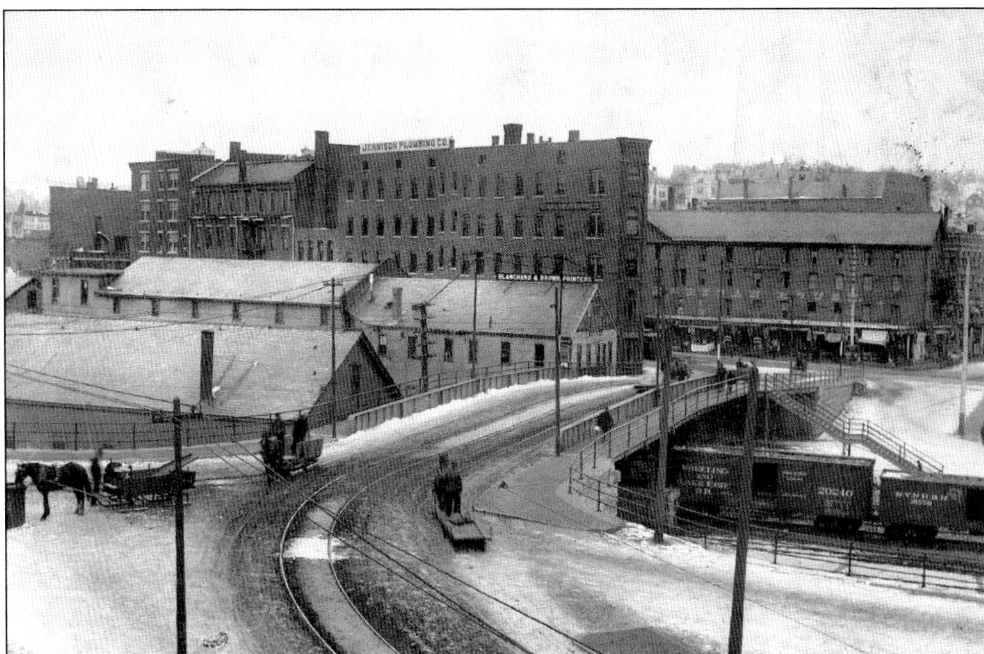

WATER STREET LOOKING TOWARD DEPOT SQUARE. This photograph of Water Street looking toward Main Street must have been taken after 1900, because the Park Building (seen here with the Jennison Plumbing sign) was built in that year. To the right of the Park Building is the American House. The horse at the left is drinking out of one of the many water troughs that were located around the city.

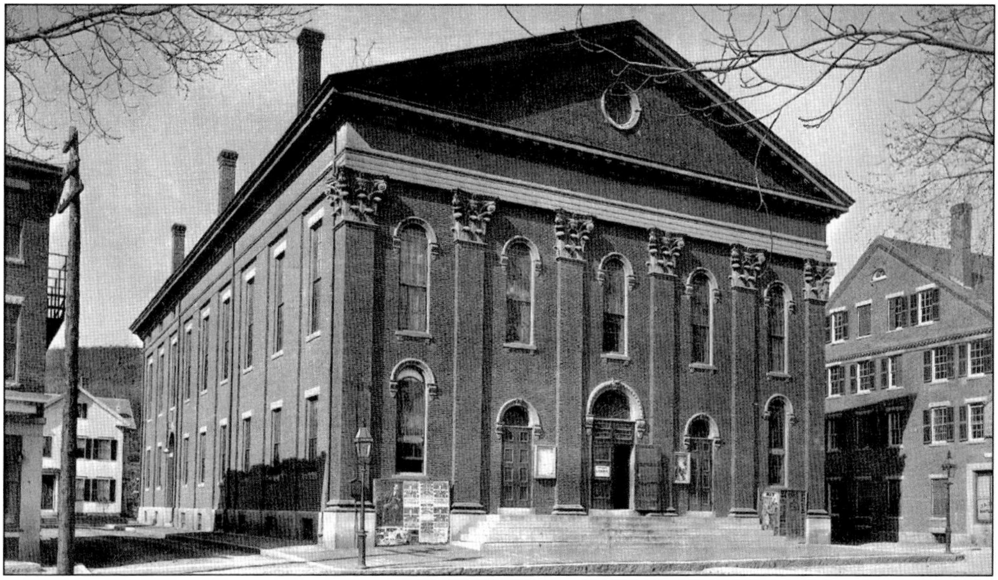

CITY HALL. City hall, built in 1852, was the center of municipal and social life in Fitchburg during the second half of the 19th century. Wendell Phillips, Ralph Waldo Emerson, Oliver Wendell Holmes, and Henry Ward Beecher lectured in the building's great hall. City hall housed the offices of city officials and was also home to the post office, the library, and the superior court before they were moved into their own buildings.

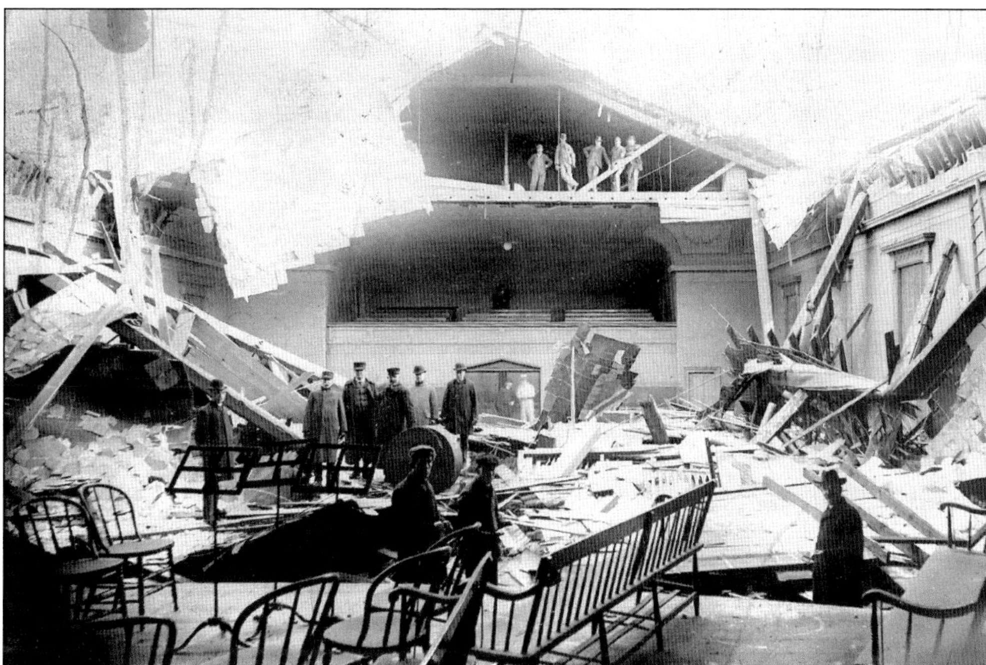

THE COLLAPSE OF CITY HALL'S ROOF. Joseph Moulton's photograph shows the collapse of the city hall roof in 1904. The city determined that the damage was due to rusted truss rods. Controversy erupted over whether the city should repair the roof or build a new city hall. The city council decided to repair the roof and install new offices, which sacrificed the assembly hall.

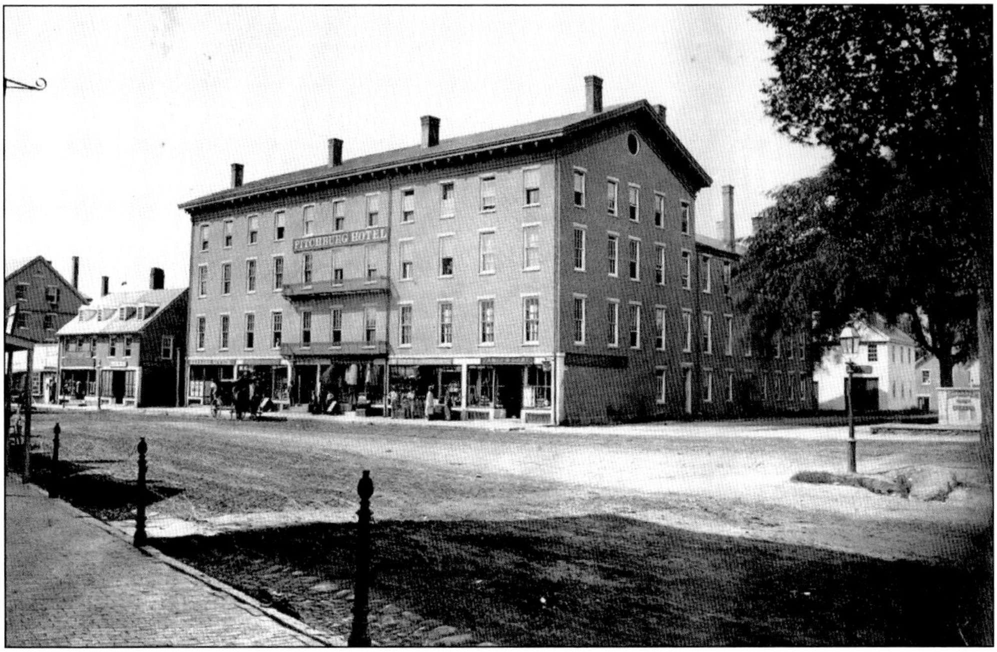

THE FITCHBURG HOTEL. The Fitchburg Hotel, located to the west of city hall, had elegantly decorated rooms. It was one of three city hotels that served temperance guests. According to the hotel's advertisements, "a good stable, Barber Shop and Billiard Hall" were connected to the hotel, and several other businesses rented space on the ground floor.

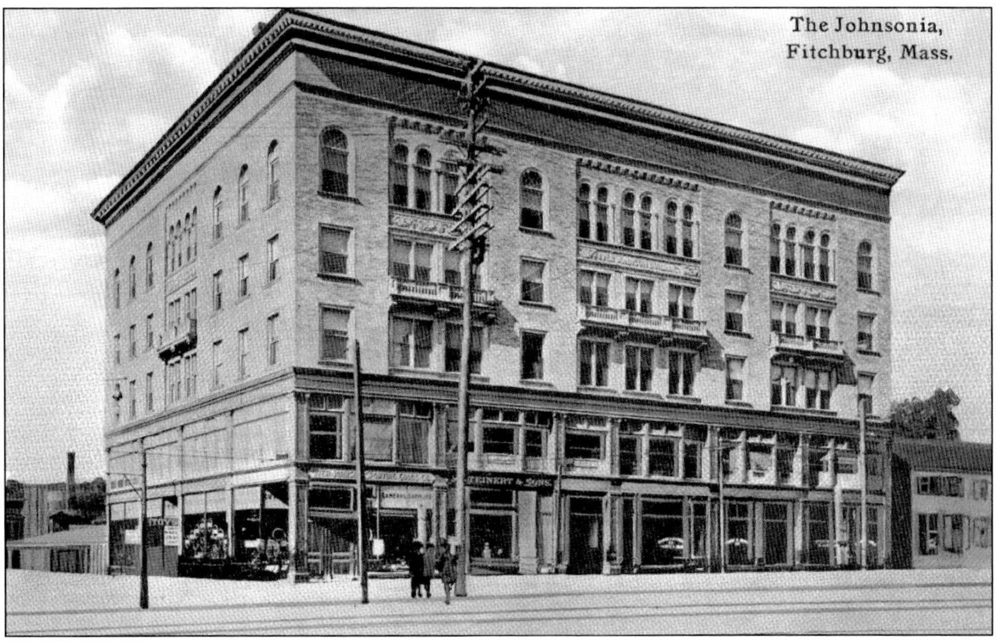

THE JOHNSONIA. Iver Johnson, a firearm manufacturer, passed away in 1895. His wife, Mary Johnson, memorialized her husband with a hotel on Main Street, which she named the Johnsonia. In the 1960s, some suggested that the building be demolished for a parking lot. Fortunately, the building was saved and still survives as a vestige of the 19th century.

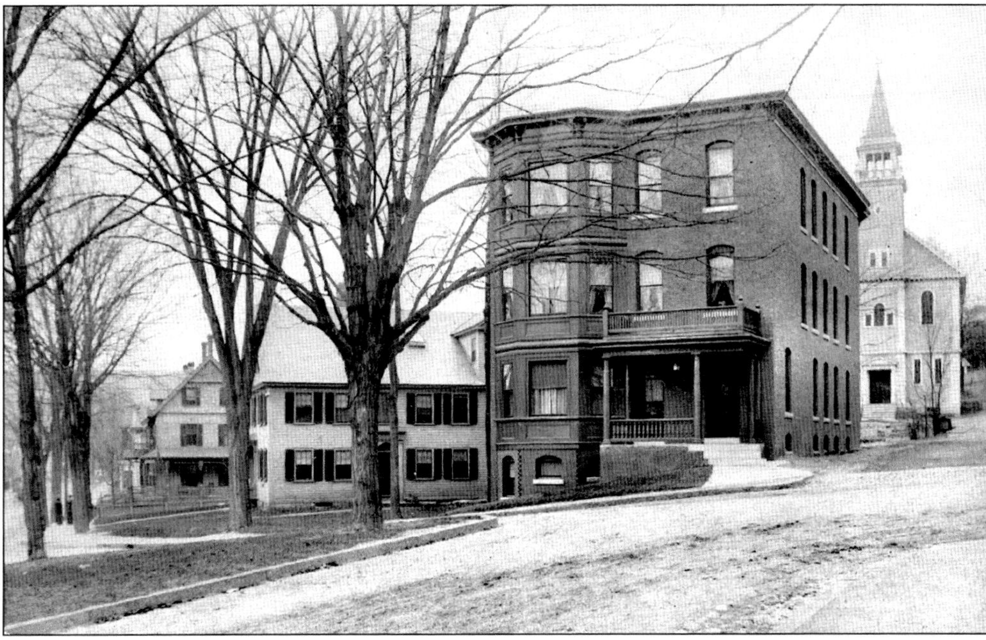

A THREE-DECKER HOUSE. As the city's immigrant population grew, three-decker housing also burgeoned. This example of a three-decker was built at the head of the Upper Common. The interior and exterior design of the houses differed depending on the ethnic groups that built them. Behind the three-decker house is the Swedish Lutheran Church, erected in 1893.

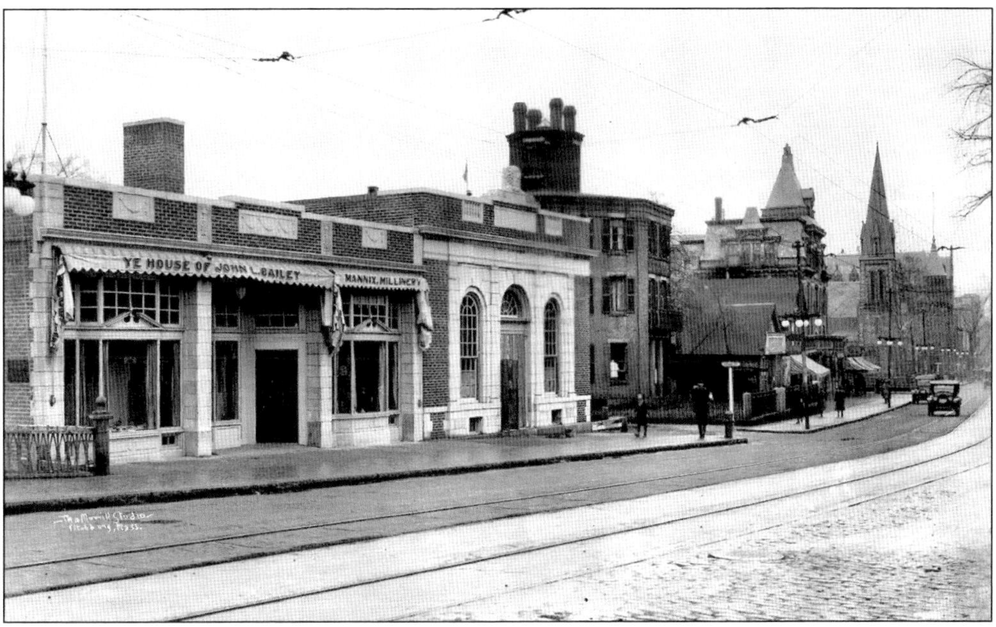

YE HOUSE OF JOHN L. BAILEY. In 1907, Bostonian John Bailey opened a candy store on the Upper Common, naming it Ye House of John L. Bailey. His apprentice, Alfred Wenzel, came to the city the following year as a candy maker. In 1920, Wenzel and David Merriam purchased the business and carried on making candy and ice cream for another 30 years. The store went out of business in 1972.

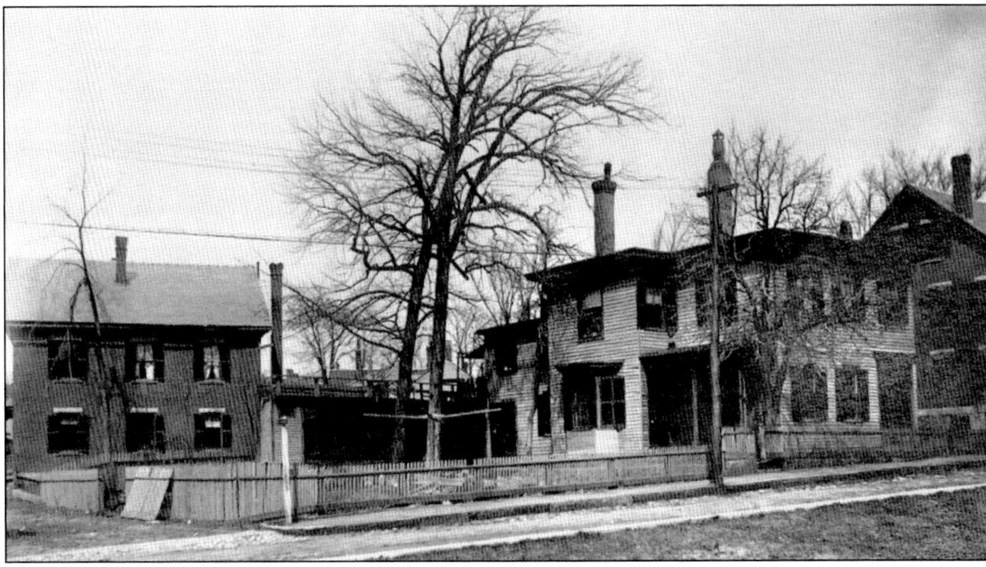

THE SITE OF THE FITCHBURG HISTORICAL SOCIETY. The Fitchburg Historical Society acquired a plot of land on Grove Street in 1911 from James Garfield. Garfield had purchased the land the year before and removed the I. C. Wright house to High Street. Many buildings were moved instead of being demolished during that time period. The brick building on the left is now the law office of Robert Ware.

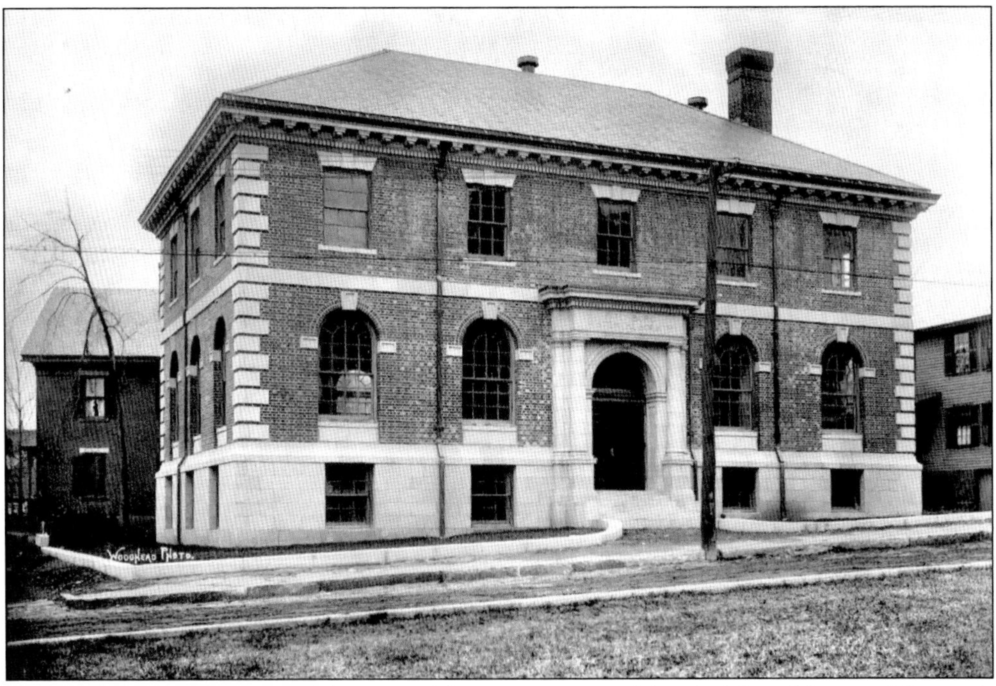

THE FITCHBURG HISTORICAL SOCIETY. The cornerstone of the Fitchburg Historical Society's building was laid on August 5, 1911. The meeting records list all the articles deposited in the cornerstone, including a 1911 city directory, the architect's specifications of the building and his card, a copy of Garfield's deed to the society, a copy of the builder's contract, and a list of the society's members.

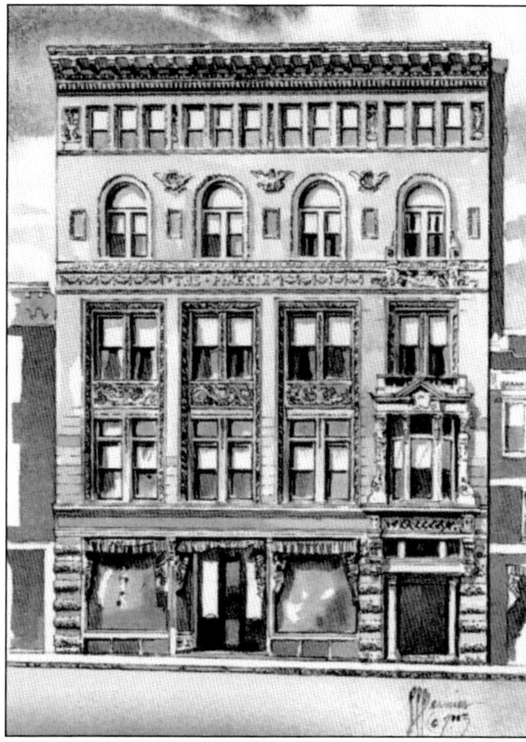

THE PHOENIX BUILDING. The Fitchburg Mutual Fire Insurance Company commissioned H. M. Francis to design a new building near the Upper Common. The Phoenix Building, in the Renaissance Revival style, was completed in 1893. The building housed retail shops on the first floor, the insurance company on the second level, and apartments on the upper floors. The Phoenix Building is the future home of the Fitchburg Historical Society. (Illustration by Robert Bernier.)

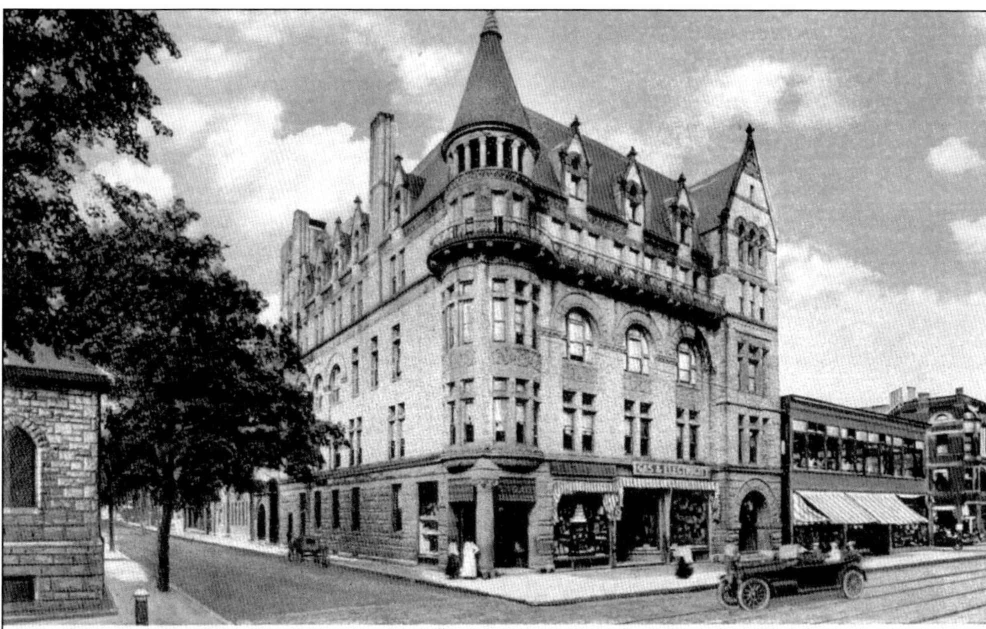

THE YMCA AT FOX AND MAIN STREETS. During the 1890s, old structures were razed along Main Street, making way for large architect-designed buildings. The YMCA was among the first of many of these new buildings to grace Main Street. Designed by the city's own prolific architect, H. M. Francis, the stone Romanesque-style building, completed in 1894, looked much like a French chateau. It is still present on Main Street, but it has been altered.

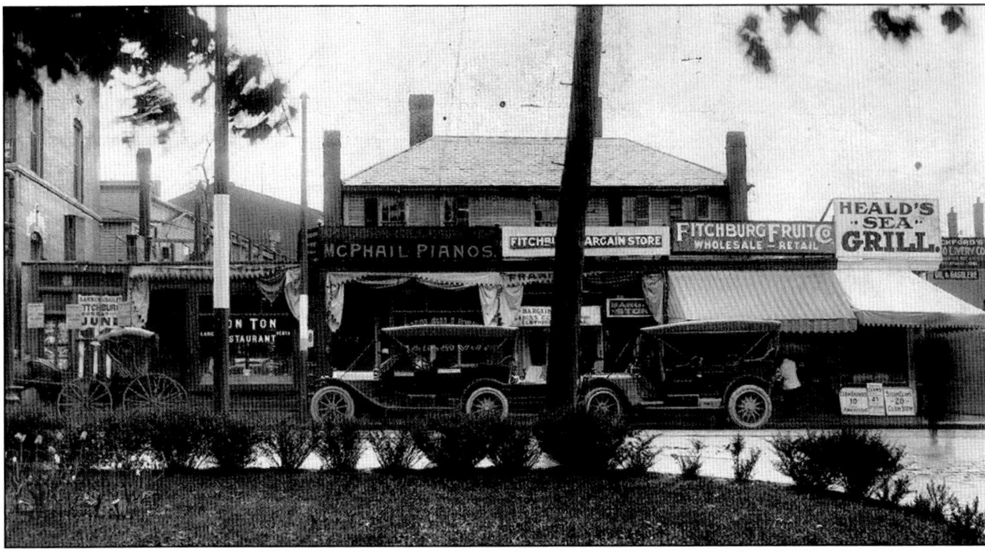

THE BON TON RESTAURANT. Directly across from Union Depot, the Bon Ton Restaurant catered to visitors coming in on the train. It was a very popular eating spot for the locals as well. The Bon Ton and the rest of the block were destroyed by fire in 1963.

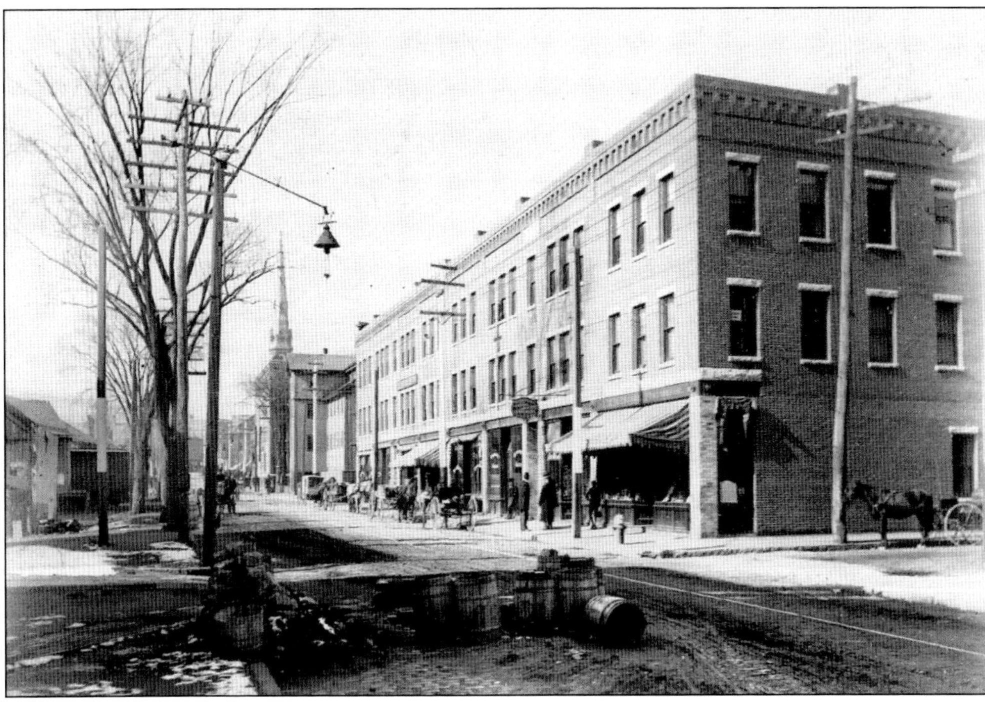

MAIN AND WILLOW STREETS. This view looks up Main Street from Willow Street. It has a feeling of both the old and the modern; horses and buggies traverse a street dotted by electric light poles. The first electric company in the city was the Wachusett Electric Light Company, established in 1883. It was purchased by the Fitchburg Gas Company in 1889, resulting in the formation of the Fitchburg Gas and Electric Company.

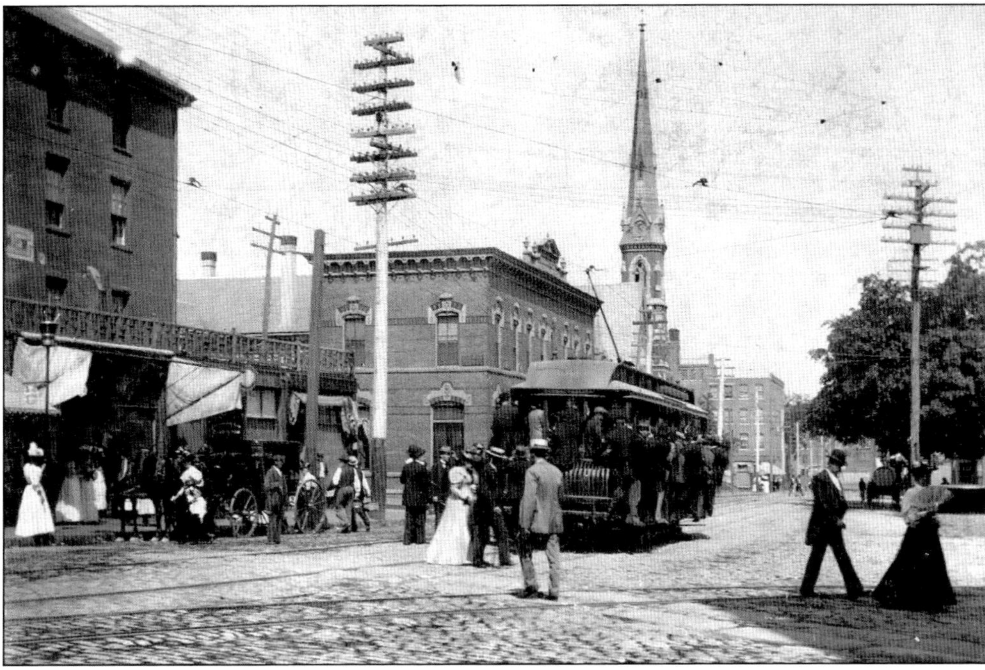

DEPOT SQUARE. Depot Square was a busy intersection in the 1890s. The steeple in the distance is the Rollstone Church.

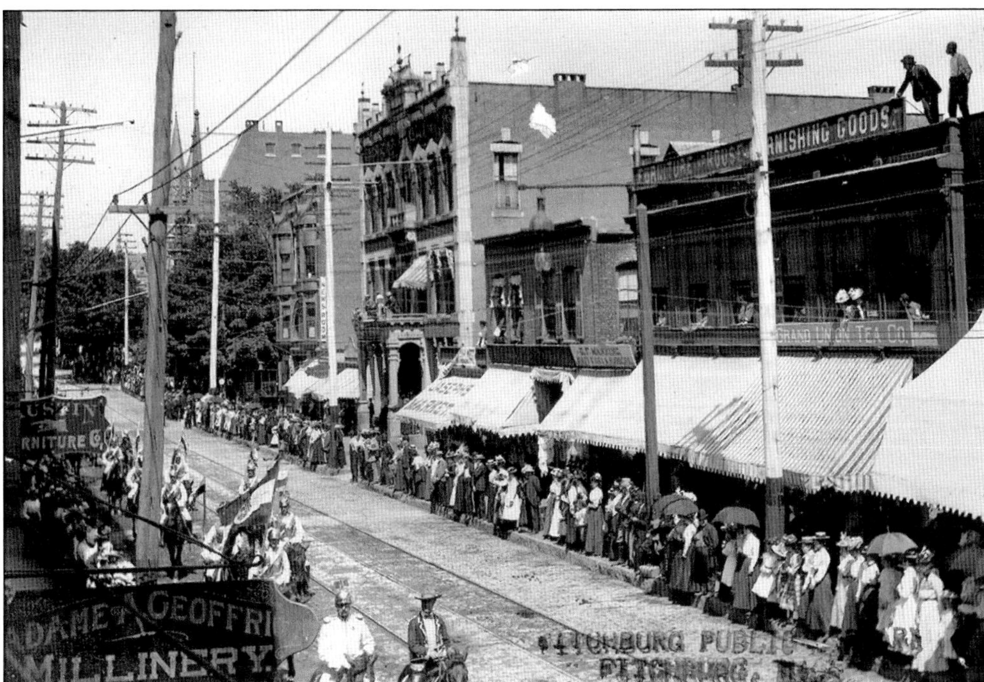

A MAIN STREET PARADE. Everybody loves a parade, and this one in 1900 was no exception. Men and women, dressed in their finest clothes and hats, crowded the street to experience the excitement. At the turn of the century, Main Street featured furniture stores, millinery shops, shoe and boot stores, and the ubiquitous F. W. Woolworth.

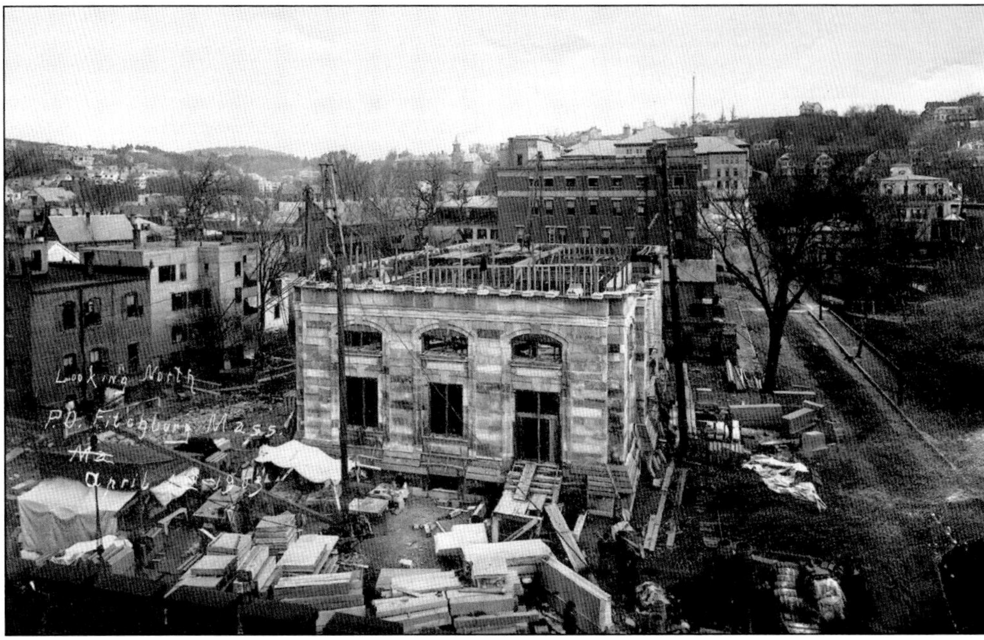

THE POST OFFICE UNDER CONSTRUCTION. In 1811, the first postmaster conducted business from his Main Street home. The post office boarded in several buildings around the city over the next 92 years until the federal government decided to build an official post office in 1902.

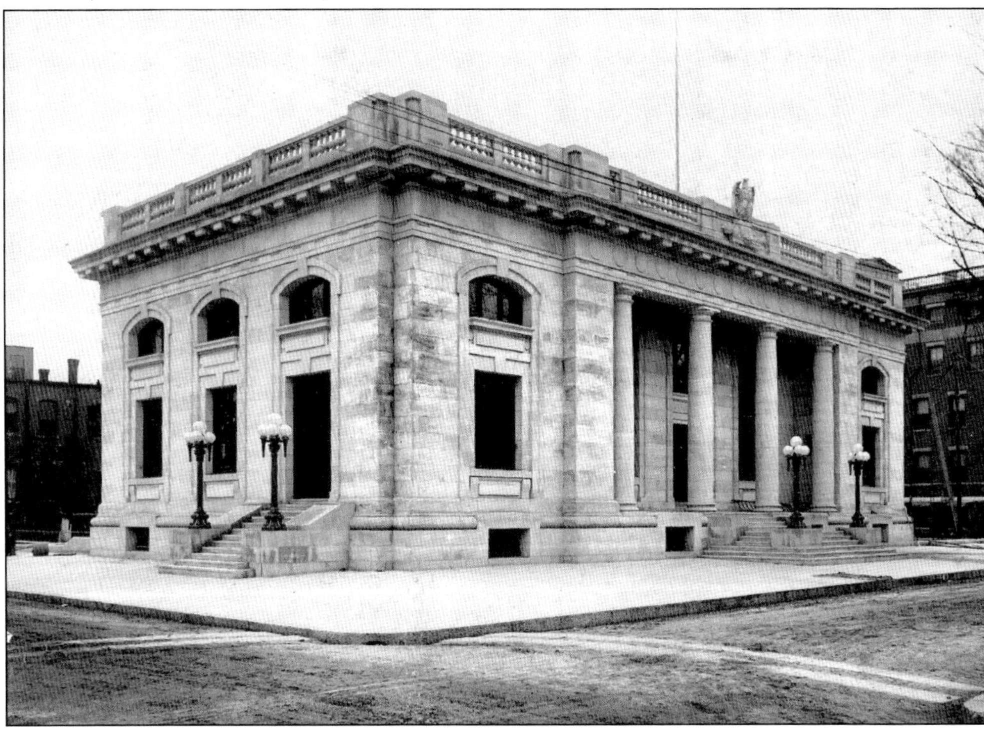

THE COMPLETED POST OFFICE. Completed in 1903, the post office was designed by a federal government architect and was built with Indiana granite. The building became the present-day courthouse.

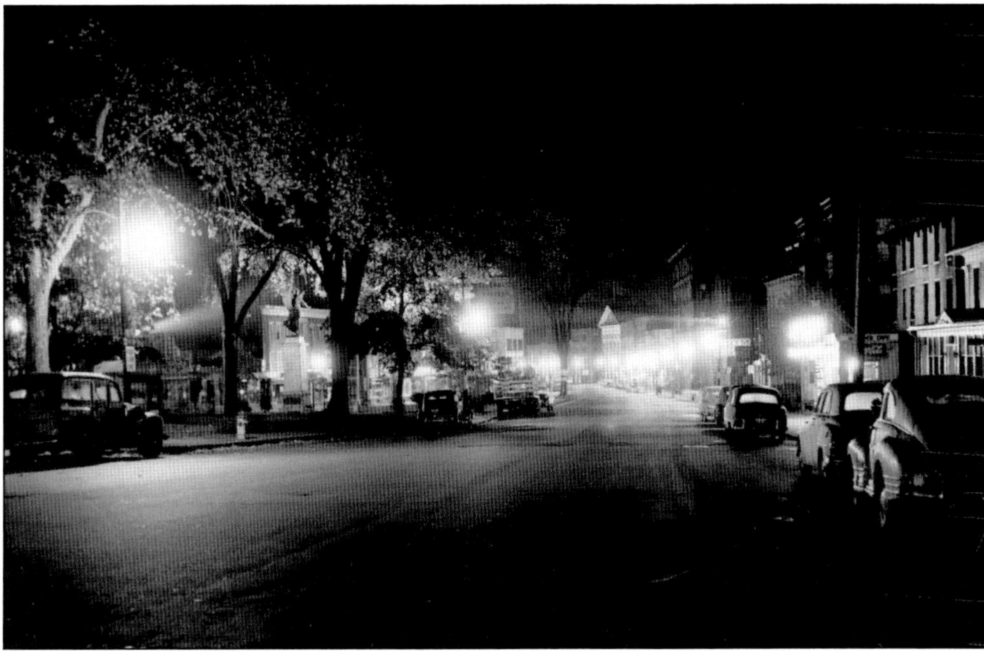

NIGHT LIGHTS IN FITCHBURG. This is a *c.* 1945 nighttime view of Fitchburg, looking east from the Upper Common, after the Fitchburg Gas and Electric Light Company had installed a total of 150 streetlights. The World War I memorial can be seen among the trees on the left.

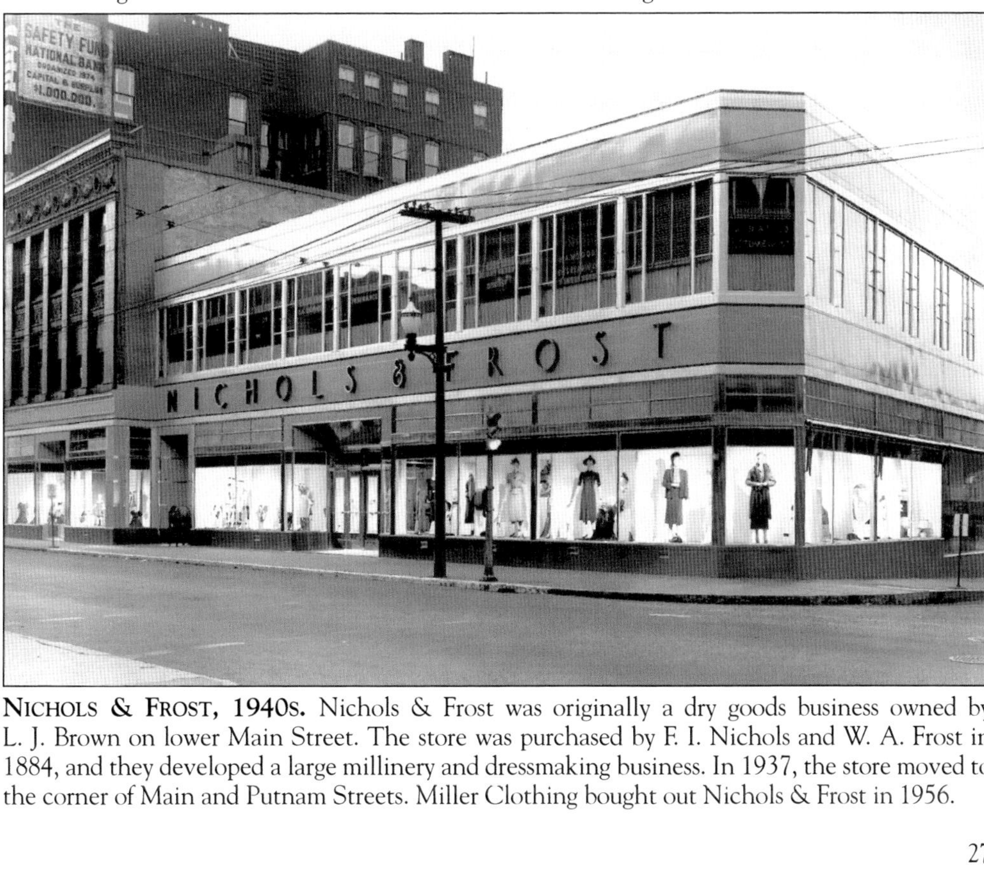

NICHOLS & FROST, 1940S. Nichols & Frost was originally a dry goods business owned by L. J. Brown on lower Main Street. The store was purchased by F. I. Nichols and W. A. Frost in 1884, and they developed a large millinery and dressmaking business. In 1937, the store moved to the corner of Main and Putnam Streets. Miller Clothing bought out Nichols & Frost in 1956.

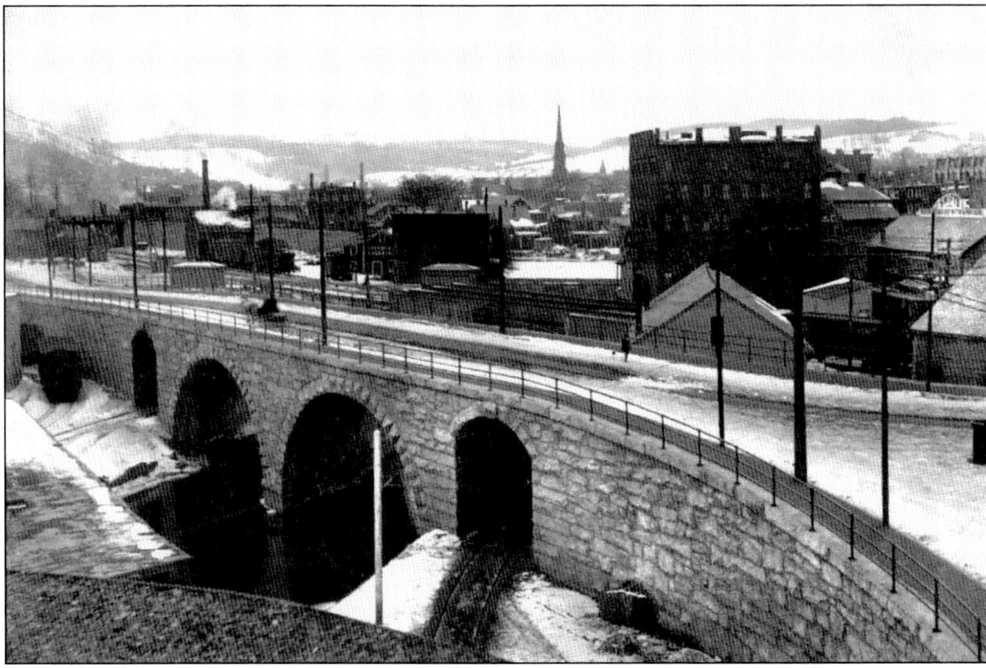

The Laurel Street Bridge. This is the Laurel Street Bridge as seen from Water Street. The Nashua River flowed under the central portion of the bridge, while train tracks passed through tunnels on either side of the river. The Rollstone Church steeple is visible in the distance.

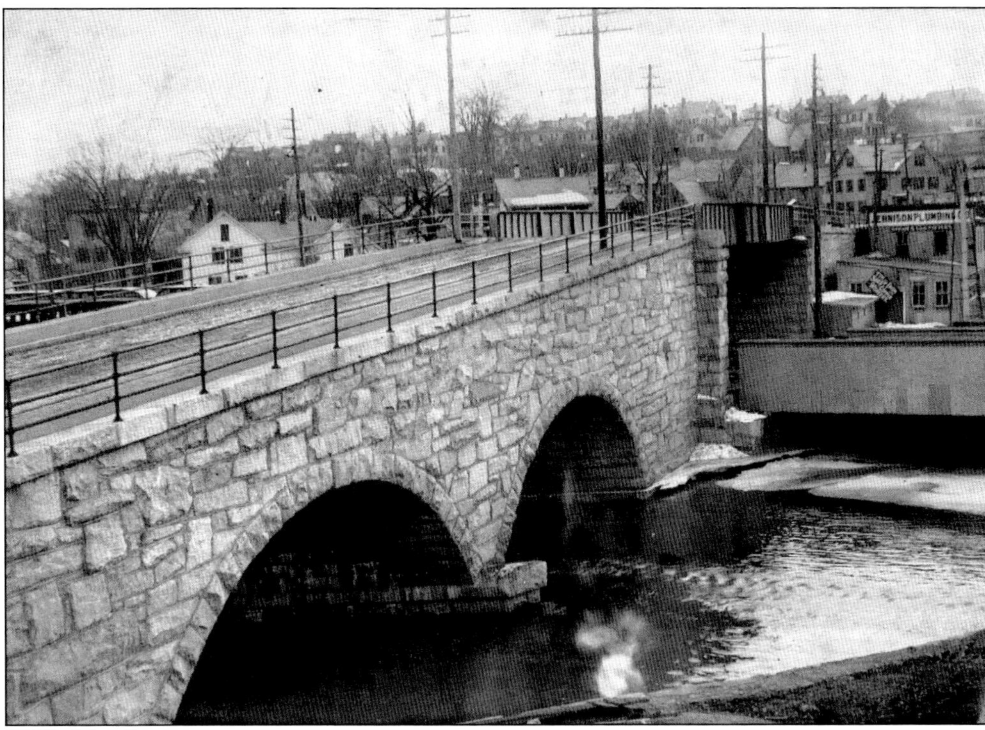

The Putnam Street Bridge. The Putnam Street Bridge is seen in this view looking toward Laurel Street. At the end of the bridge is the Jennison Plumbing Company office.

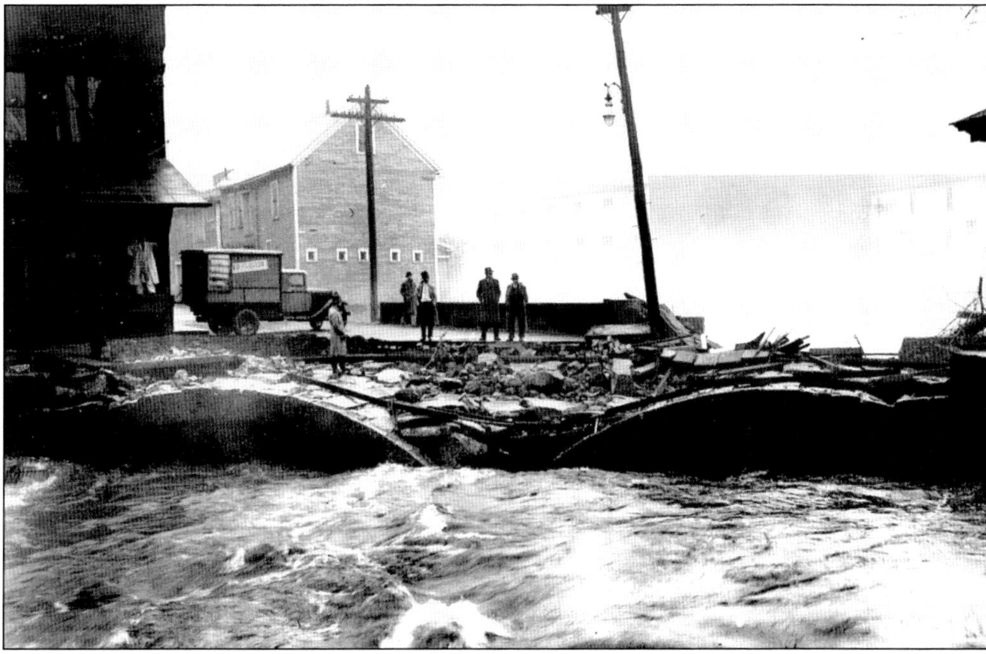

FLOOD DAMAGE AT CUSHING DAM. On March 18, 1936, a flood hit the city of Fitchburg. The Nashua River and its tributaries, swollen by two days of rain and melting snow, burst their banks and roared through Fitchburg, causing more than $2 million in damage. In this photograph, men are inspecting the flood damage at Cushing Dam.

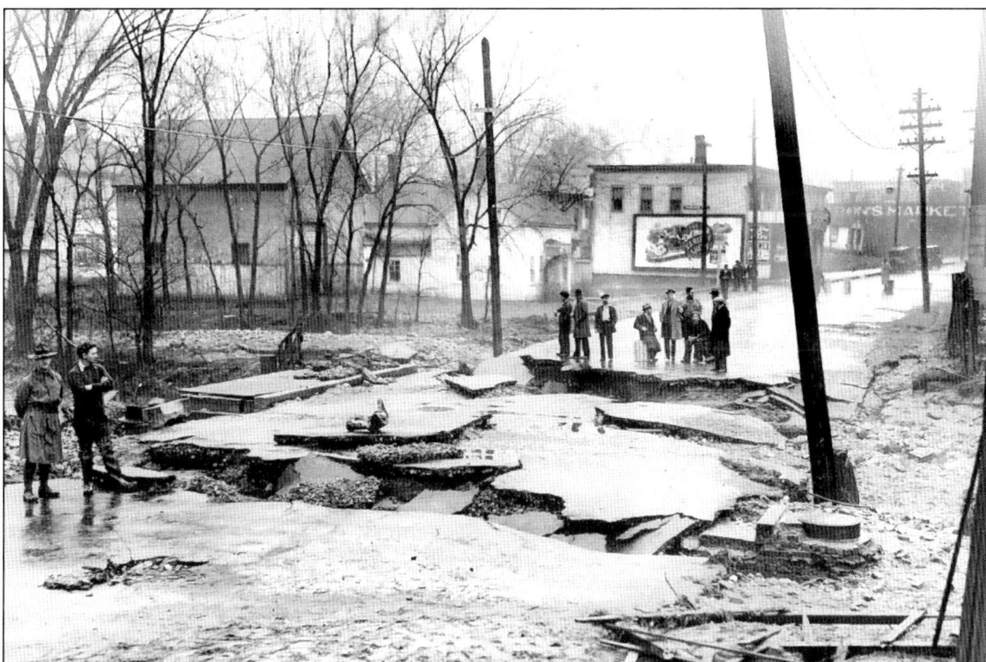

FLOOD DAMAGE AT BEMIS ROAD. Fitchburg Works Progress Administration workers were responsible for cleaning up after the flood. They rebuilt many of the city's bridges.

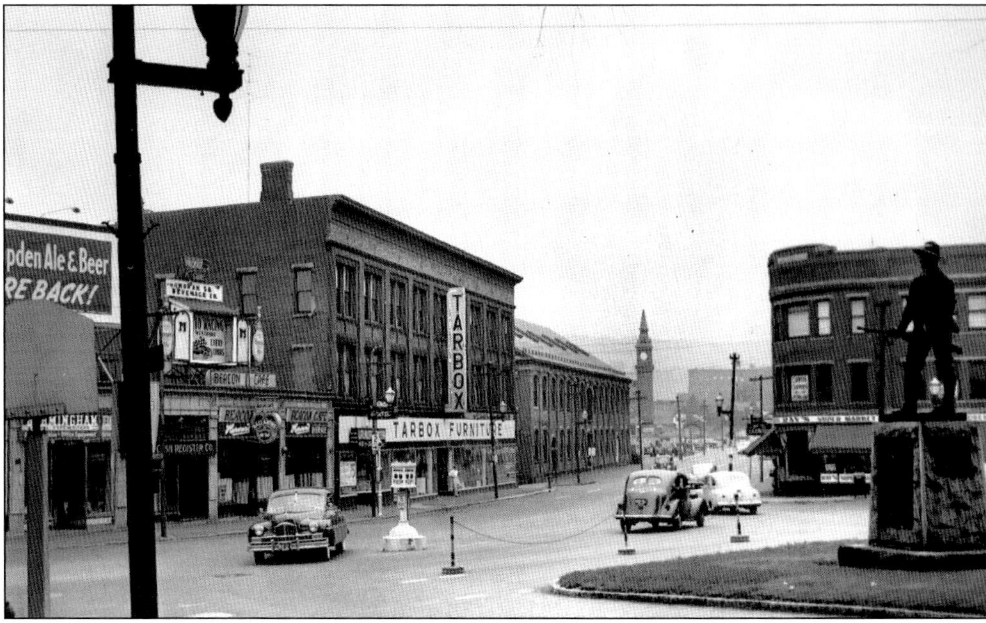

MORAN SQUARE, LOOKING WEST. The Tarbox Furniture Company opened its doors at 10 Main Street on Moran Square in 1924. In 1946, the company suffered a devastating fire, but it quickly rebuilt. On the right is the Spanish-American War memorial. The railroad depot clock tower is clearly visible. Today 10 Main Street is the home of Harper Furniture.

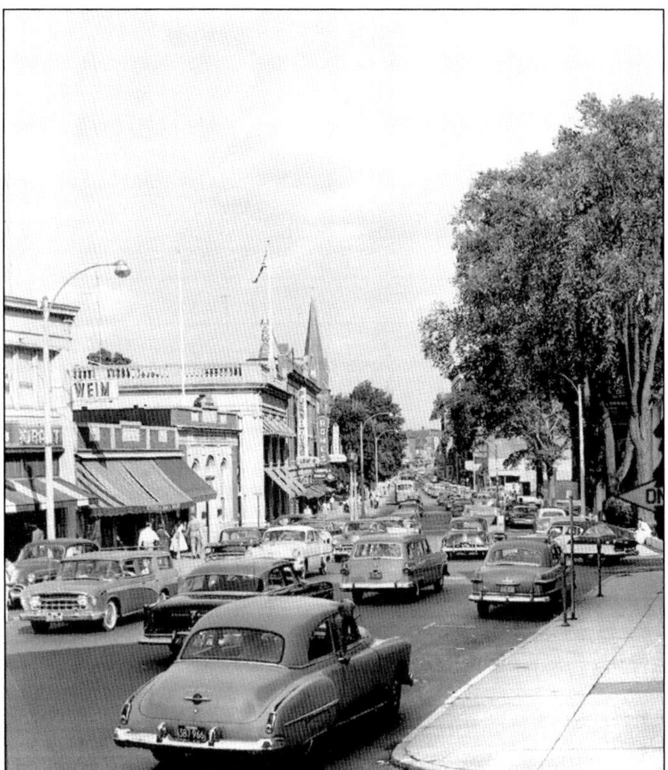

MAIN STREET, 1950S. The Octagon House disappeared from Main Street in 1925, replaced by a modern office building erected for the Fitchburg Gas and Electric Company. The company later relocated to the John Fitch Highway.

Two

People and Homes

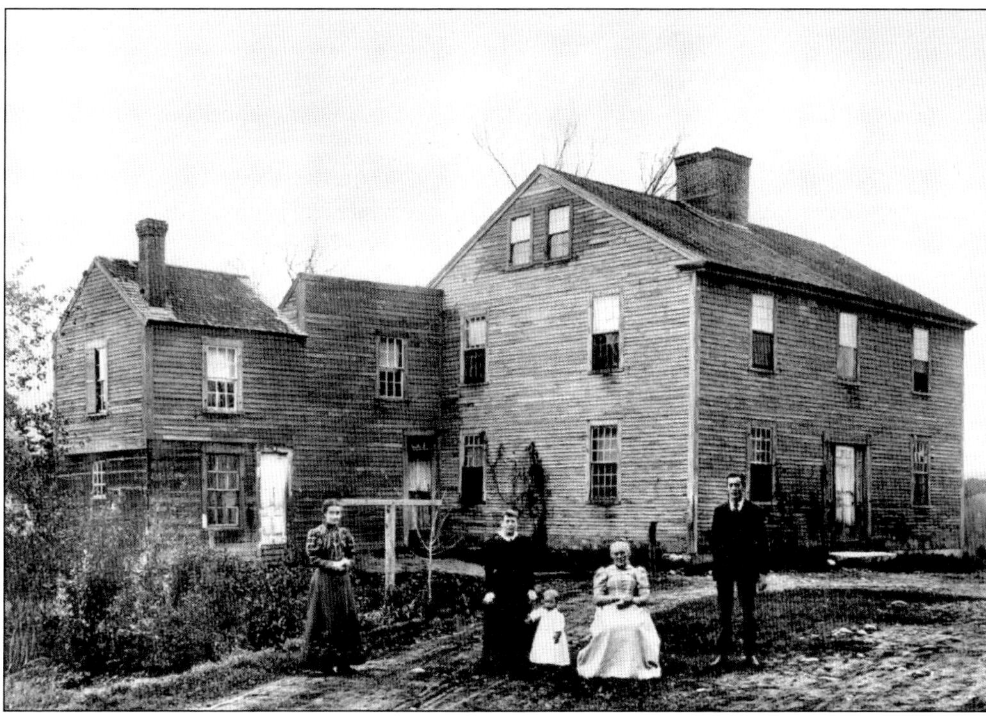

The Garfield House. The Garfield house, at the corner of Pearl and East Streets, was built by Elijah Garfield around 1752 and still stands on its original site. This photograph was taken around 1895.

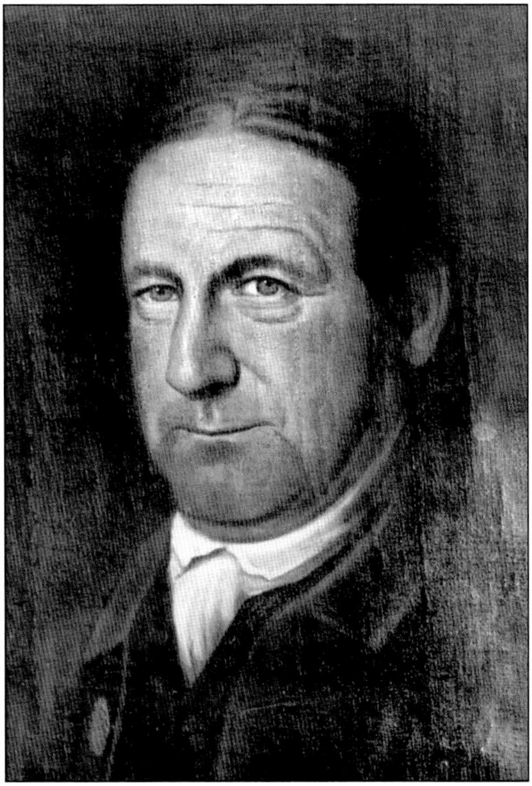

CAPT. THOMAS COWDIN. Capt. Thomas Cowdin came to Fitchburg in 1764. He was chosen as selectman at the first town election, and he held that post until the Revolution. Cowdin was an officer in the French and Indian War. He was an obedient soldier, although not a willing subject of the king, and he was suspected as a Tory until he was cleared by a Boston court. In 1779, he was commissioned as a captain and joined a New York regiment.

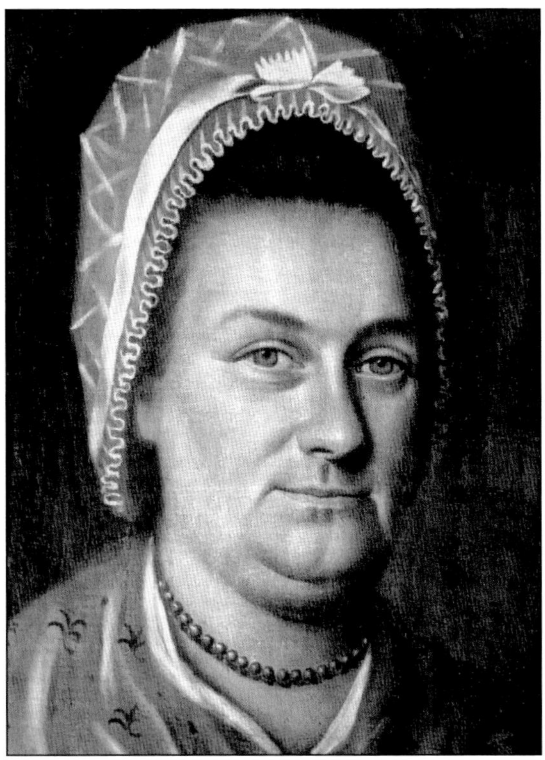

HANNAH COWDIN. Thomas and Hannah Cowdin owned a tavern on Pearl Street. Because Thomas was so active in civic and military service, it is believed that Hannah kept the tavern and raised the children. Thomas gave land at the corner of Crescent and Blossom Streets for Fitchburg's first meetinghouse. It was used for religious services as well as for town meetings.

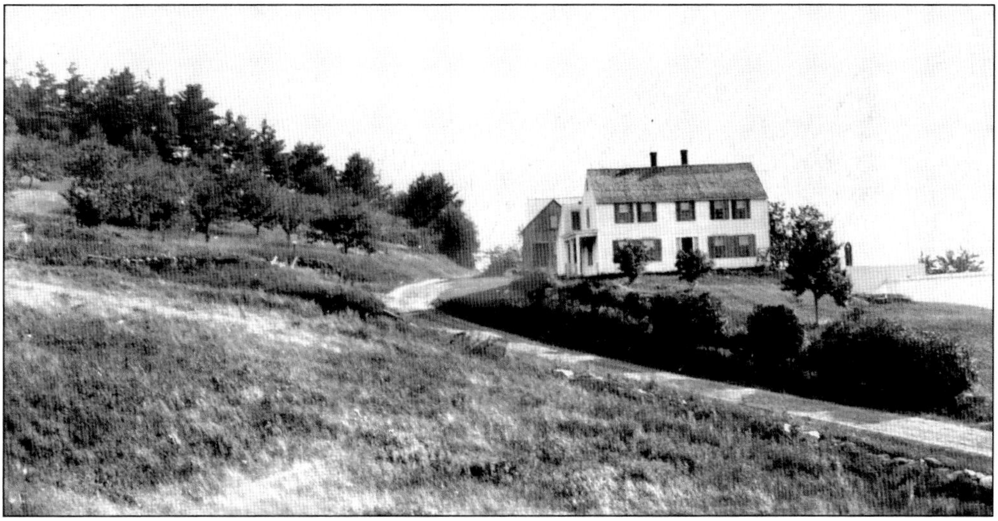

THE GIBSON GARRISON. Isaac Gibson and three of his sons, John, Nathaniel, and Jonathan, were among the Minutemen of Fitchburg who set out for Concord on the morning of April 19, 1775. The Gibson men were known for their size and strength; Isaac is said to have wrestled a mother bear who was defending her cub. This 1897 photograph shows "the Old Gibson Place" on top of Pearl Hill, surrounded by fields and an apple orchard.

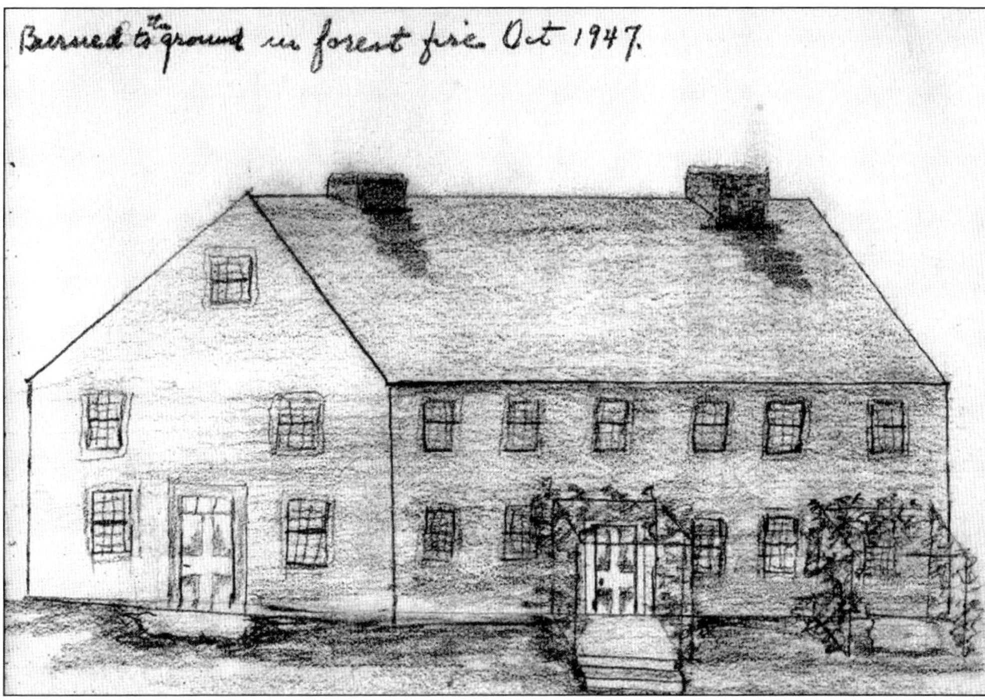

THE THURSTON FARMSTEAD. Asa Thurston was born in 1787 in this house, which his father, Thomas, built in 1780. After surviving typhoid fever, Asa entered the ministry and became Hawaii's first missionary in 1820. He created the Hawaiian alphabet, taught reading and writing, and established a church that is still active. The house, seen here in a sketch from 1897, burned in 1947. It is currently the site of an archaeological dig sponsored by the Fitchburg Historical Society.

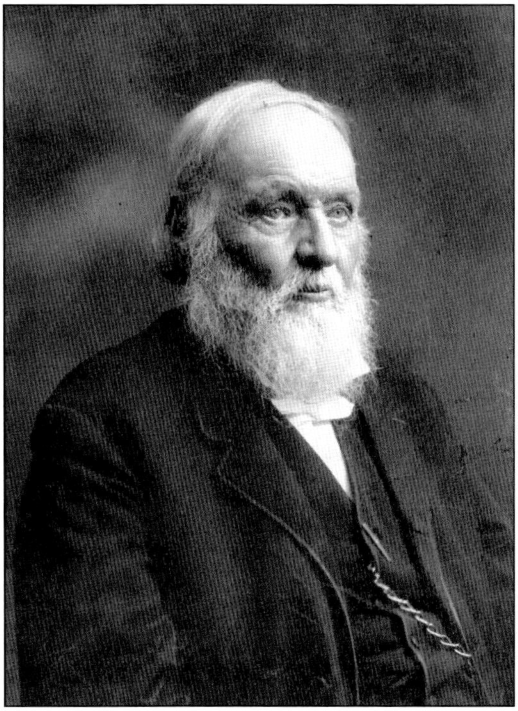

DR. THOMAS PALMER. Dr. Thomas Palmer (1820–1907) was a dentist and a pioneer in the use of ether. He was a friend of Dr. William Morton, who is credited with discovering ether's use as an anesthetic. Morton taught Palmer how to use an inhaler, and Palmer applied the knowledge in his Fitchburg dentistry practice in 1846. Palmer also corresponded about a "gas machine" with Hiram Maxim, the inventor of the machine gun, who visited Fitchburg on occasion.

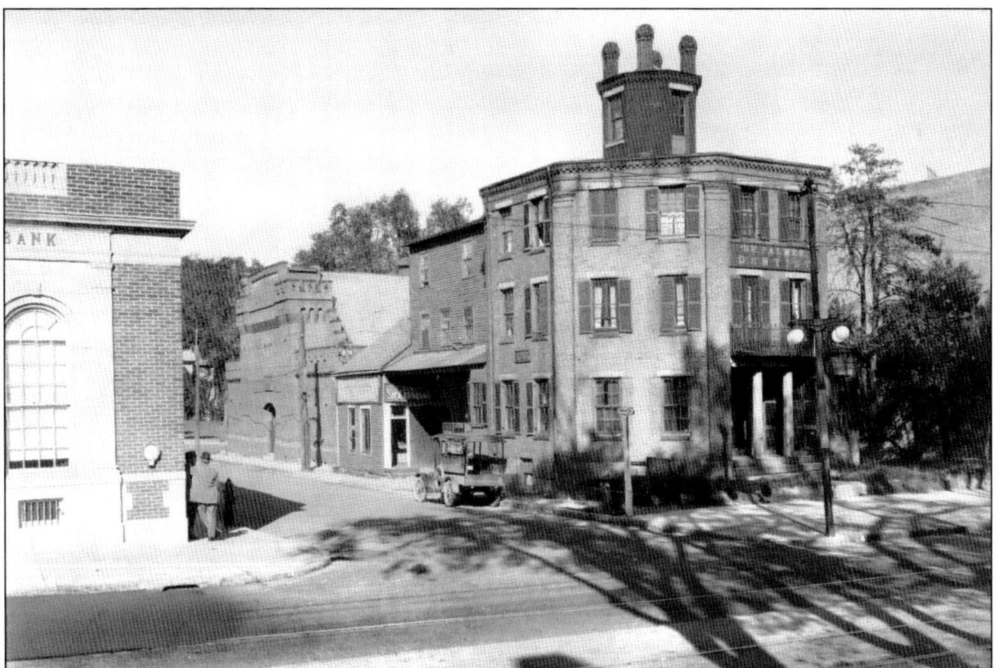

PALMER'S OCTAGONAL HOUSE. Four years after beginning his dentistry practice, Dr. Thomas Palmer purchased land at the corner of Main and Grove Streets to construct an unusual house. Dr. Palmer was convinced that an octagonal house would get more sunshine and air. The house was finished in the spring of 1849, and Palmer moved his practice to the new house and made it his home as well. The armory is to the rear of the house.

CAROLINE MASON. Caroline Mason (1823–1890) was a talented poet, and her poems were published in *Atlantic Monthly*. Her poem "Ode to Fitchburg" was a must for memorization among 19th-century Fitchburg schoolchildren. She supported causes such as the abolition of slavery, the establishment of women's rights, and the prevention of cruelty to animals. She suffered deep depression for most of her life and succumbed to mental illness at the end of her days.

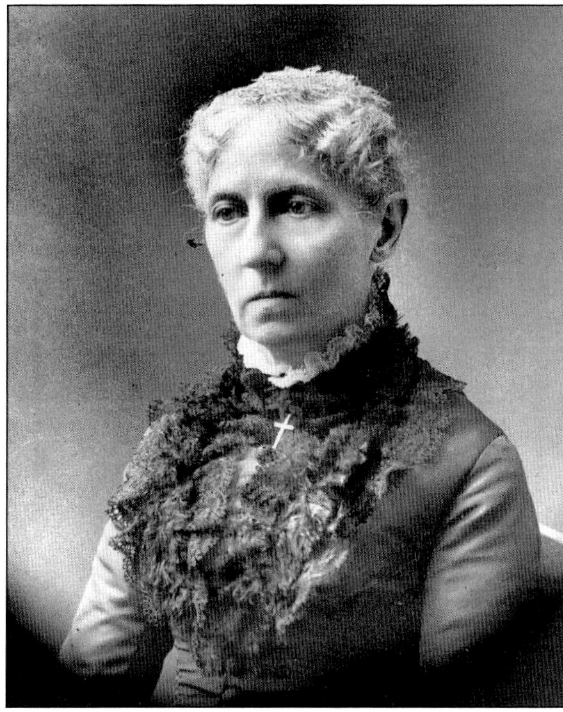

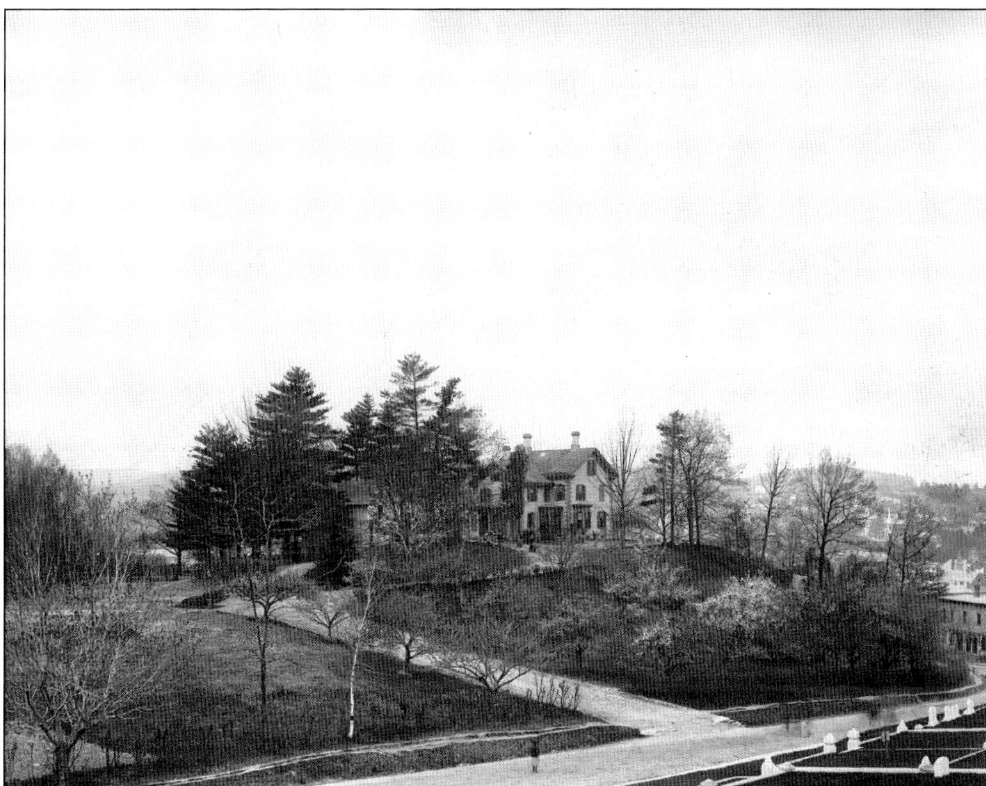

THE MASON HOUSE. This was Charles and Caroline Mason's home on Laurel Hill.

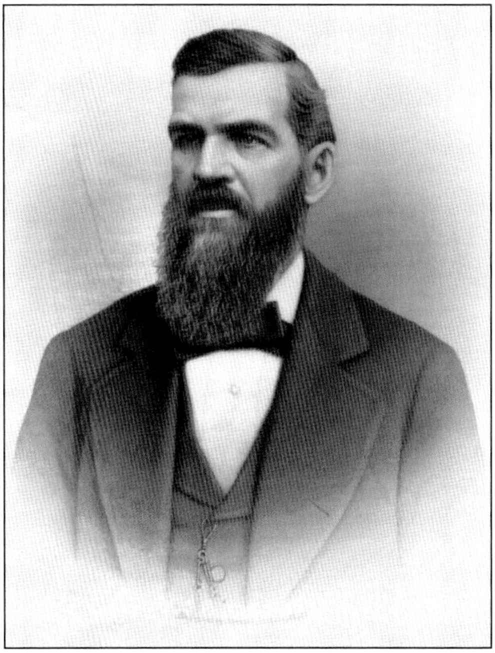

CHARLES BURLEIGH. Charles Burleigh moved to Fitchburg in 1850. At the end of the Civil War, while working for Putnam Manufacturing, he was approached by Alvah Crocker to design a drill that would hasten tunneling through the Hoosac Mountain. Burleigh invented a rock drill that used steam and an air compressor for power. Burleigh established his own company to sell the drill, which was also used for mining. He died in 1883.

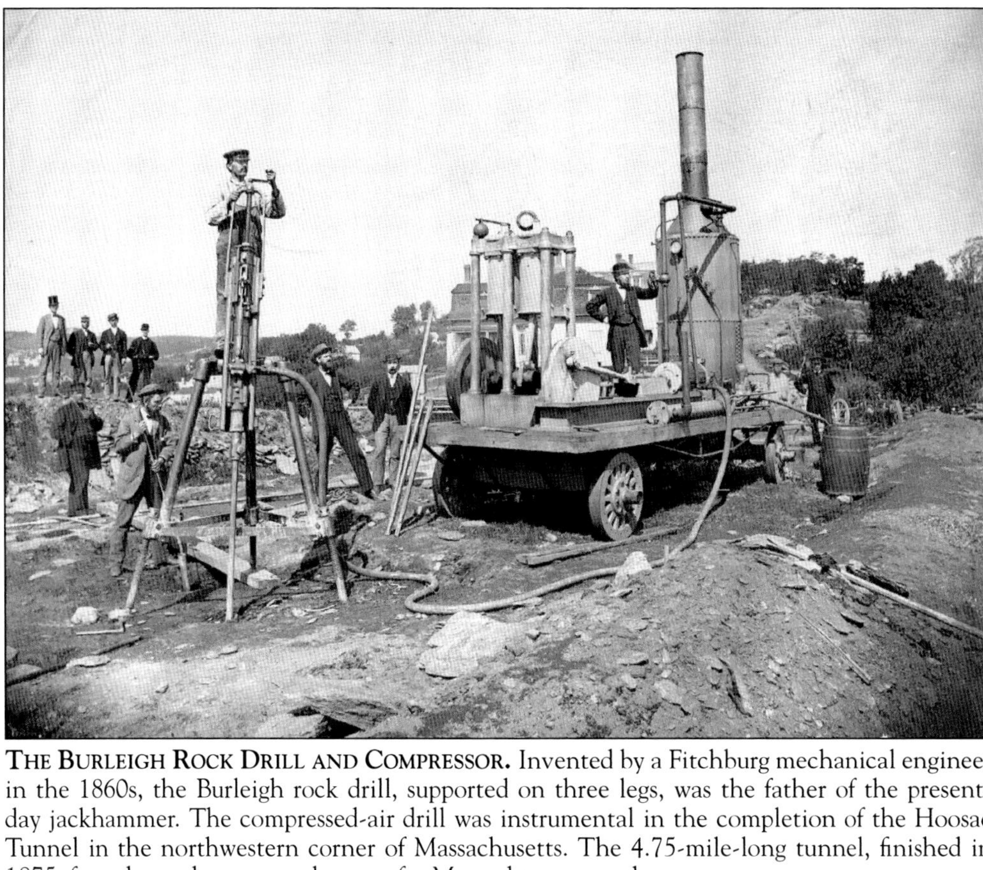

THE BURLEIGH ROCK DRILL AND COMPRESSOR. Invented by a Fitchburg mechanical engineer in the 1860s, the Burleigh rock drill, supported on three legs, was the father of the present-day jackhammer. The compressed-air drill was instrumental in the completion of the Hoosac Tunnel in the northwestern corner of Massachusetts. The 4.75-mile-long tunnel, finished in 1875, forged a trade route to the west for Massachusetts goods.

EBENEZER FOSTER BAILEY WITH HIS PATENTED PRUNER. Fitchburg citizens have patented hundreds of inventions, from simplistic apple peelers to intricate designs for steam engines, guns, and rock drills. Joseph Brown invented a machine that was able to fill small bags; the new machines were used by the Burpee Seed Company. Ebenezer Butterick came up with the idea for paper patterns to facilitate making clothes. Here, Ebenezer Foster Bailey poses with his tree pruner, which he patented in 1881.

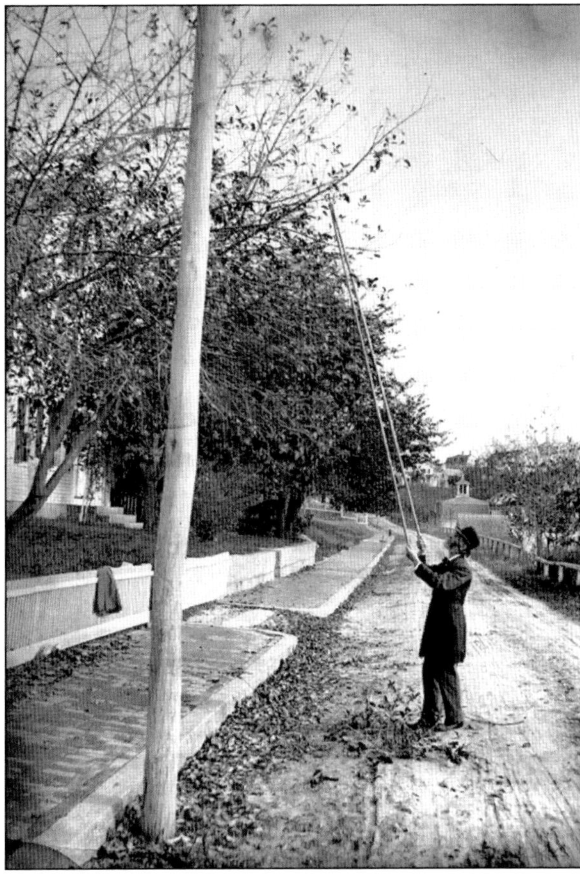

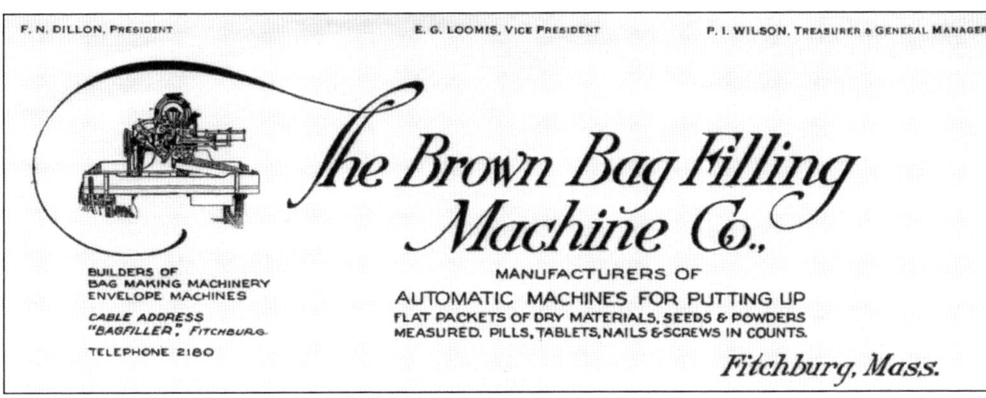

A BILLHEAD. This is a 1930 billhead from the Brown Bag Filling Machine Company.

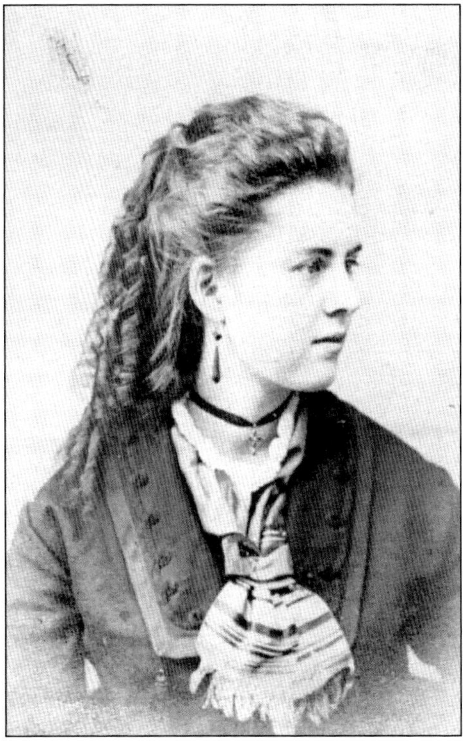

ELEANOR NORCROSS. Eleanor Norcross was an unusual woman for her time. Born in 1854, the daughter of the city's first mayor, she received her education at Fitchburg Academy, Wheaton Seminary, and the Massachusetts Normal Art School. An accomplished artist, she spent much of her life in Paris collecting art objects and painting. Upon her death in 1923, she made a bequest to found an art center in Fitchburg, now the Fitchburg Art Museum.

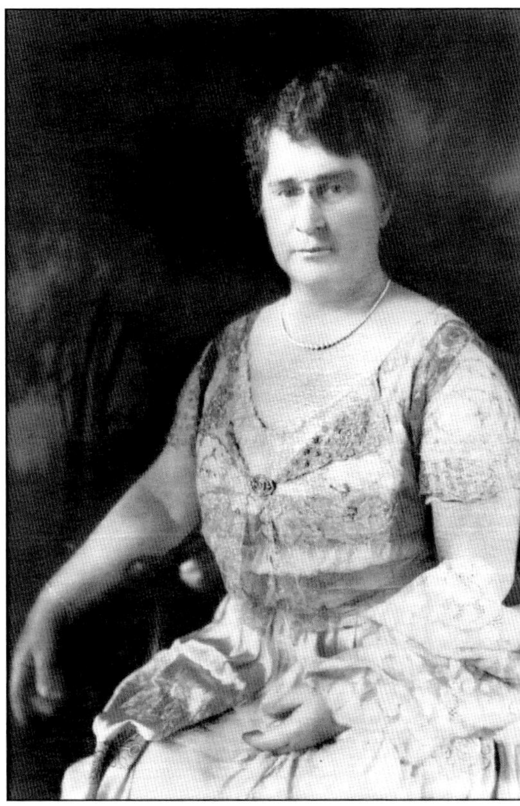

LUCY FAY GRIFFETH. Lucy Fay Griffeth was known as the wealthiest heiress in Massachusetts at the turn of the century. Her father, George Flagg Fay, earned a fortune by investing in local railroads, and Lucy was his only heir. The first gift she made upon inheriting the estate was an organ given to Christ Episcopal Church as a memorial. She was also instrumental in establishing a home for working girls. Her last charitable contribution was a $580,000 donation to Burbank Hospital.

A VICTORIAN PARLOR. This photograph provides us with an intimate view of a Victorian parlor in the 1890s, complete with plants, small furnishings, and a piano, an instrument that was dear to Victorians.

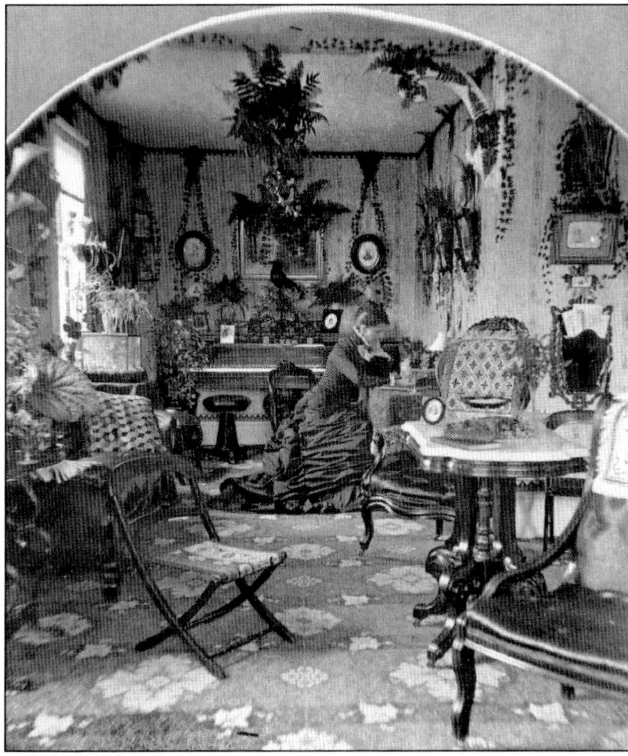

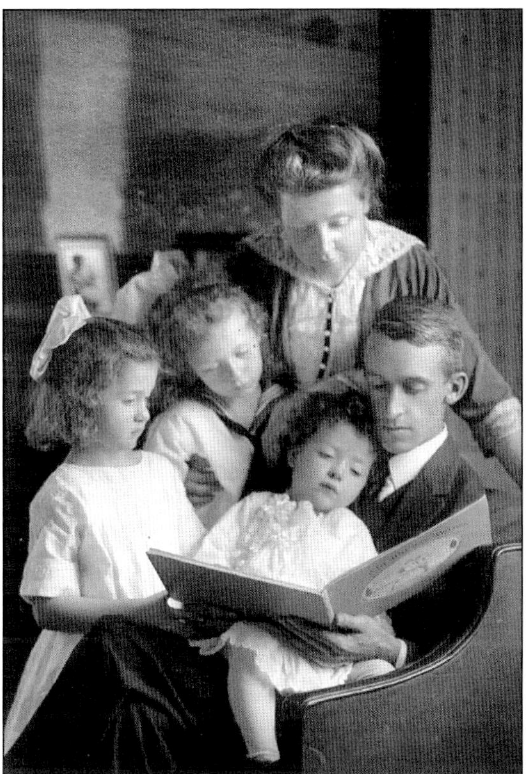

THE FALCONER FAMILY. The Falconer family enjoys some quiet time for reading.

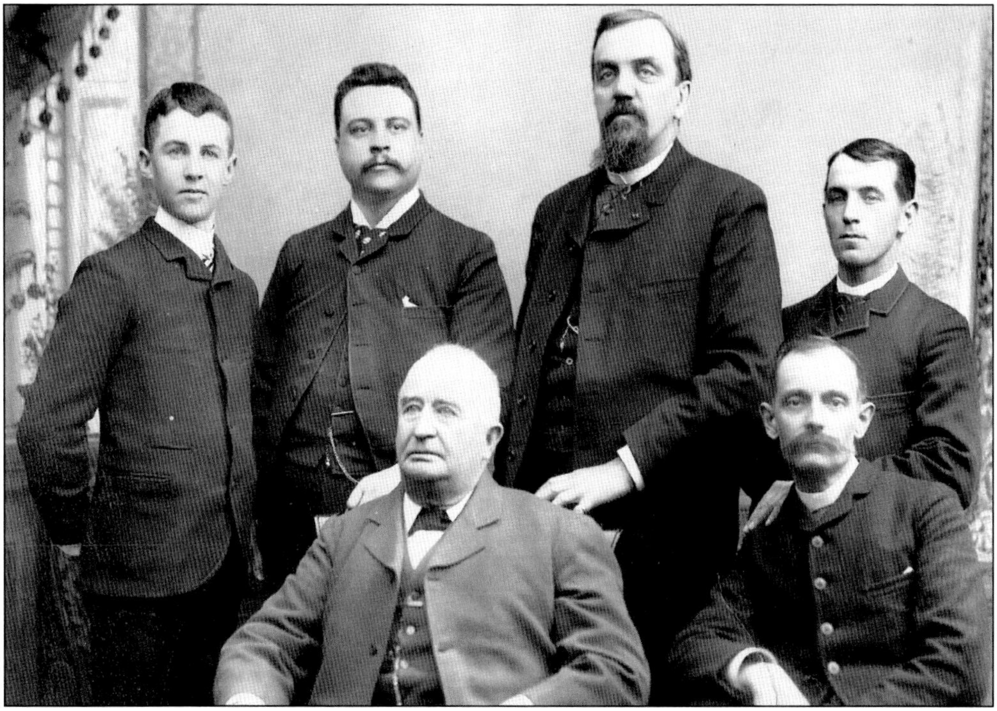

JOSEPH CUSHING. In 1868, Joseph Cushing (1817–1894) purchased the Old Stone Mill located at Laurel, Mill, and Putnam Streets, which today is the site of Riverside Park. Joe Cushing and his partners became dealers in flour, grain, and lumber. In this photograph, Joe Cushing is seated front and center. To his left is Herbert C. Hawley. Standing, from left to right, are Milton M. Cushing (Joseph Cushing's son), Edward M. Graves, Maj. Nelson F. Bond, and E. F. Marble (Joesph Cushing's nephew).

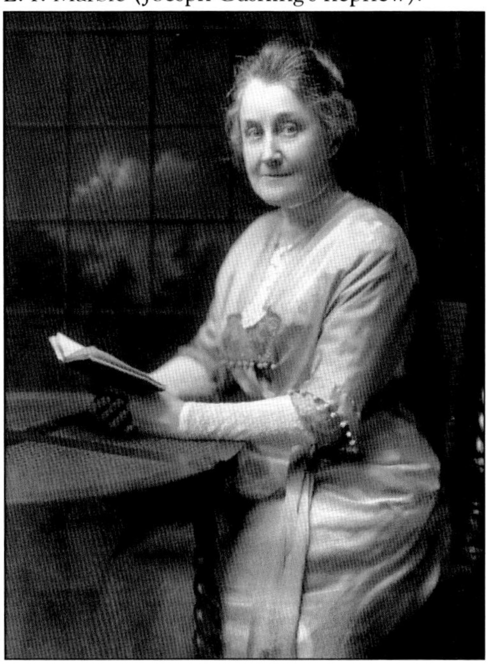

SUSAN CUSHING DICKINSON. Susan Cushing Dickinson was the daughter of Joseph Cushing and the wife of Charles Porter Dickinson. She inherited the Cushing family home at 37 Holt Street upon the death of her father. Dickinson established the Union Aid Home for orphaned children in the Holt Street house.

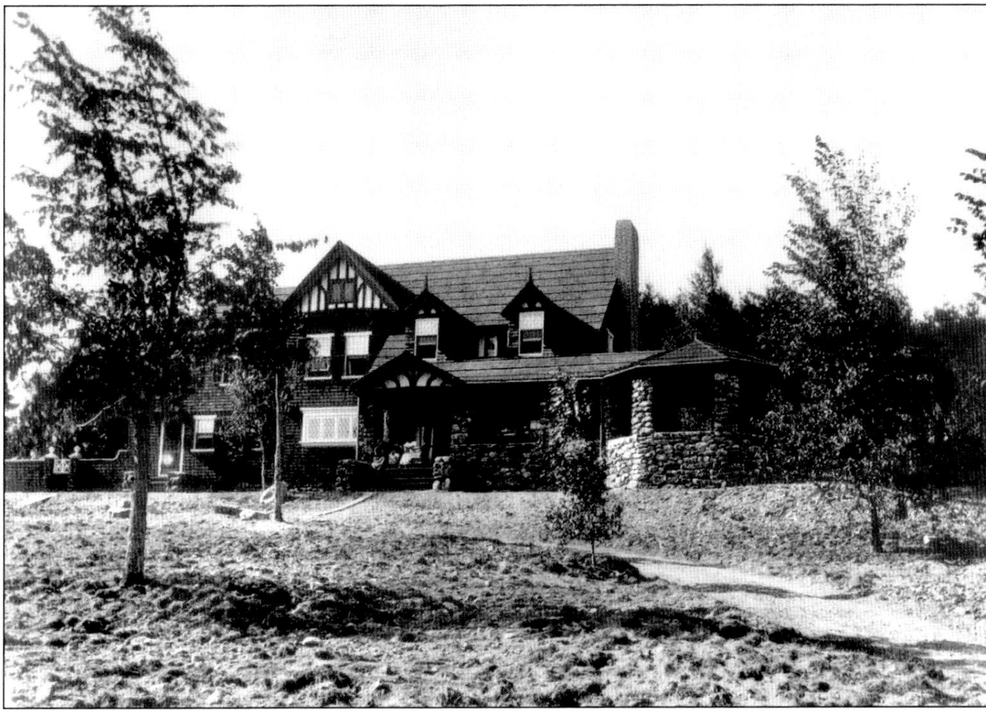

MILTON L. CUSHING. Milton L. Cushing, Joseph Cushing's grandson, bought land from James Garfield at the top of a dirt road called Blossom Street and built this house, which still stands. His family moved in on July 29, 1899. Oscar A. Thayer, an associate of H. M. Francis, was the architect. The home is listed in the Massachusetts Historical Register. Today, deer can be seen roaming the fields behind the house. (Courtesy of Stuart McDermott.)

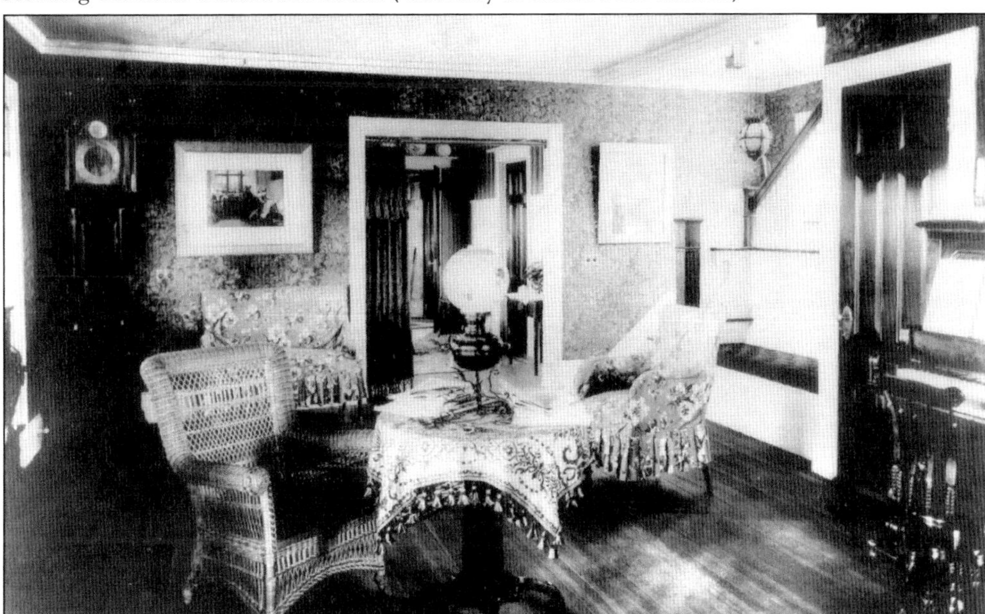

THE CUSHING PARLOR. This 1905 photograph shows the parlor of the Cushing residence. (Courtesy of Stuart McDermott.)

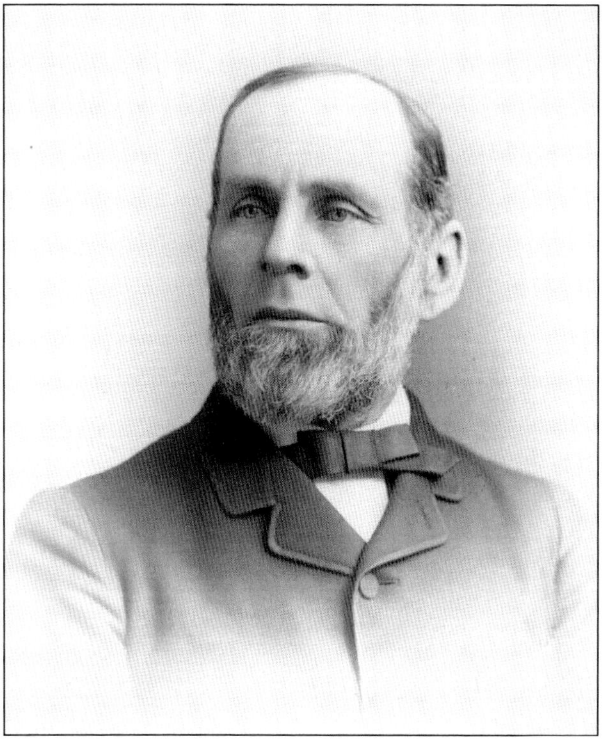

JAMES F. D. GARFIELD. Born in 1828 in New Hampshire, James F. D. Garfield, seen here in 1887, was a founder of the Fitchburg Historical Society, and for a time he was publisher of the *Fitchburg Sentinel*. A distant cousin of Pres. James Garfield, James F. D. Garfield collected presidential signatures, which are now in the Fitchburg Historical Society's collection. He died in 1911.

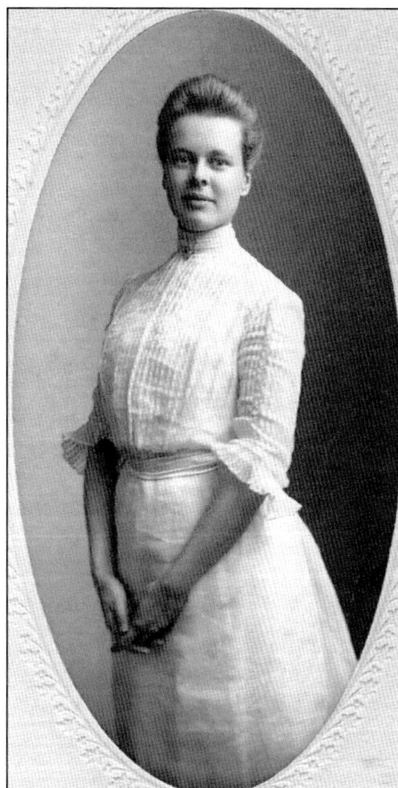

THERESA GARFIELD. Theresa Garfield (1879–1972) was a young girl of 13 when the Fitchburg Historical Society was begun at her father's home on the night of February 3, 1892. Her father passed away just before the opening of the society's new building on Grove Street in 1912. Theresa took over her father's post as librarian that year, and she remained the overseer of the society's collection for the next 60 years.

JOSEPH EDGERLY. Joseph Edgerly spent 47 years in education. He championed the establishment of the Fitchburg Normal School, now Fitchburg State College, in 1894. After graduating from Dartmouth in 1867, he became superintendent of schools in Manchester, New Hampshire. In 1875, he was hired for the position of superintendent of schools in Fitchburg, a job that he held until his retirement in 1910. He died at his Atlantic Avenue home in 1922.

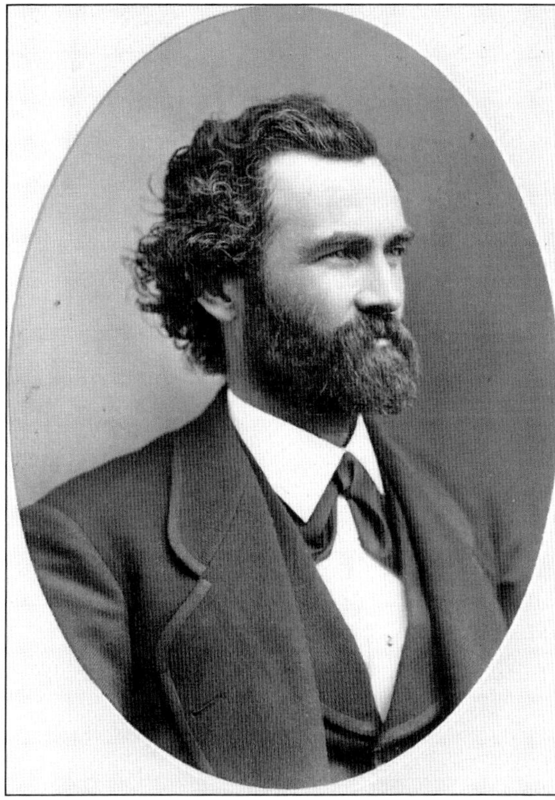

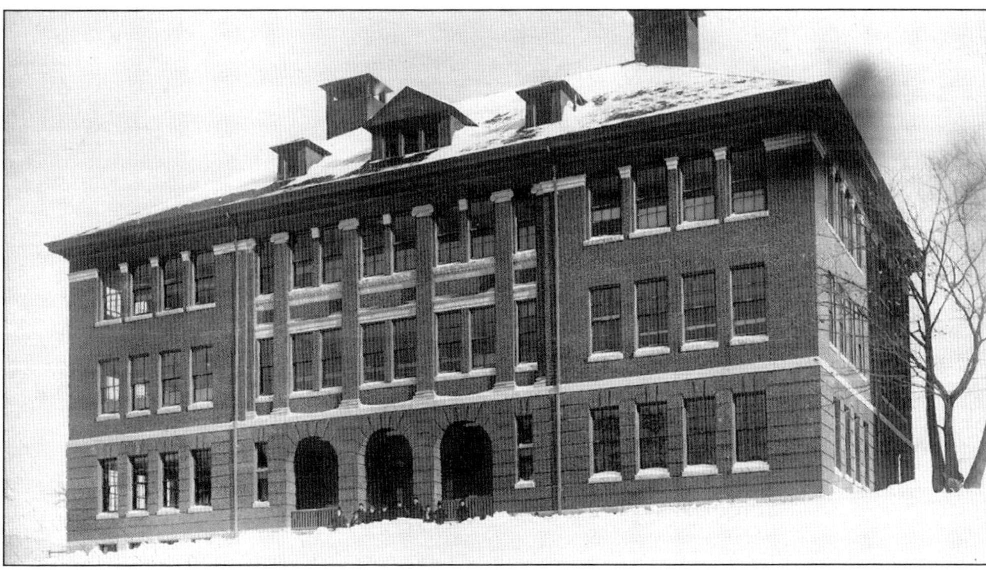

THE EDGERLY BUILDING. Joseph Edgerly realized that there was a shortage of qualified teachers in the educational system. He believed that there should be more formal training for teachers, and to that end he lobbied hard for a normal school to be located in Fitchburg. There were five other normal schools in the state, and most graduates preferred to stay in the communities in which they were trained. The second building constructed at the Fitchburg Normal School was named in his honor.

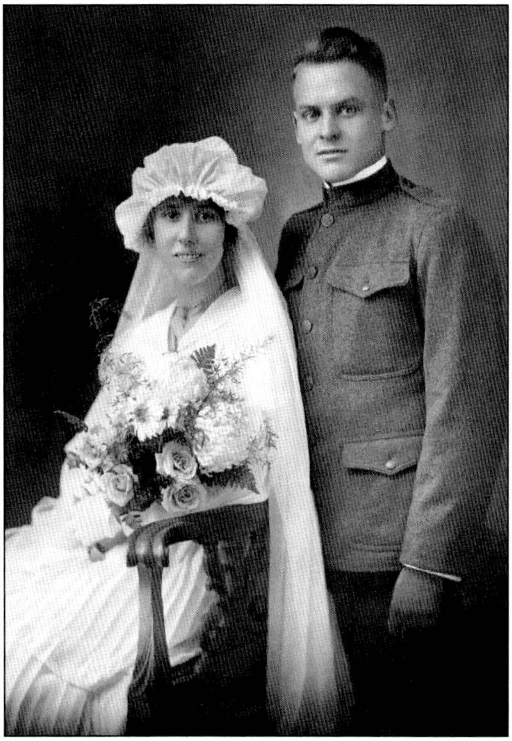

LOUIS P. BOIVIN AND FLORIDA DELODGE BOIVIN. The October 29, 1917, nuptials of Louis "Drinkwine" Boivin and his bride, Florida DeLodge, was one of the city's most prominent weddings of the season. Nearly the entire World War I Company M of the Fifth Massachusetts Infantry attended the wedding at Immaculate Conception and the home reception at 436 Fifth Mass Turnpike. That house has remained in family hands from 1780 to the present. (Courtesy of Hillary Keating.)

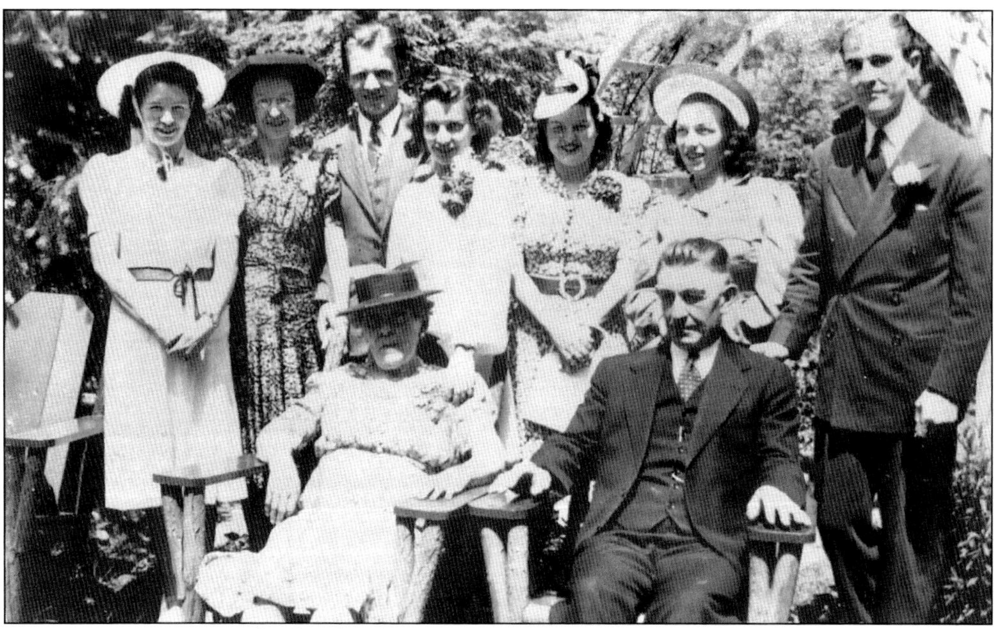

GERALD P. LOMBARD. The family of state representative Gerald P. Lombard gathers for a family wedding photograph sometime during the 1940s. Lombard (on the far right) served as a pilot in World War II; he was shot down and was a prisoner of war for 14 months. He later received the Distinguished Flying Cross. Lombard served as a state representative for 32 years. (Courtesy of Nancy Chrostowski.)

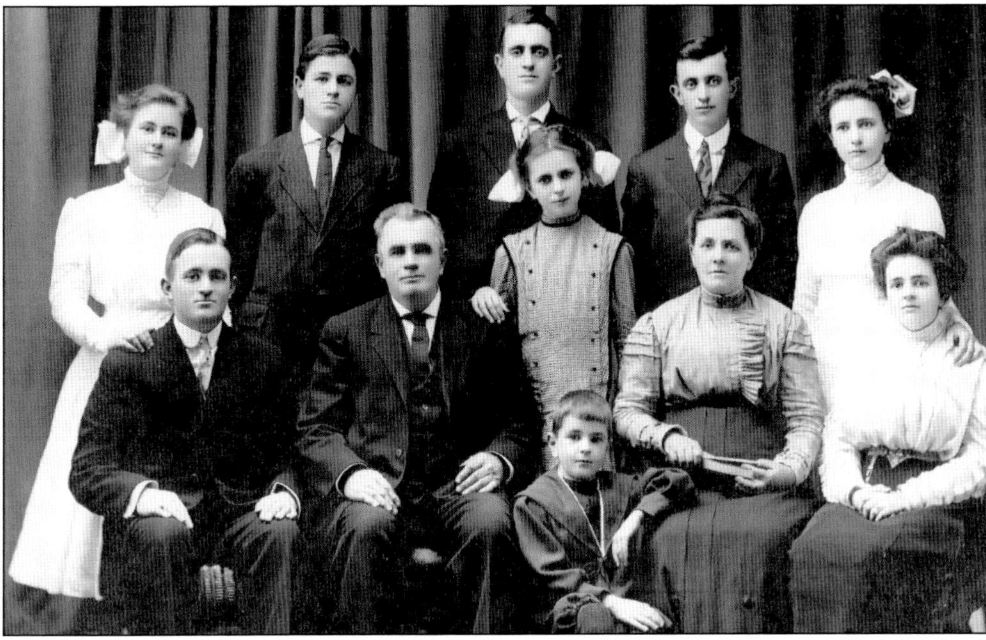

THE BEAUCHEMIN FAMILY. Pierre and Exilda Beauchemin were married in Woonsocket, Rhode Island, in 1881. Shortly thereafter, they moved to Fitchburg, where their nine children were born. In 1910, the family gathered for a photograph. Seen here, from left to right, are the following: (seated) Wilfred, Pierre, George, Exilda, and Aurore; (standing) Germaine, Hector, Joseph, Aldei, and Albanie. Cecile is standing behind George. Aldei was the first secretary and treasurer of the Immaculate Conception (IC) Credit Union, founded in 1928. (Courtesy of Anne Beauchemin.)

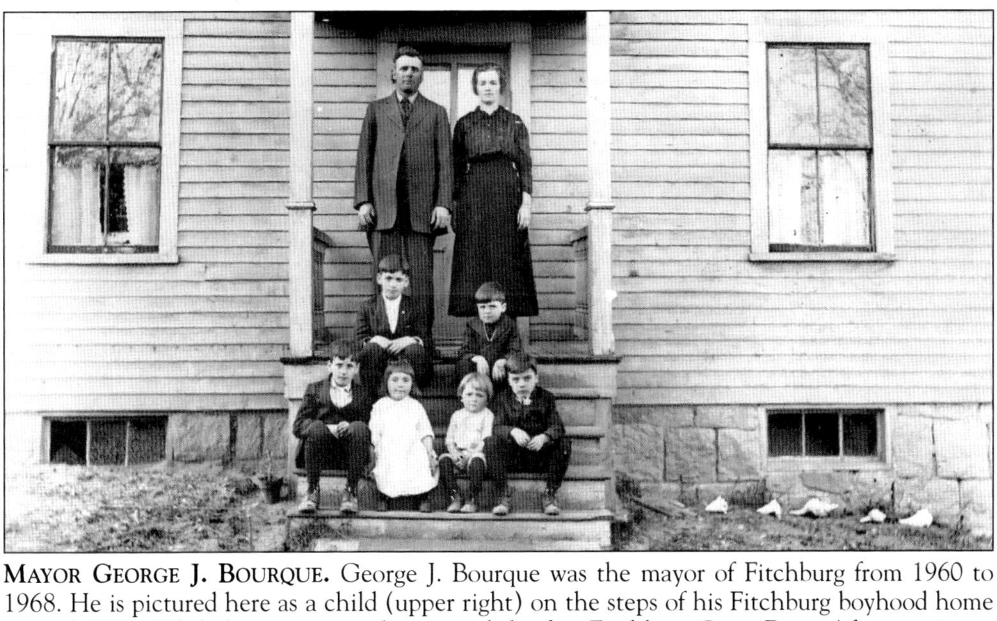

MAYOR GEORGE J. BOURQUE. George J. Bourque was the mayor of Fitchburg from 1960 to 1968. He is pictured here as a child (upper right) on the steps of his Fitchburg boyhood home around 1918. While he was mayor, he created the first Fitchburg Civic Days. After serving as mayor, Bourque served 11 terms as state representative from the third district of Worcester. He ran for a 12th term in 1990 but was narrowly defeated.

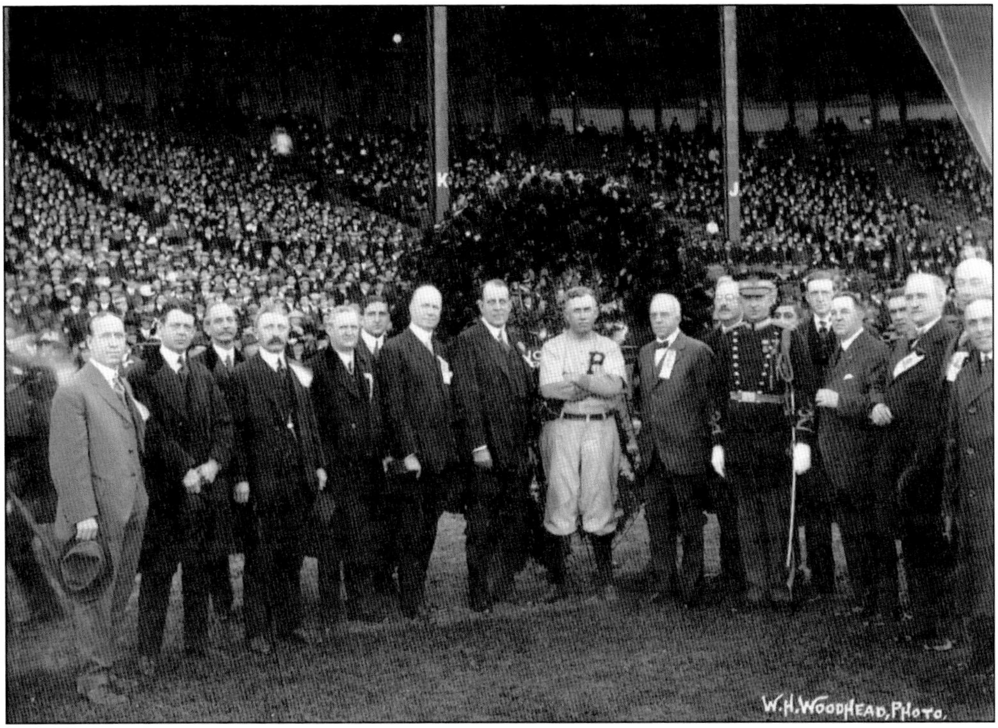

PAT MORAN DAY AT FENWAY PARK. September 29, 1915, was Pat Moran Day at Fenway Park. Born in Fitchburg, Moran played for Boston, Chicago, and Philadelphia teams during his 14-year career. In 1919, he managed the Cincinnati Reds and led them to their first pennant. The Reds were considered underdogs, but they defeated the Chicago White Sox. It was later discovered that eight of the Sox players, including Shoeless Joe Jackson, conspired to throw the World Series.

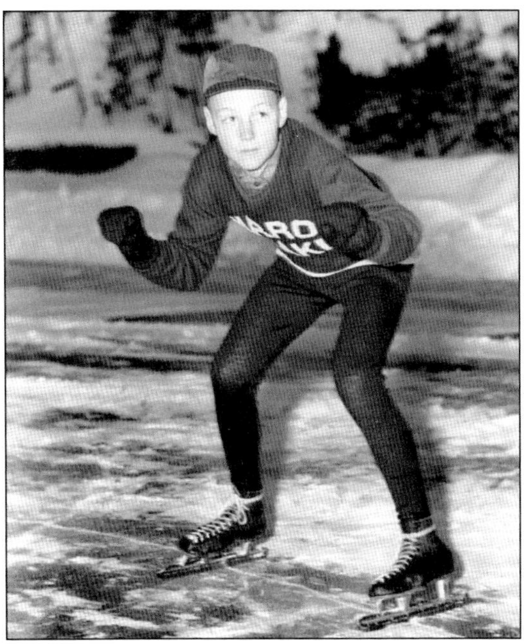

ARTHUR LONGSJO. Arthur Longsjo was the first American to compete in both the Summer and Winter Olympics in the same year. In 1956, Longsjo competed as a member of the U.S. Olympic team in both speed skating and cycling. Longsjo died in a car crash in 1958 at the age of 26. The Arthur Longsjo Memorial Race is a nationally recognized bicycle race that has been held in Fitchburg since 1960. Longsjo was 13 years old when this photograph was taken. (Courtesy of Theresa Longsjo.)

Three

Business and Industry

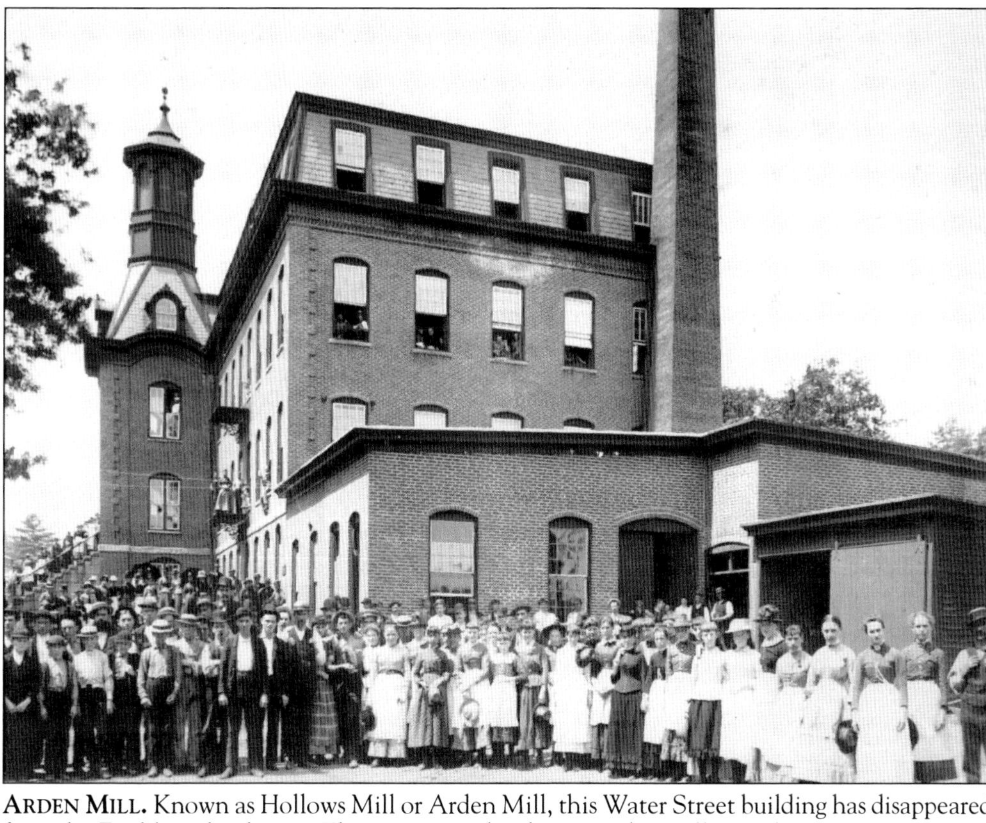

Arden Mill. Known as Hollows Mill or Arden Mill, this Water Street building has disappeared from the Fitchburg landscape. The site was utilized as a woolen mill as early as 1854. American Woolen Company occupied the building from 1900 until the mid-1950s, producing tropical worsted and gabardine for men's clothing. Great American Plastics used the building from 1957 until 1988, when an explosion brought about the company's demise.

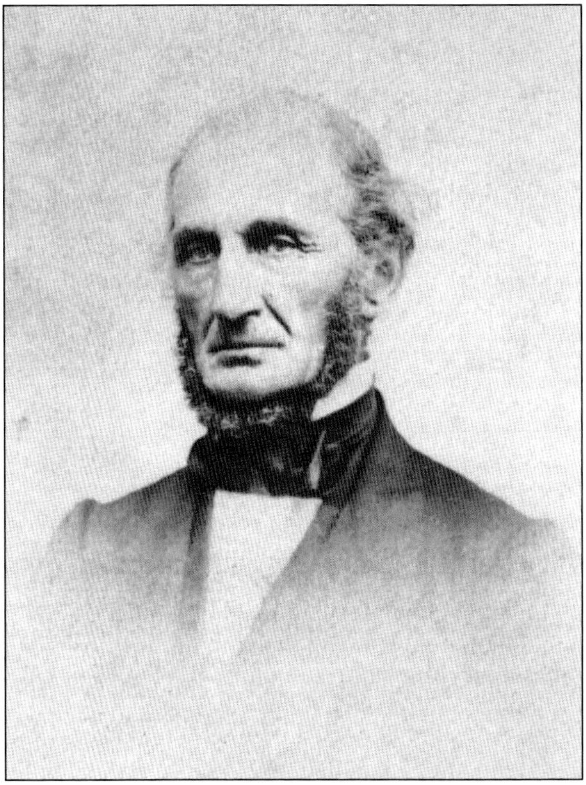

ALVAH CROCKER. Alvah Crocker (1801–1874) became one of Fitchburg's leading citizens. Crocker had a great mind for business, and he established a paper company that brought him immense wealth. He was also a visionary, succeeding in bringing the railroad to Fitchburg and building the Hoosac Tunnel. He served his community as a state legislator, a director of banks and an insurance company, and a benefactor to a church.

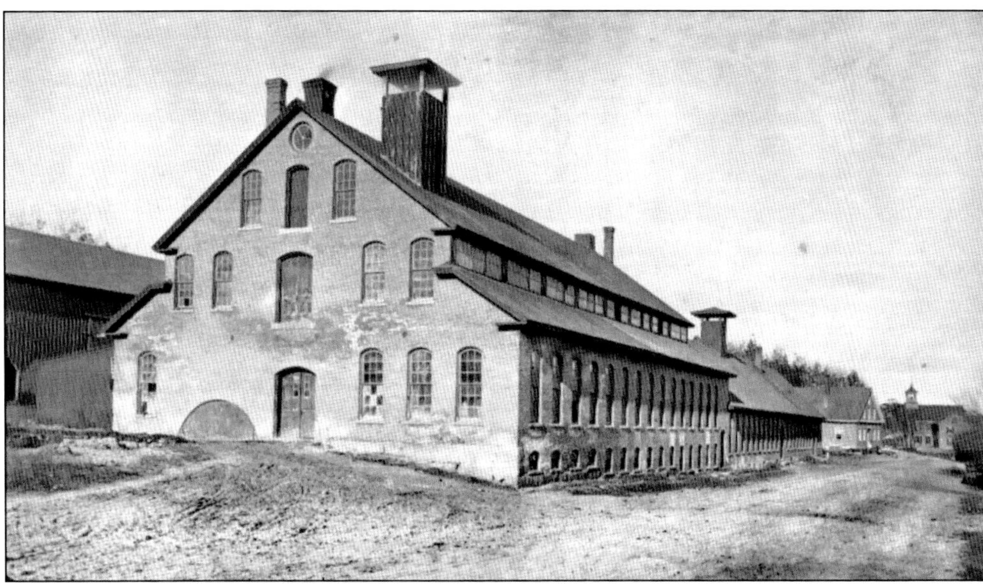

CROCKER, BURBANK AND COMPANY. The Hanna Mill, built in 1852, was one of eight papermills owned by Crocker, Burbank and Company in the 19th century. Alvah Crocker purchased the mill from Samuel Hanna in 1860. By the time of the Civil War, the mill was producing newspaper for the *New York Herald*. The West Fitchburg mill has been torn down and replaced by a pizza parlor.

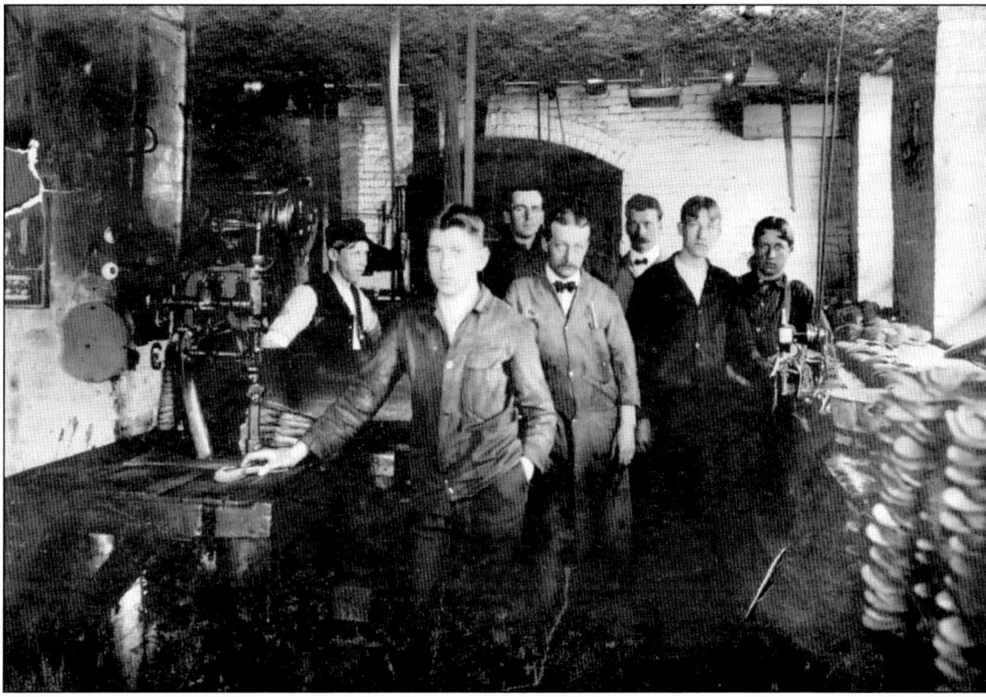

INTERIOR OF A SHOE FACTORY, 1903. Elijah Dickinson brought his shoe manufacturing business to Fitchburg in 1854. He became partners with Edgar Belding in 1880. The factory at North and Main Streets produced 1,200 pairs of shoes daily, which were sold to foreign and domestic markets. Dickinson erected a building on Main and Mill Streets in 1890, and he gave a library to his hometown of Northfield.

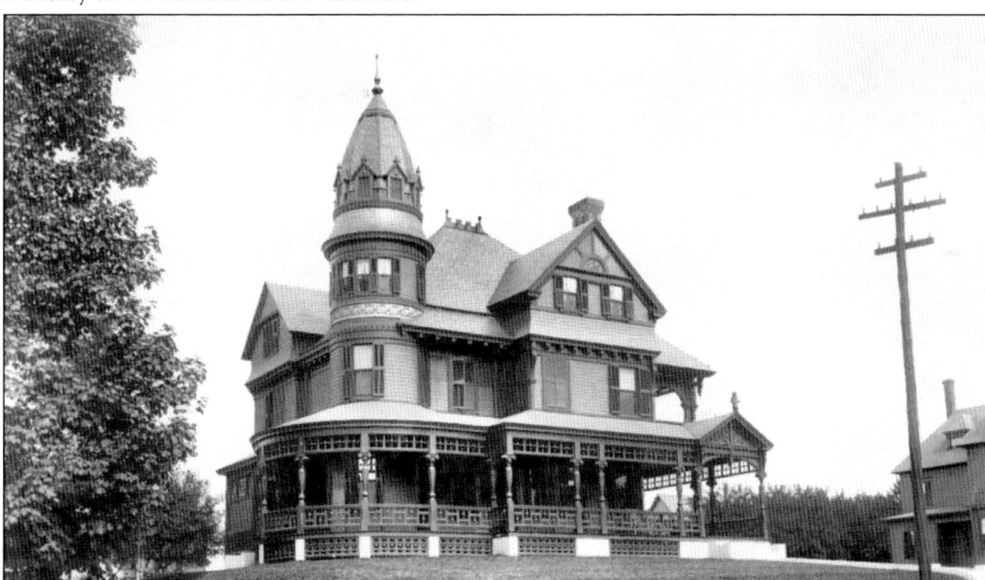

EDGAR BELDING'S HOUSE. H. M. Francis designed Edgar Belding's elegant Queen Anne–style house on Summer Street in 1888. It had elaborate architectural details, a stately tower, and stained-glass windows. It was razed in the 1980s, but its stable still stands on Bluff Avenue.

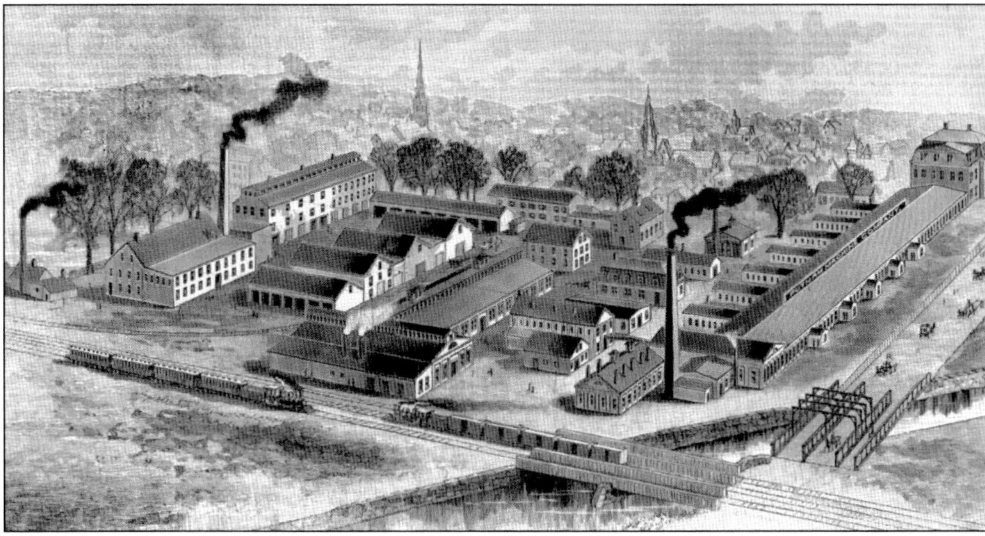

THE PUTNAM MACHINE COMPANY. In the last quarter of the 19th century, the Putnam Machine Company covered a 20-acre site that extended from Main Street to the Nashua River along Putnam Street. The 37,000-square-foot floor space was lighted by 284 windows during the day and 500 gaslights at night. The factory had six miles of steam piping, and the complex contained brass and iron foundries.

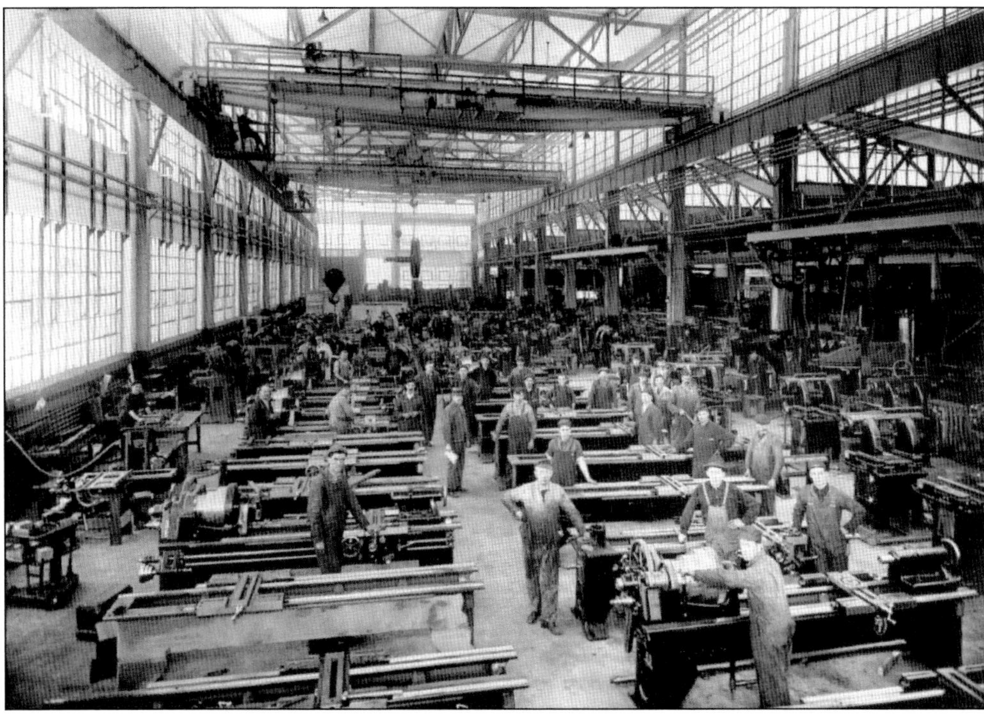

AN INTERIOR VIEW OF MANNING, MAXWELL & MOORE. This is an interior view of the Manning, Maxwell & Moore factory on Broad Street. Manning, Maxwell & Moore absorbed the Putnam Machine Company in October 1913 and immediately designed new machinery that was specially adapted for railroad work. The Fitchburg plant closed in 1930 at the start of the Great Depression.

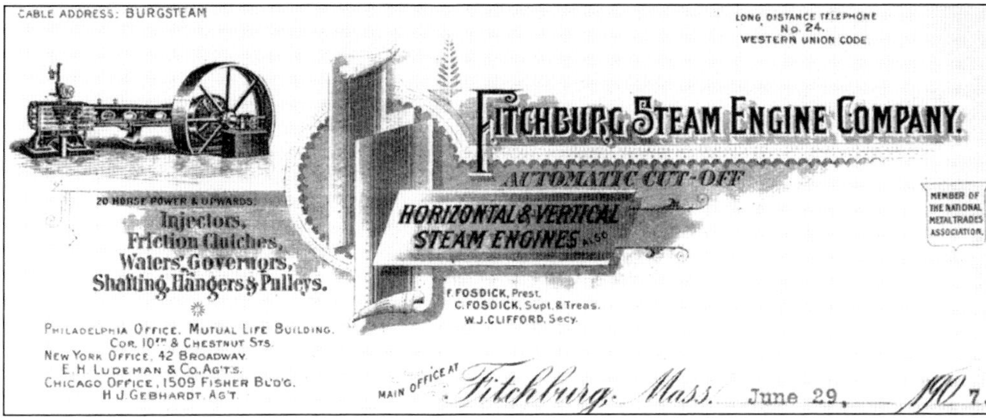

THE FITCHBURG STEAM ENGINE COMPANY. In 1876, Hale W. Page took over the Haskins Steam Engine Company, renaming it the Fitchburg Steam Engine Company. The company's steam engines supplied power to the machinery of papermills, textile factories, and shoe factories, and they generated electricity for hotels and libraries. Electrical power eventually overtook steam, and the company folded in 1929. This billhead is from 1907.

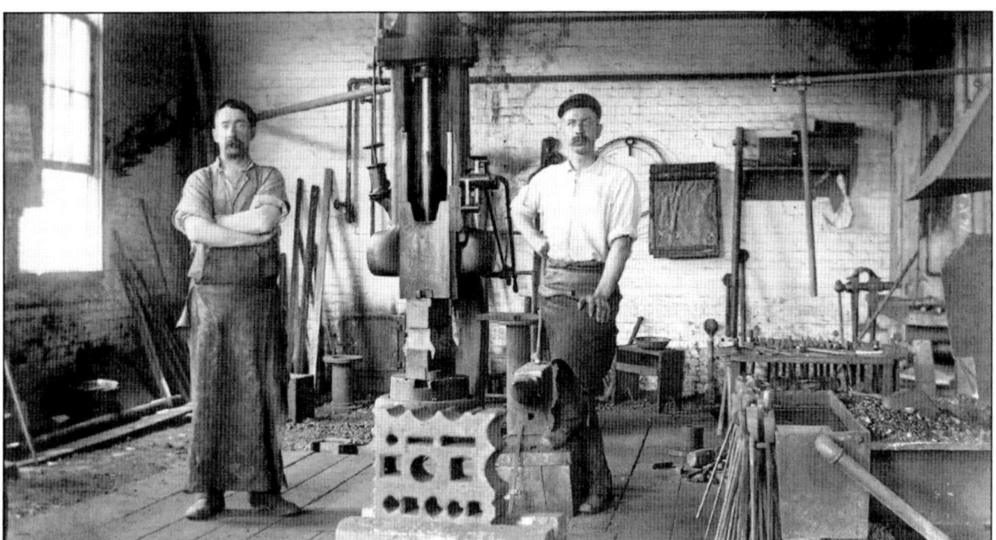

BLACKSMITHS AT THE FITCHBURG STEAM ENGINE COMPANY. Pictured here in 1892 is a blacksmith shop owned by the Fitchburg Steam Engine Company. The blacksmiths are C. E. Taylor and Joseph Bray.

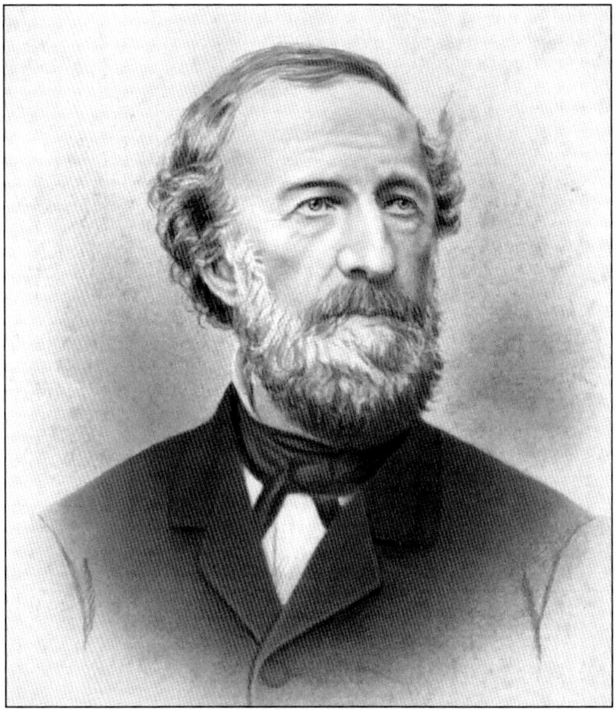

WALTER HEYWOOD. Walter Heywood and his four brothers learned to make chairs by hand in their father's barn. Heywood Manufacturing, on Water Street, produced 500 chairs a day using machine technology during the height of the industrial age.

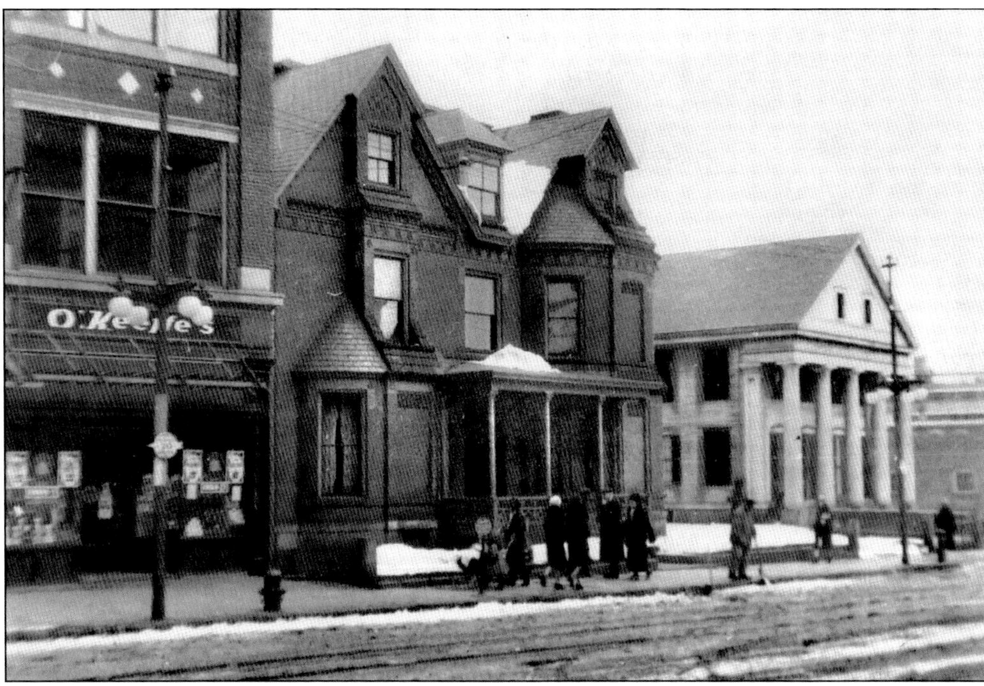

WALTER HEYWOOD'S HOME ON MAIN STREET. Heywood was a wealthy man, and his elegant white home graced Main Street, not far from his factories. In 1927, the house was demolished, and the area became the site of the Fitchburg Theater (now closed). The brown house to the left of Heywood's home was moved to Elm Street and is now the Sawyer-Miller Masciarelli Funeral Home.

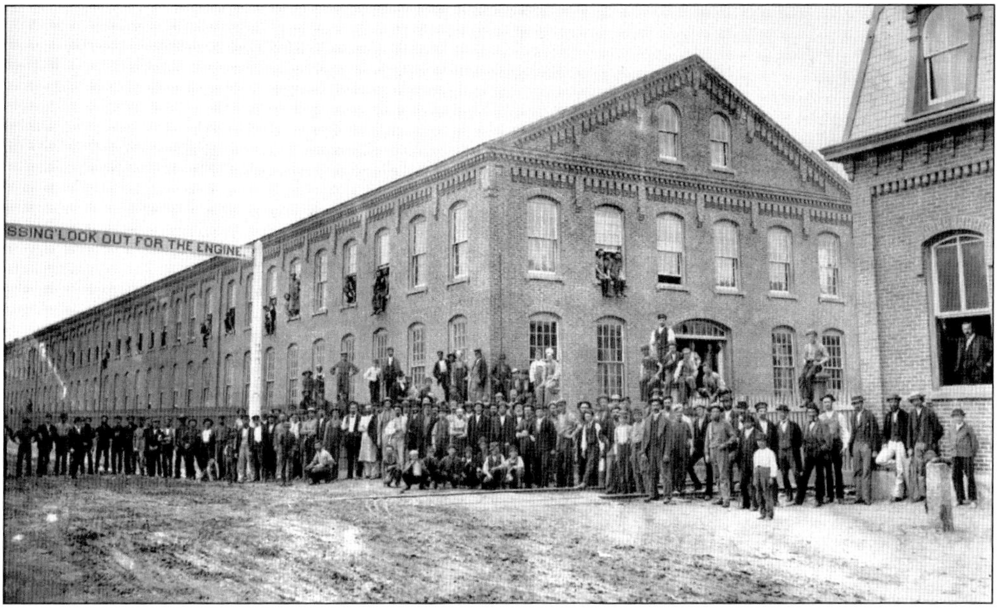

THE WALTER HEYWOOD CHAIR FACTORY ON RIVER STREET. Walter Heywood left Gardner's Heywood-Wakefield chair manufacturers, the business he had started with his brothers, in 1841. He began his own chair company in Fitchburg, and by 1856 his chairs were being sold worldwide. After several fires destroyed his other business locations, Heywood built a factory on River Street in 1870.

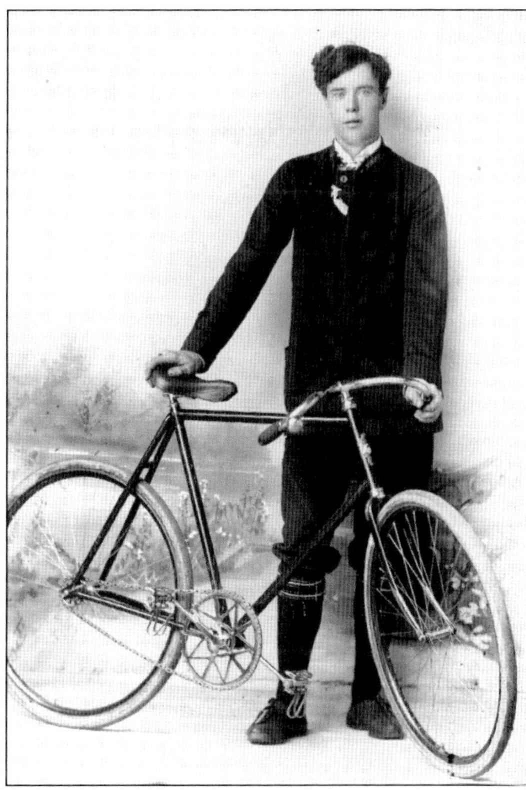

IVER JOHNSON'S ARMS AND CYCLE WORKS BICYCLE. Iver Johnson's Arms and Cycle Works moved from Worcester to the vacant Heywood factory in 1891. This young man's bicycle is a "gentlemen's roadster" made by Iver Johnson's Arms and Cycle Works in 1898. World War II brought an end to the company's bicycle production in 1941. (Courtesy of Barbara Edsall.)

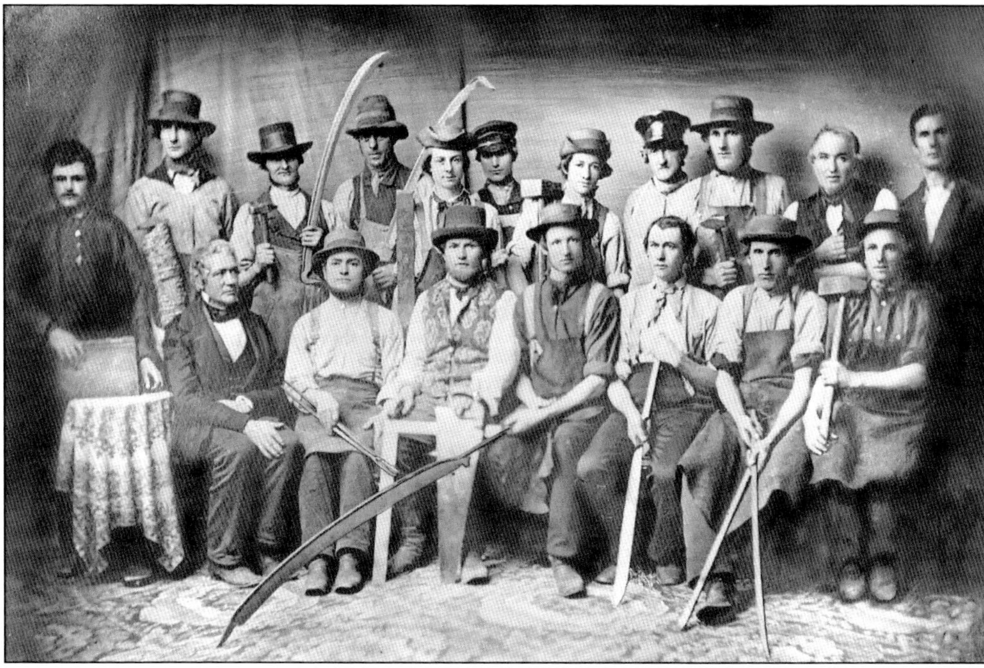

ABEL SIMONDS. Abel Simonds (at left in the front row) poses here with his employees in 1850. Abel started manufacturing scythes in 1832 under the name J. T. Farwell Company. During the Civil War, the company name was changed to Simonds Brothers and Company, and the company began making knives and reaper sections.

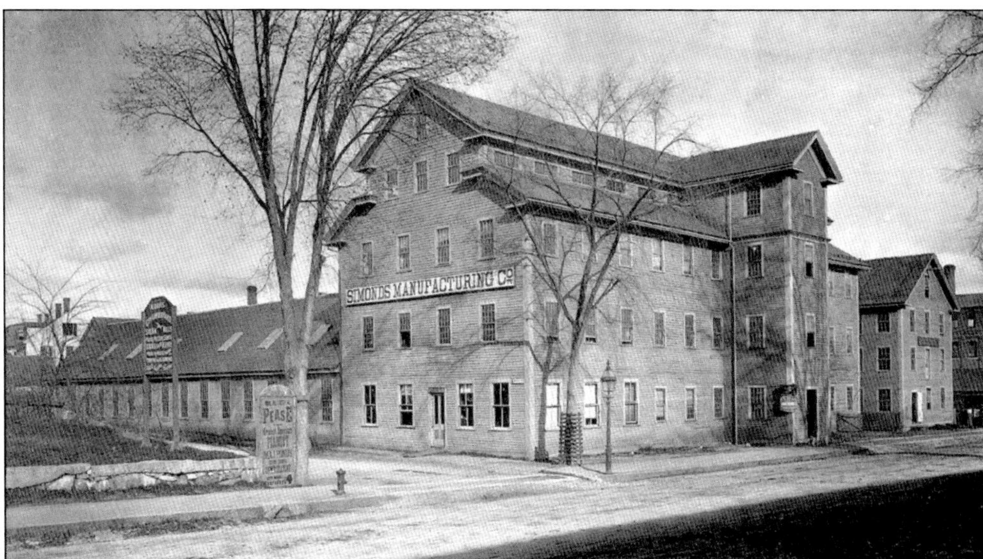

SIMONDS MANUFACTURING COMPANY. In 1868, the company moved to North Street and changed its name to Simonds Manufacturing Company. A few years later, the company began to produce cross-cut, band, and hand saws.

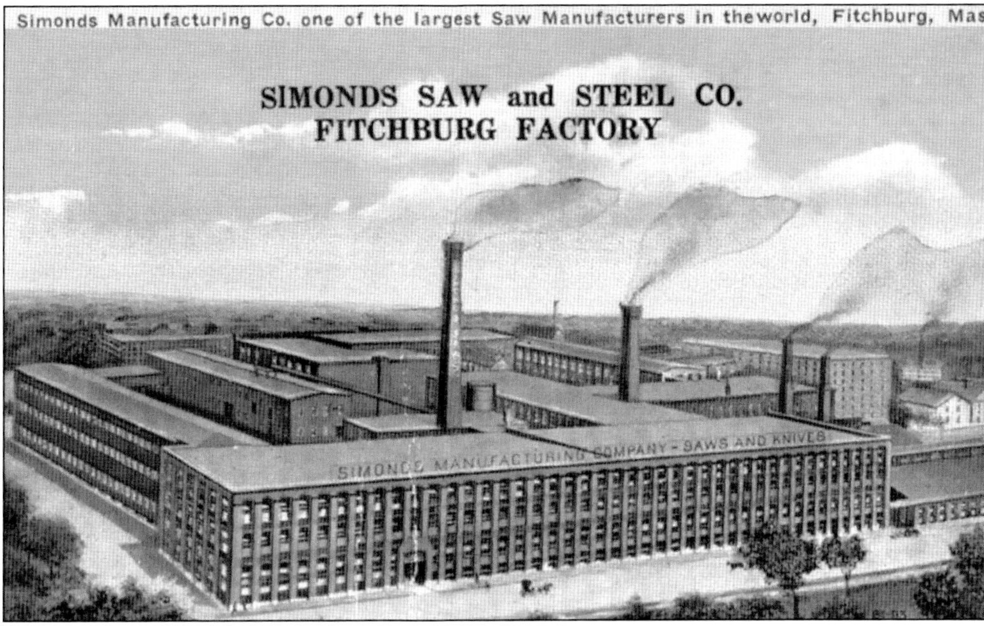

SIMONDS SAW AND STEEL COMPANY. In 1922, the company name was changed to Simonds Saw and Steel Company. A vintage postcard shows the large factory on Main and North Streets. Today it is the location of the Fitchburg Fire Department and retail businesses. Abel Simonds would be pleased to know that his business still exists, although it is no longer family owned. The company was sold in 1965 to the Wallace Murray Corporation.

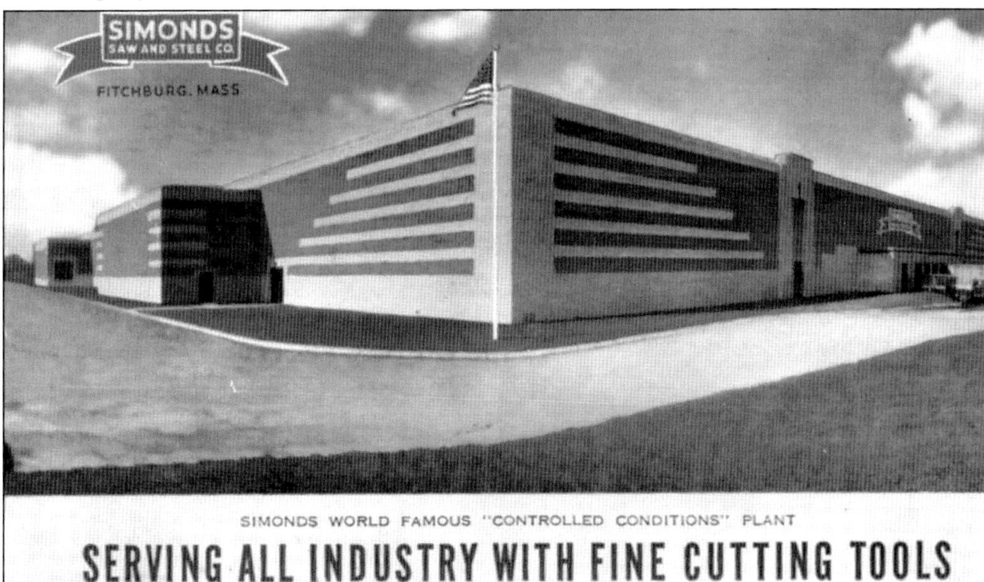

THE FIRST WINDOWLESS FACTORY. The Simonds Saw and Steel Company made architectural history when it built a windowless factory on Bemis Road in 1929. It was the first single-level factory anywhere in the world that encompassed five acres of floor space, was completely air-conditioned, and was artificially lit without a single window. It was a radical design at the time, and many businessmen questioned its workability. Today, Simonds products are still made at the windowless factory.

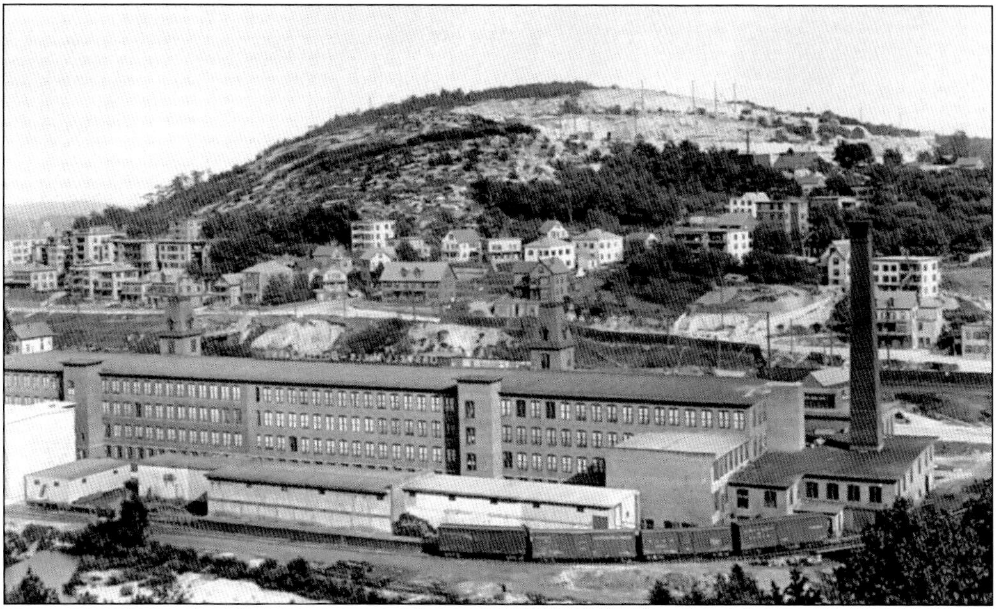

ORSWELL MILLS AND ROLLSTONE HILL. This postcard from the turn of the century shows the Orswell Mills on River Street in the foreground and Rollstone Hill in the background. The bare patch on the hill is the Rollstone Quarry. The Irish were the first ethnic group employed at the quarry. Later the Finns and the Italians worked the hilltop until the quarry closed in 1941.

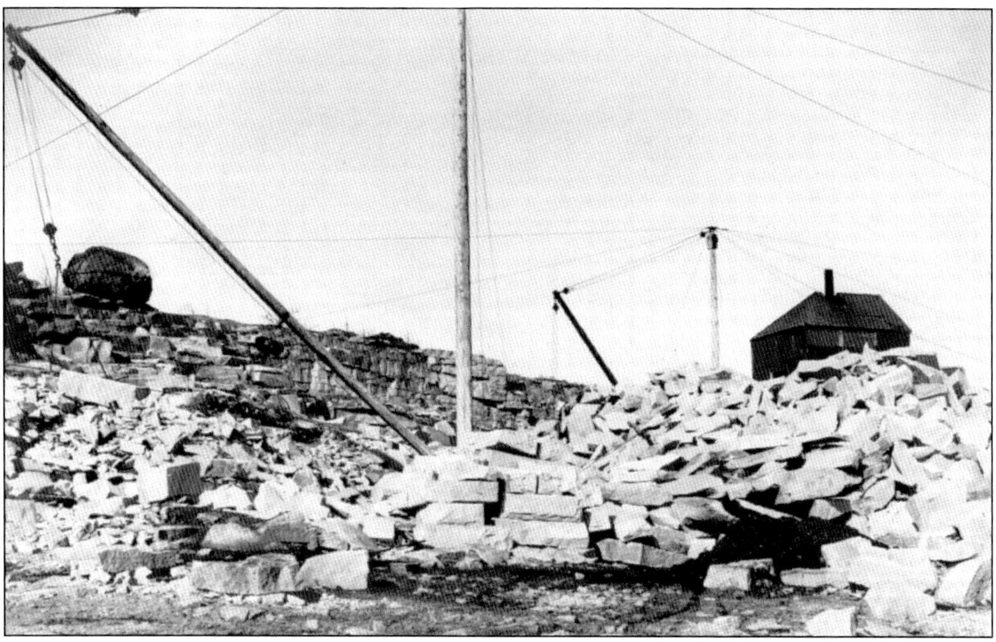

ROLLSTONE HILL. Granite quarried from Rollstone Hill was sold locally and nationally in the 19th and early 20th centuries. The First Parish Church, built in 1837, features Doric columns hewn from 20-ton blocks of Rollstone granite. The stone was also used in five bridges that cross the Hudson River, including the George Washington Bridge. The city of Fitchburg employed masons to build bridges over the Nashua River and retaining walls for hillside streets using Rollstone granite. Note the Rollstone Boulder to the left.

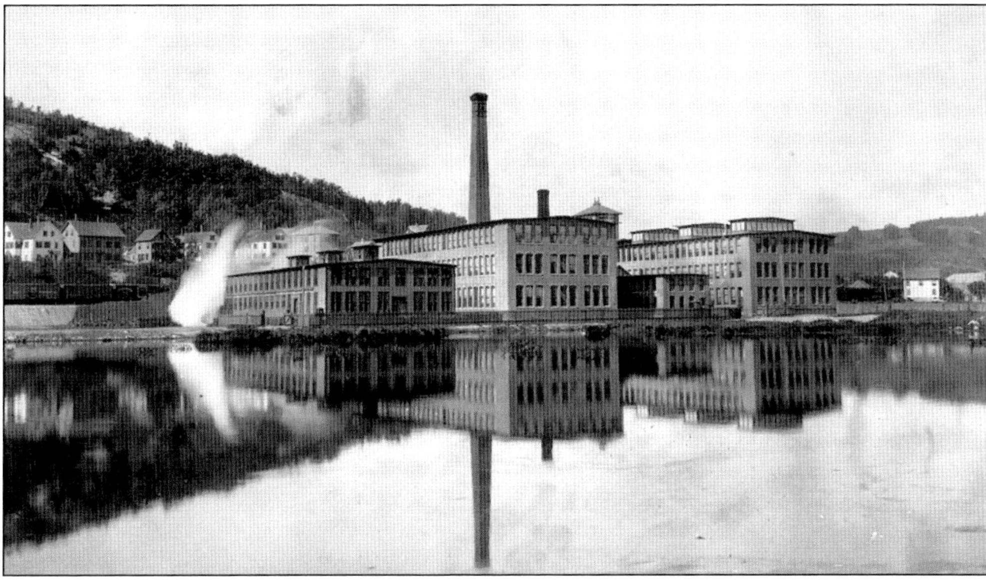

PARKHILL MANUFACTURING COMPANY. By 1907, textile manufacturing was Fitchburg's largest industry. John Parkhill purchased the Alonzo Davis Chair Factory in 1879 and began making fine ginghams. In the early 1880s, the company had 40 looms; by the 1890s, it had 4,000 looms.

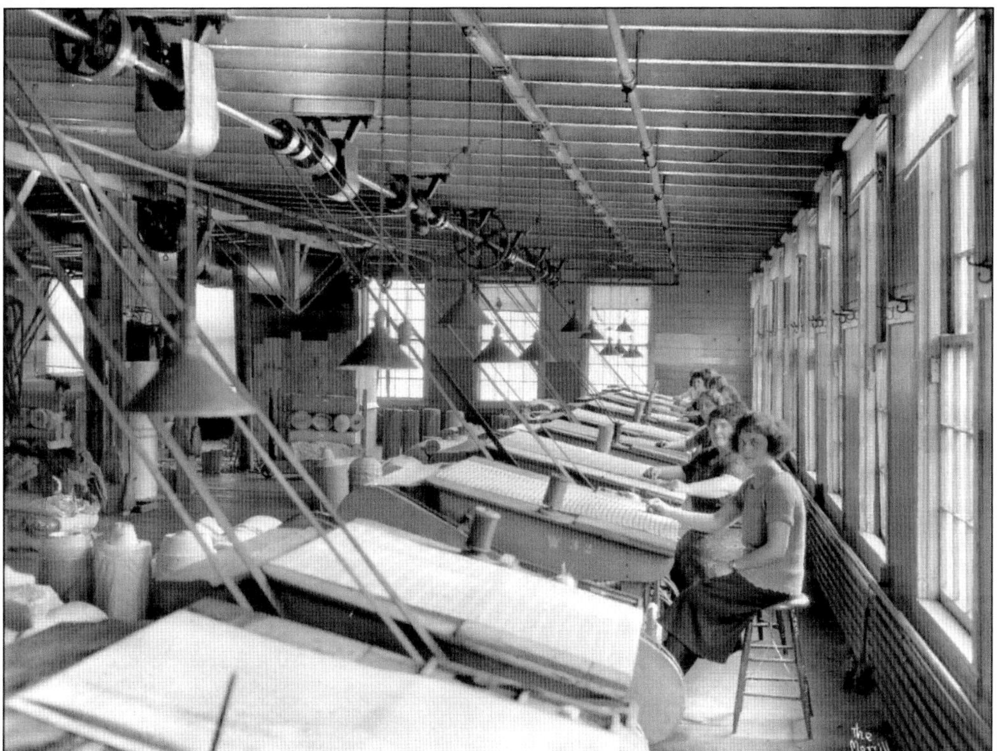

INSPECTING CLOTH AT PARKHILL MANUFACTURING COMPANY. These young ladies are inspecting cloth in the Parkhill mill. In the early years of the 20th century, the company had the largest payroll in the city.

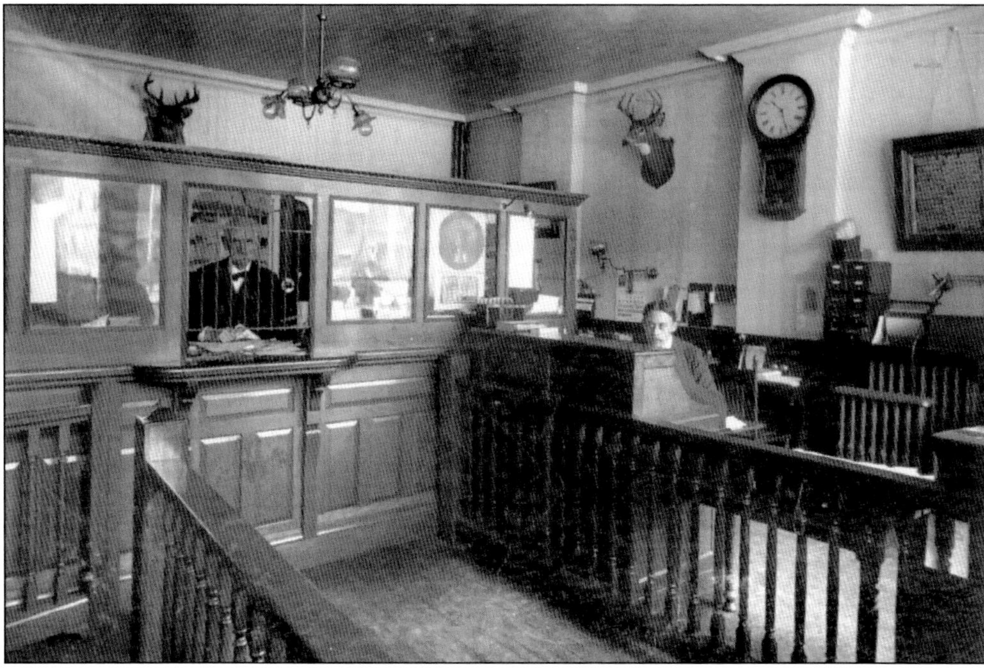

THE *FITCHBURG SENTINEL*. The *Fitchburg Sentinel* began publication in 1838. It published an average of 5,052 copies per day in 1912, when this photograph was taken. Subscription rates were $5.00 per year. This image shows the business office of the newspaper.

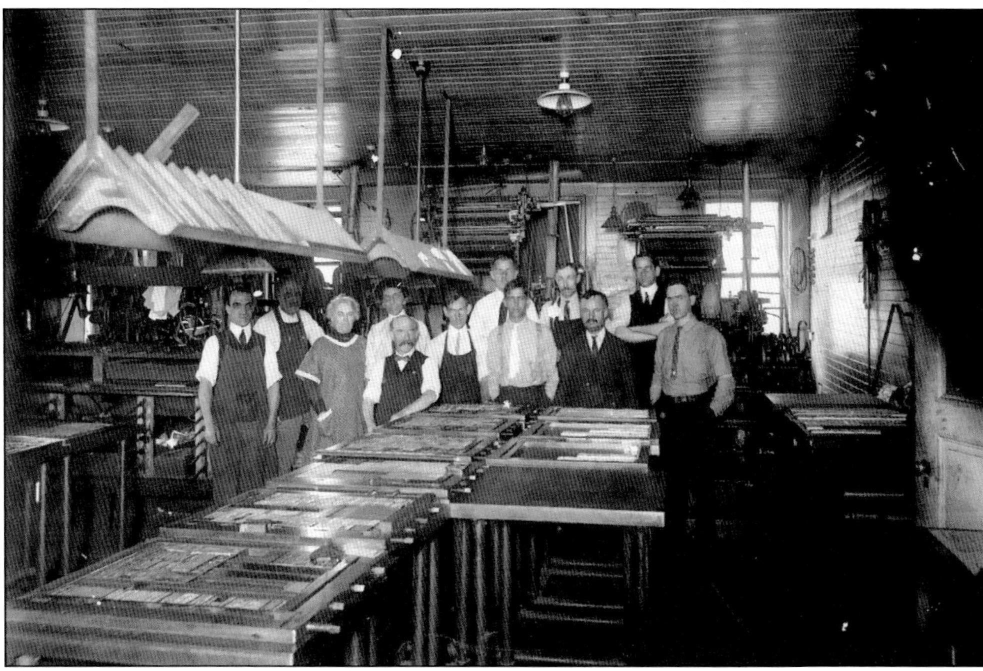

THE *FITCHBURG SENTINEL* COMPOSING ROOM. These employees are, from left to right, as follows: (first row) David Wood, George F. Bills (foreman), Mary Jacquith, Mabel Morse, William F. Lawrence, Andrew Tate, George W. Smith, Herbert L. Hill, and R. Stanley Pearson; (second row) Thomas Hannan, Edward Watson, and William F. Byrnes.

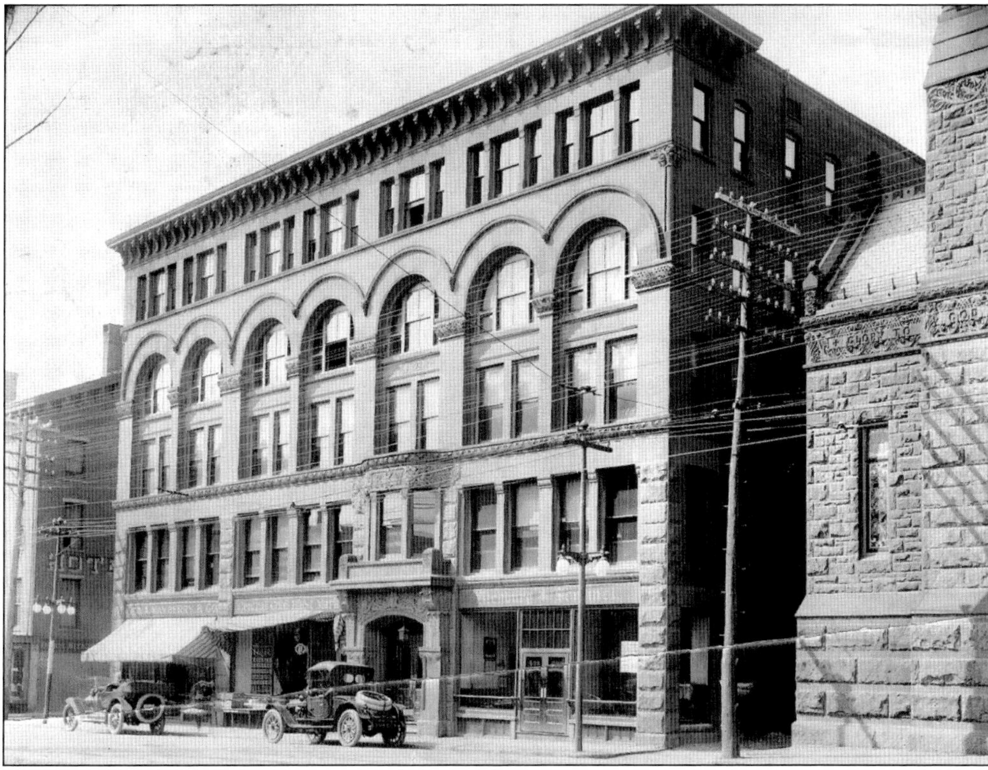

THE WALLACE BUILDING. Rodney Wallace commissioned H. M. Francis to build the Wallace Building in 1893. The building was later razed and is now the site of the Fitchburg Sentinel and Enterprise office building.

THE FITCHBURG ATHLETIC CLUB. The Fitchburg Athletic Club constructed its Wallace Avenue building in 1891. The club roster contained the elite of the city. By 1905, the club was renting the building to Dawson Business College. The *Raivaaja*, a Finnish newspaper, occupied the building from 1911 until its demolition in 1972. The Worker's Credit Union's original home was on the first floor of the building.

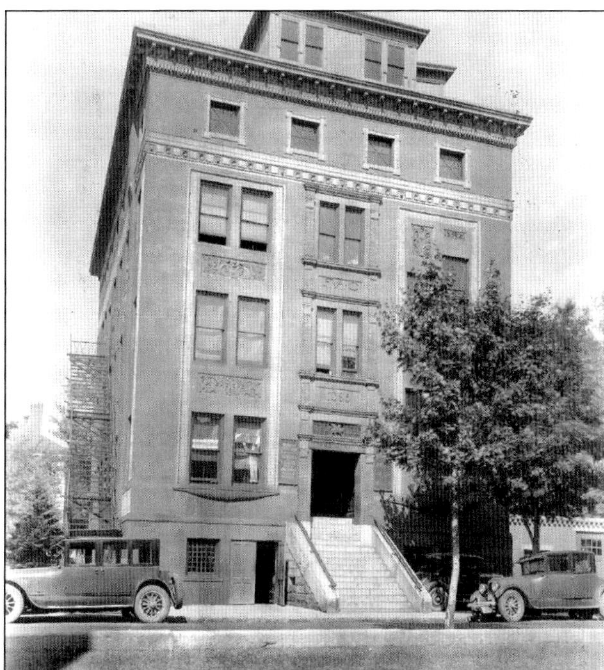

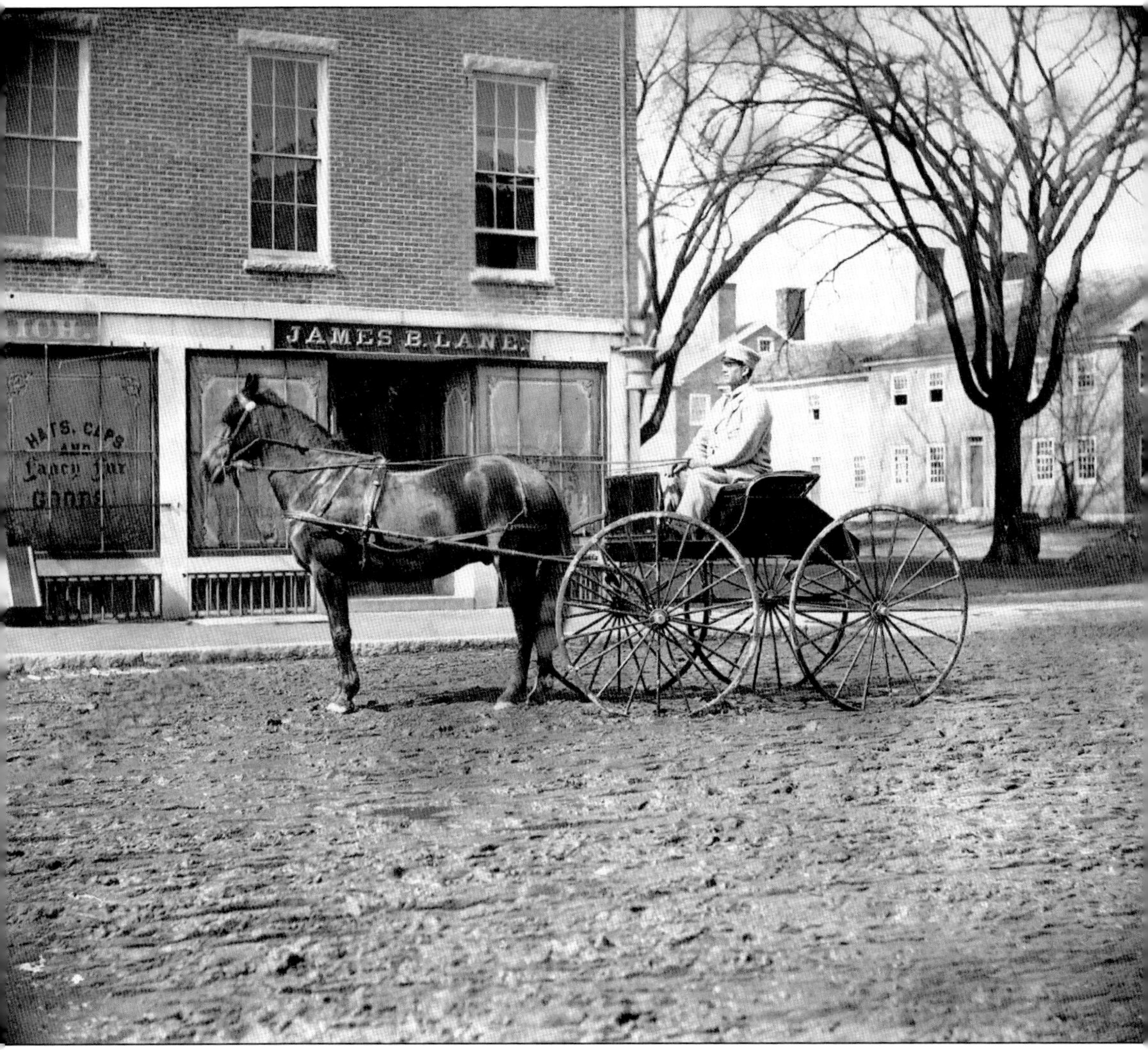

THE LANE DRUGSTORE. This drugstore was at the corner of Factory Square in the area of the present-day Fitchburg Savings Bank. The man sitting in the buggy is unidentified, but he may be a deliveryman for the James B. Lane Drug Store. Note the mortar and pestle sign hanging at the corner of the building.

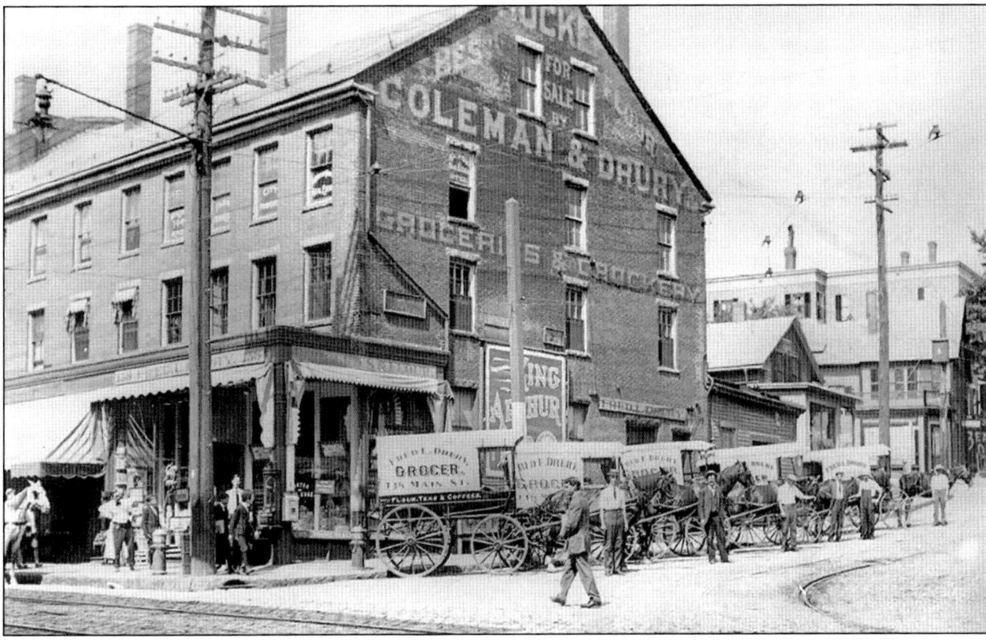

COLEMAN AND DRURY GROCERS. In 1891, Coleman and Drury bought the largest grocery store in town from W. P. Guy. Known for its groceries, crockery, silver-plated tin, and woodenware, the business thrived at the corner of Blossom and Main Streets. The market and its fleet of horse-drawn wagons moved to the Upper Common after Fred Drury bought out his partner. The store was still well known five decades later for its imported biscuits, teas, and Scotch kisses.

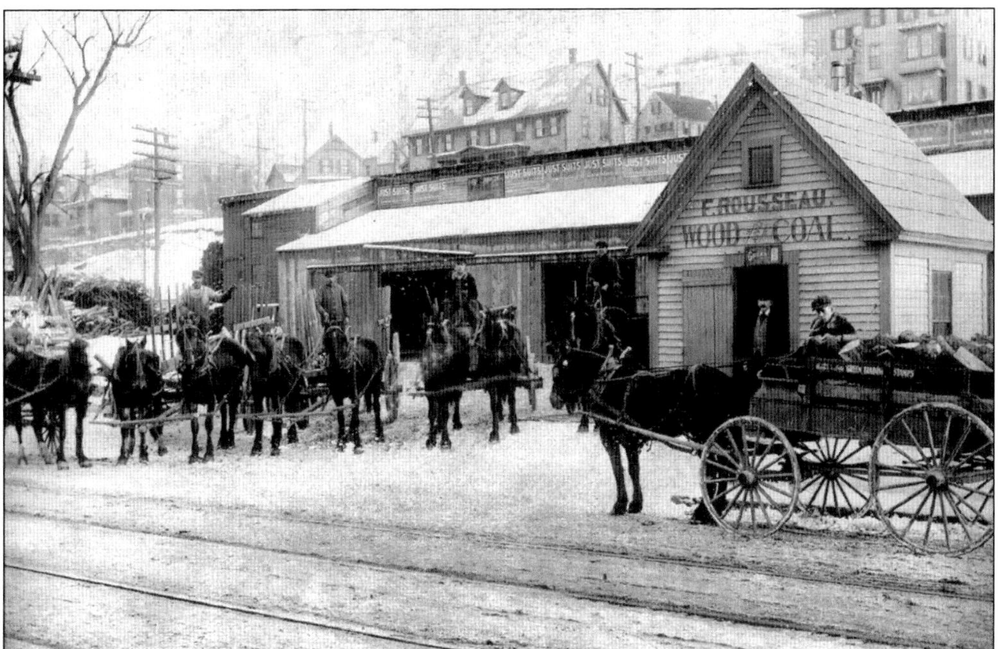

FERDINAND ROUSSEAU'S WOOD AND COAL YARD. Rousseau was one of the city's many dealers in coal and wood in the early part of the 20th century. His business was located on River Street opposite Orswell Mills, now the Premier Box Company.

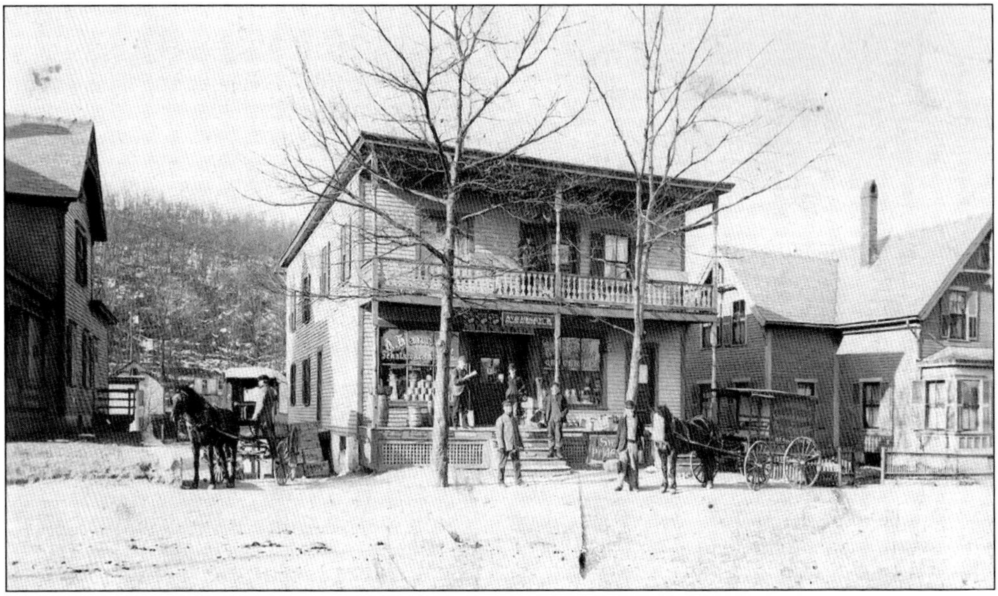

HANNULA'S GROCERY. Grocery stores serving different ethnic groups flourished at the beginning of the 20th century in Fitchburg. There was an Italian store, a German store, and three Finnish stores selling meats, staples, and ethnic specialty foods. They also sold steamship tickets. Andre Hannula's grocery, shown in this photograph, was at 157 Rollstone Street.

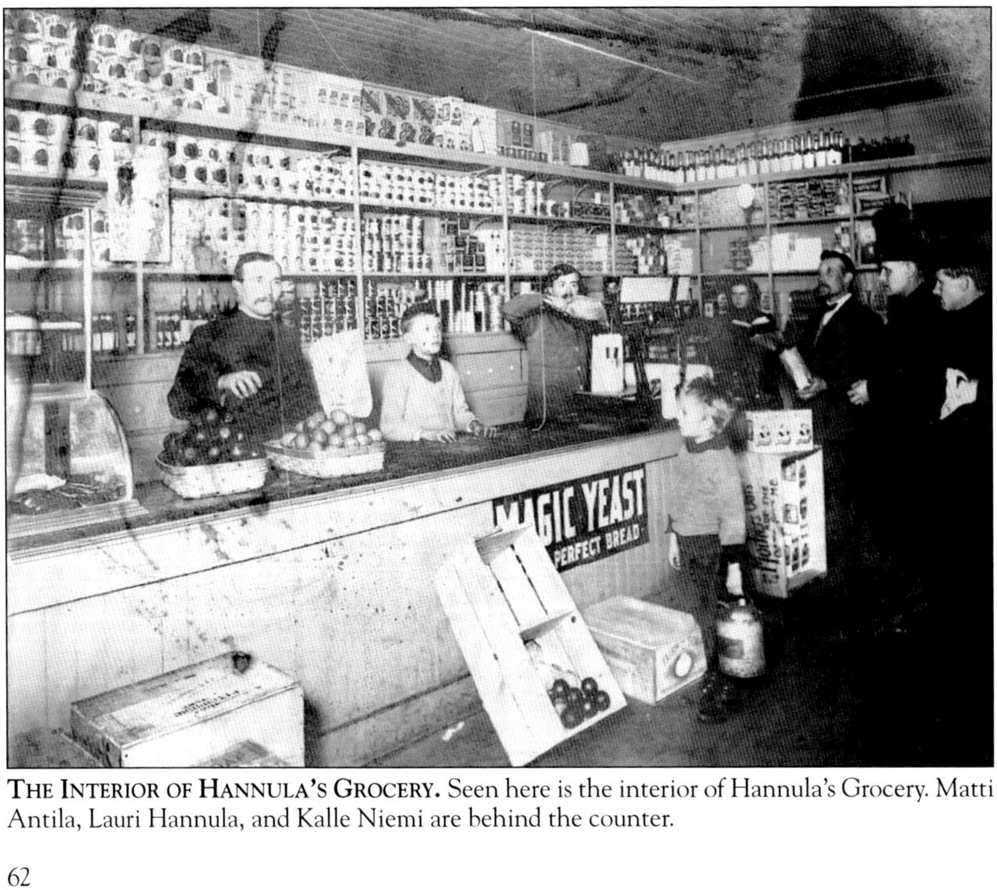

THE INTERIOR OF HANNULA'S GROCERY. Seen here is the interior of Hannula's Grocery. Matti Antila, Lauri Hannula, and Kalle Niemi are behind the counter.

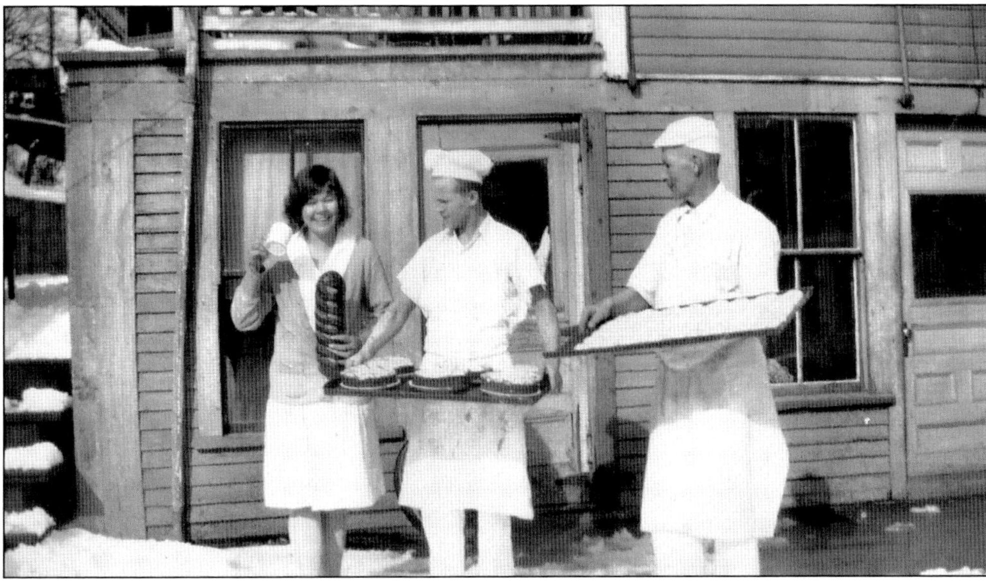

THE HIGH STREET BAKERY, 1930. Vieno Koski Linnus, Urho Lehtonen, and Antti (Andrew) Siitonen of the Finnish-owned High Street Bakery are seen here around 1930. Linnus holds a loaf of "Kahvileipa," Finnish coffee bread. Lehtonen has a tray of "Reikleipa" or "hole bread," rye bread made with a hole in the middle. Siitonen has raspberry jelly doughnuts. The bakery delivered goods all over New England and sold flour to those who could not afford bread.

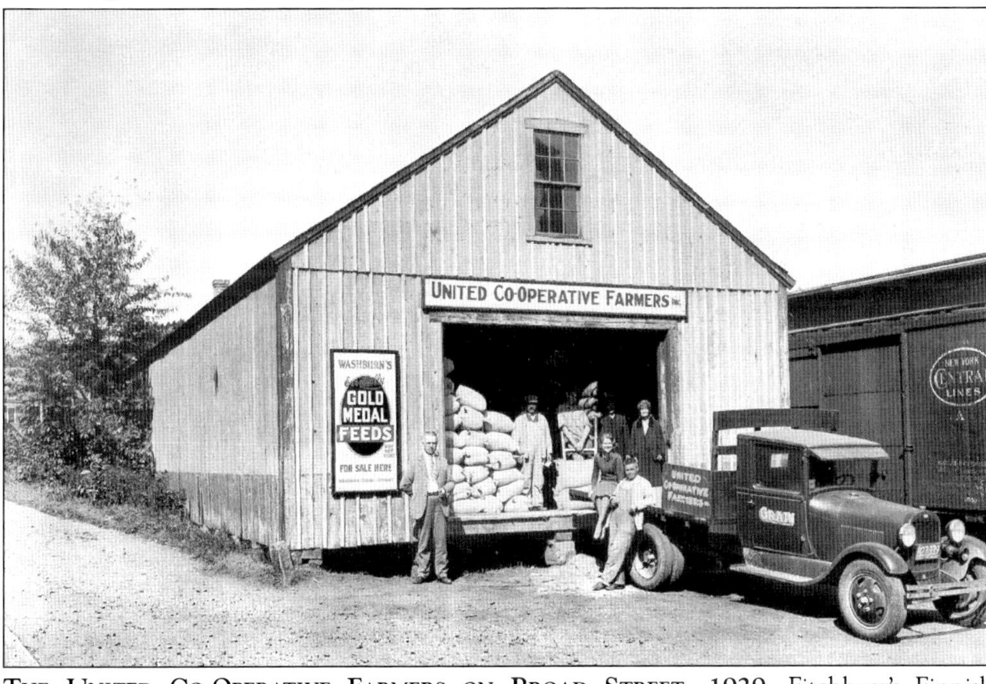

THE UNITED CO-OPERATIVE FARMERS ON BROAD STREET, 1929. Fitchburg's Finnish immigrants brought the concept of the cooperative movement to the city at the close of the 19th century. Finnish-American blueberry growers of New Ipswich, New Hampshire, formed a farmer's cooperative in 1926 to gain an advantage in selling their fruit. In 1928, the United Co-Operative Farmers was established in Fitchburg to buy and sell farm products.

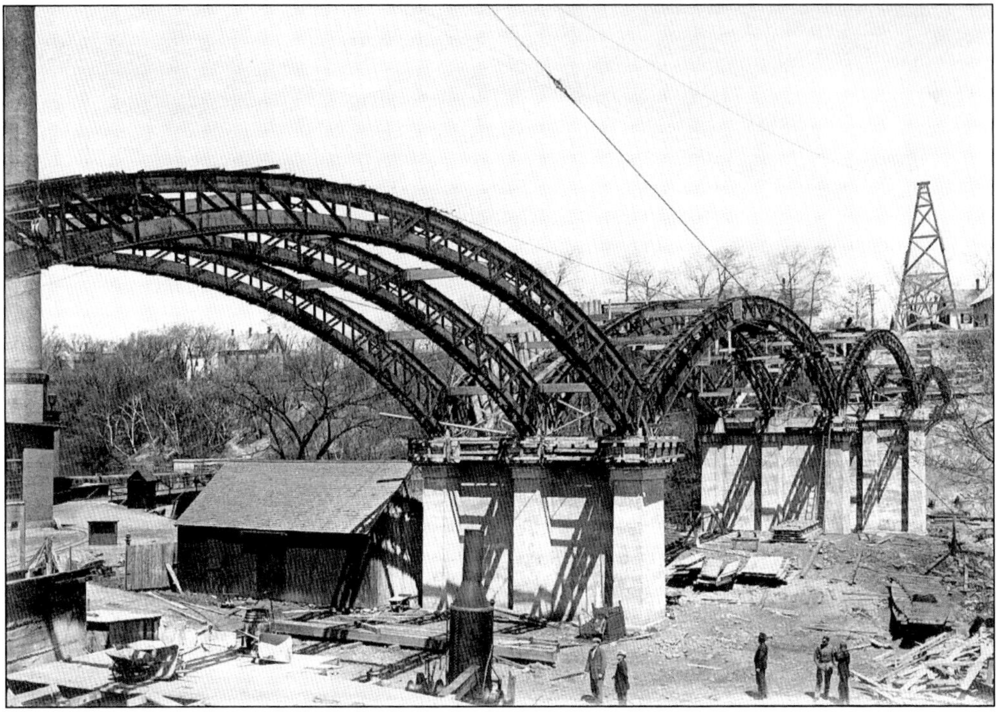

THE FIFTH STREET BRIDGE UNDER CONSTRUCTION, 1912. The Fifth Street Bridge, of steel and overhead construction, was built in 1912 to connect Water and Summer Streets. It crossed the Nashua River and the Boston and Maine Railroad tracks.

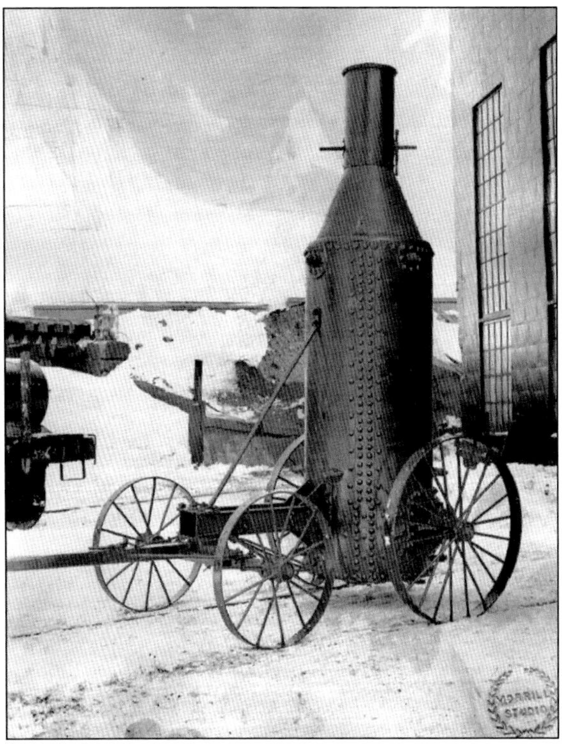

DILLON BOILERS, C. 1912. In the foreground of the construction site of the Fifth Street Bridge sits a Dillon boiler. The portable boiler provided steam to run machinery. David Dillon, a Canadian immigrant, started Dillon Boiler Works in 1870 in Fitchburg. He became a leading manufacturer of stationary steam boilers when steam, not electricity, propelled industry.

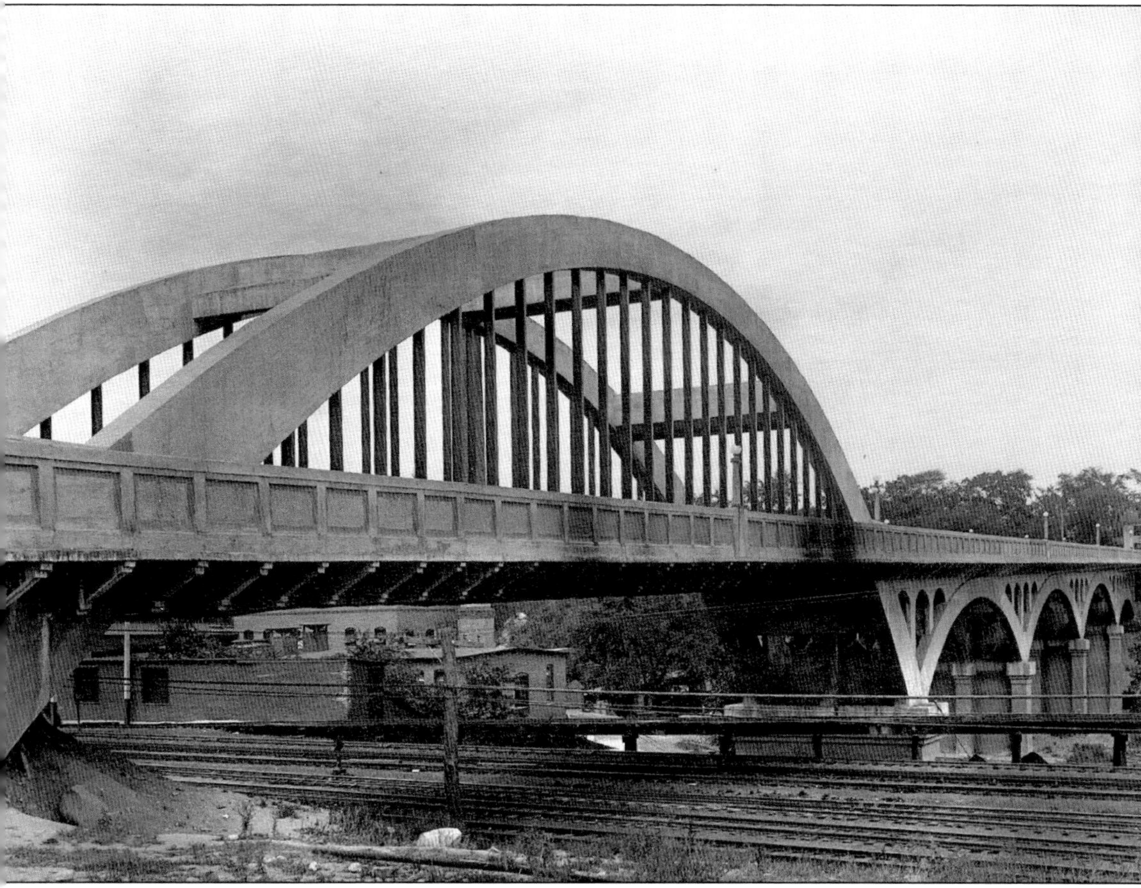

THE COMPLETED FIFTH STREET BRIDGE. In the early 1990s, the Fifth Street Bridge was declared unsafe, and it was demolished in the late 1990s. A new bridge opened in 2003 on the same site. It was named the Arthur J. DiTommaso Memorial Bridge.

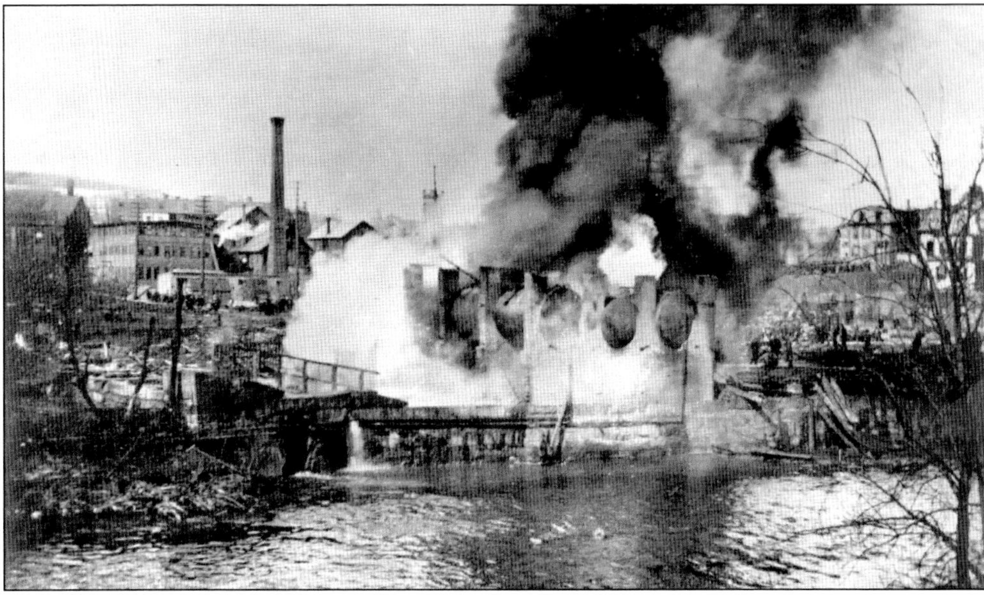

A TANK EXPLOSION AT C. A. CROSS. An oil tank explosion in 1904 at the C. A. Cross oil business killed two men and broke windows along Main, Summer, and North Streets. The roof of the building was blown more than 100 feet in the air. Cross established the business in 1883, bringing in tank cars filled with kerosene from Pennsylvania. An entrepreneur, Cross also started a wholesale grocery specializing in teas and coffees in 1885.

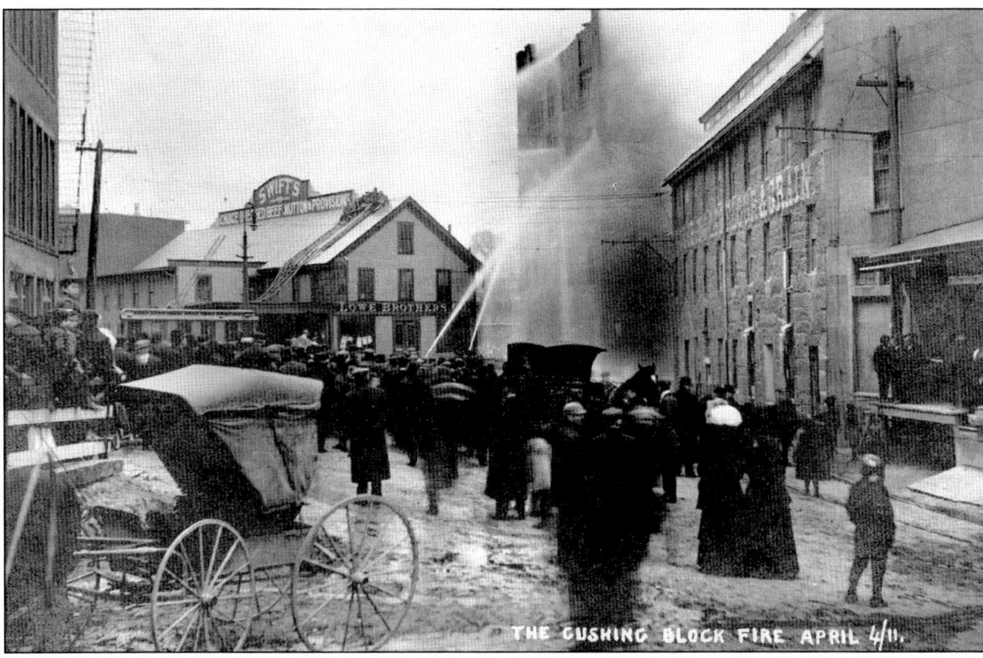

THE CUSHING BUILDING FIRE. In 1911, the worst fire that Fitchburg had seen swept through the four-story Cushing Building. Charles W. Grinnell, the city's first firefighter to die in the line of duty, was killed by falling debris during an explosion. He was taken to Burbank Hospital in George R. Wallace Jr.'s racing automobile. The owners of the block did not witness the fire. Milton Cushing was out west, and Charles Dickinson was in Havana.

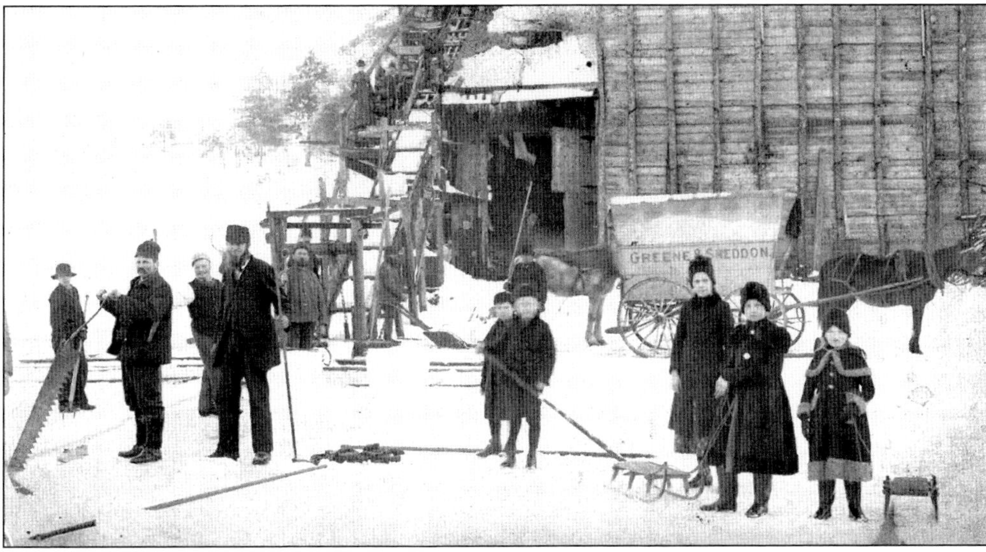

GREENE AND SHEDDON. Ice is such a common thing today that we give little thought to the days when it was harvested from ponds and lakes, stored in straw, and delivered to people's houses to refrigerate food. Fitchburg residents displayed large numbered cards in their windows to inform the ice delivery man what size ice block they needed. Note the elevator lifting blocks of ice into the building.

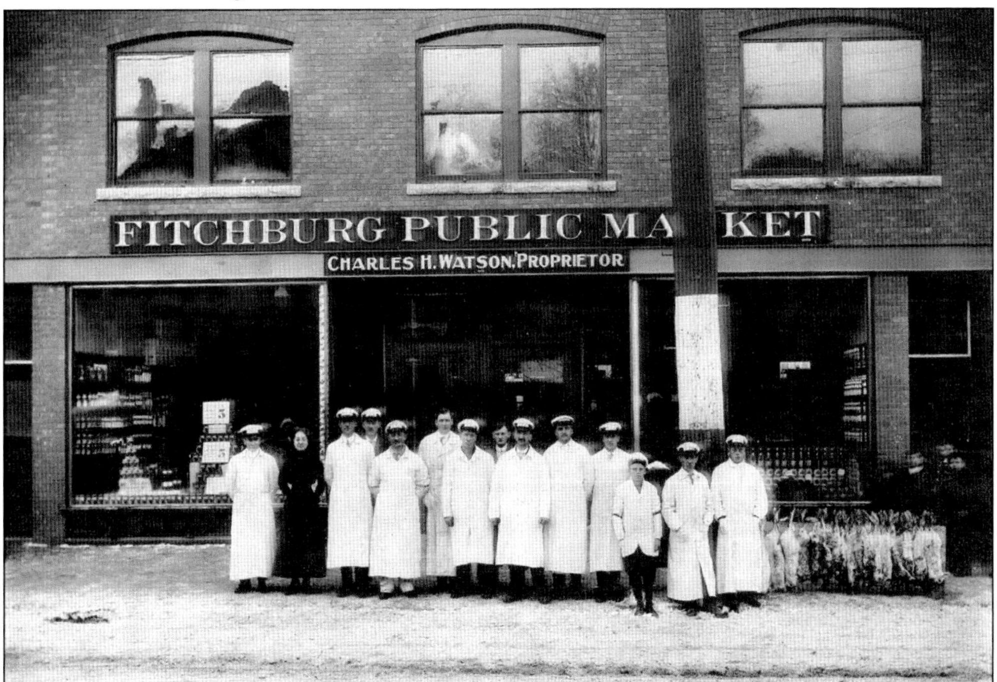

THE FITCHBURG PUBLIC MARKET. Charles H. Watson was born in Maine shortly after the Civil War and came to Fitchburg as a teenager. At first he went house-to-house selling meat from a cart. In 1890, he purchased a meat business at the corner of Main and River Streets and renamed it the Fitchburg Public Market. After 27 years at that location, he sold the market to Brockelman Brothers and relocated to Pearl Street.

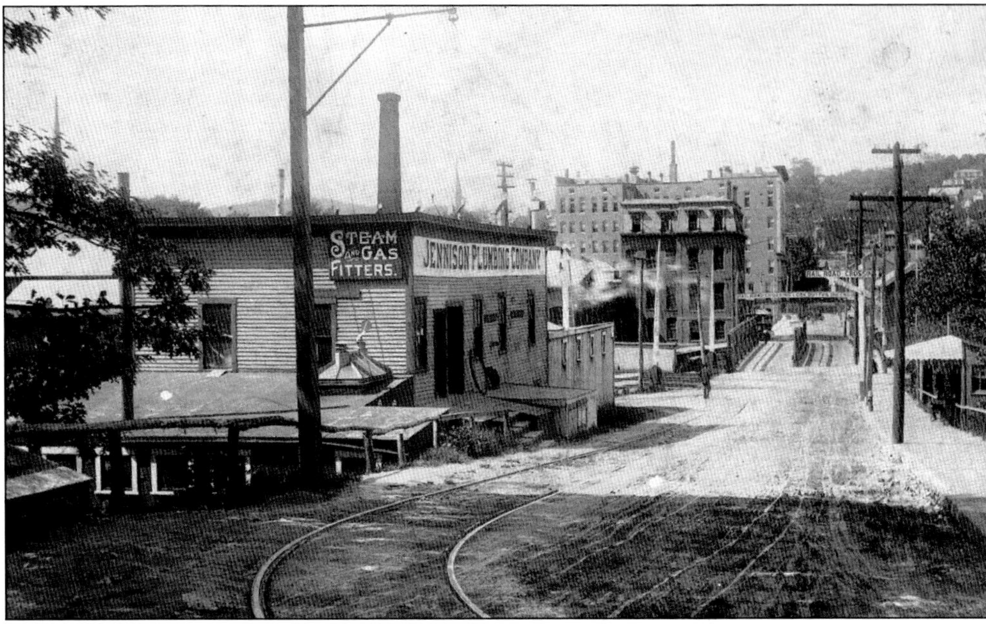

THE JENNISON PLUMBING COMPANY. In 1906, the Jennison Plumbing Company moved from Main Street to Putnam Street near the Putnam Street Bridge. William H. Dolan joined Herbert E. Jennison as a partner in 1900, and the company expanded into heating, ventilating, plumbing, and industrial installations of piping and heating systems. During World War I, the company operations were absorbed into large government building programs.

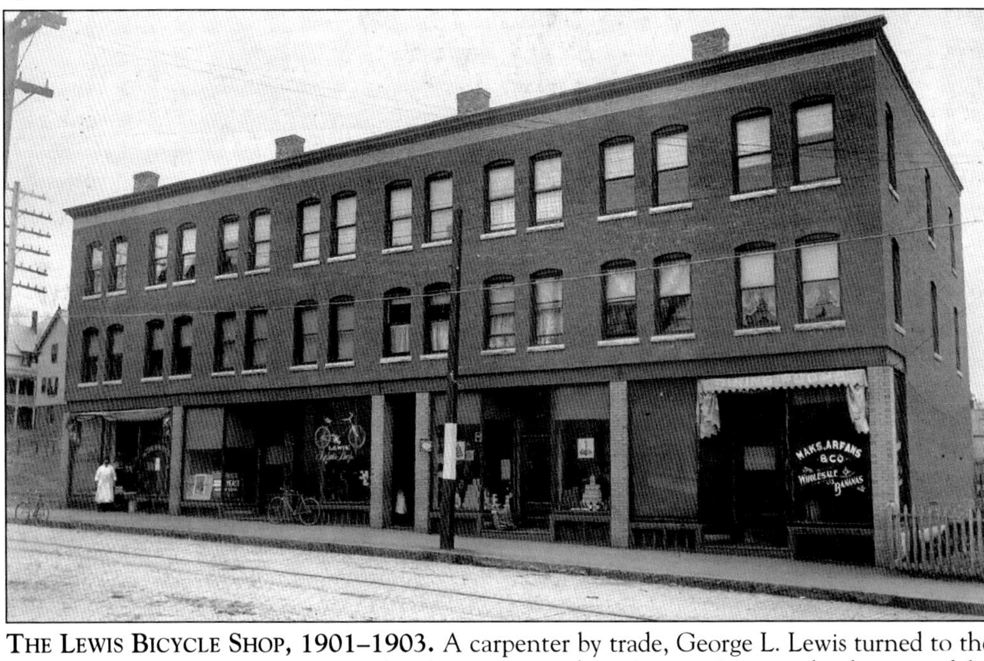

THE LEWIS BICYCLE SHOP, 1901–1903. A carpenter by trade, George L. Lewis turned to the sale and repair of bicycles in 1901 at his shop on Lunenburg Street. However, by the turn of the century, bicycles were no longer the craze, as people had become enamored with automobiles. Lewis made the transition to automobile sales and repairs in 1904, but he continued to sell and repair bicycles.

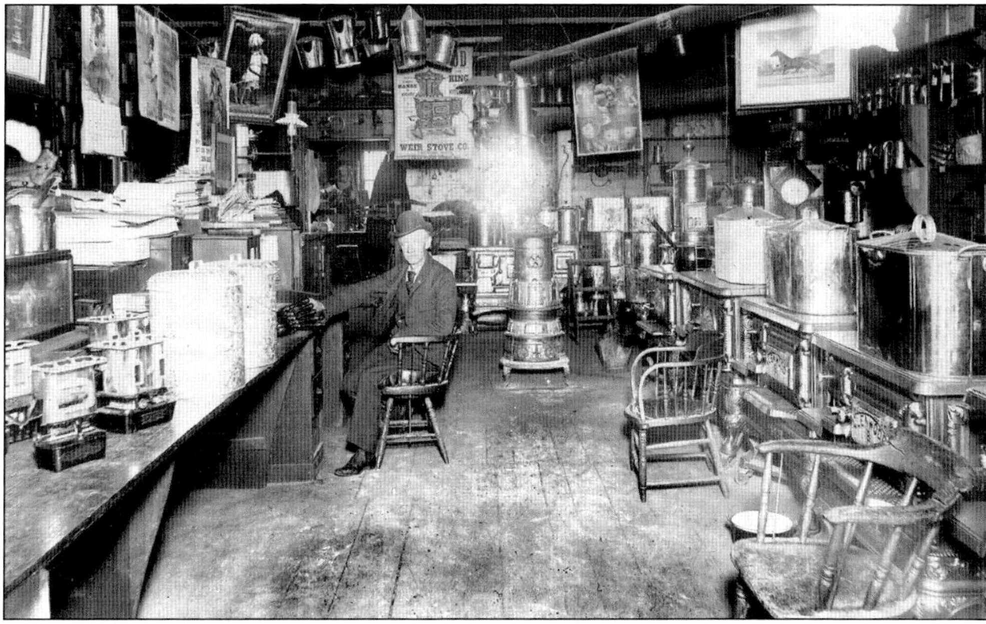

THE INTERIOR OF LYMAN PATCH'S TIN SHOP, MAIN STREET. A native of New Hampshire, Lyman Patch came to Fitchburg in 1852. On the day of his arrival, he married Catherine Davis of Templeton. Patch started a tinware business on Main Street and eventually employed as many as a dozen traveling tin peddlers. He also added stoves, glassware, and woodenware to his inventory.

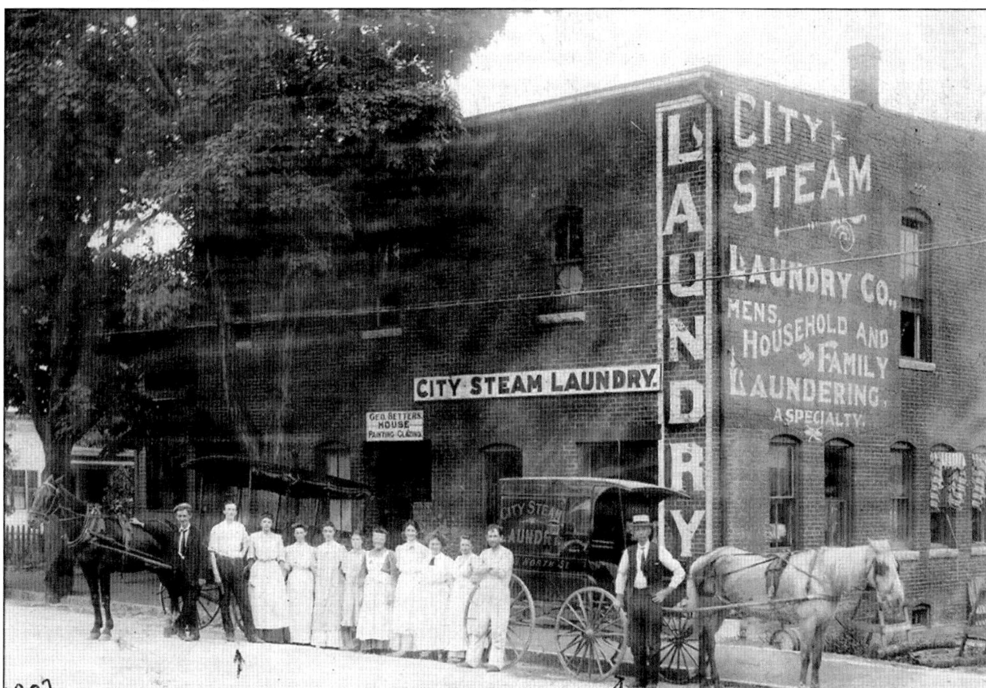

THE CITY STEAM LAUNDRY, 1907. The City Steam Laundry operated for over 70 years at different locations, finally evolving into a dry cleaner in 1960. In 1888, the newspaper reported that the laundry would take family washings at 50¢ a week during the fall and winter.

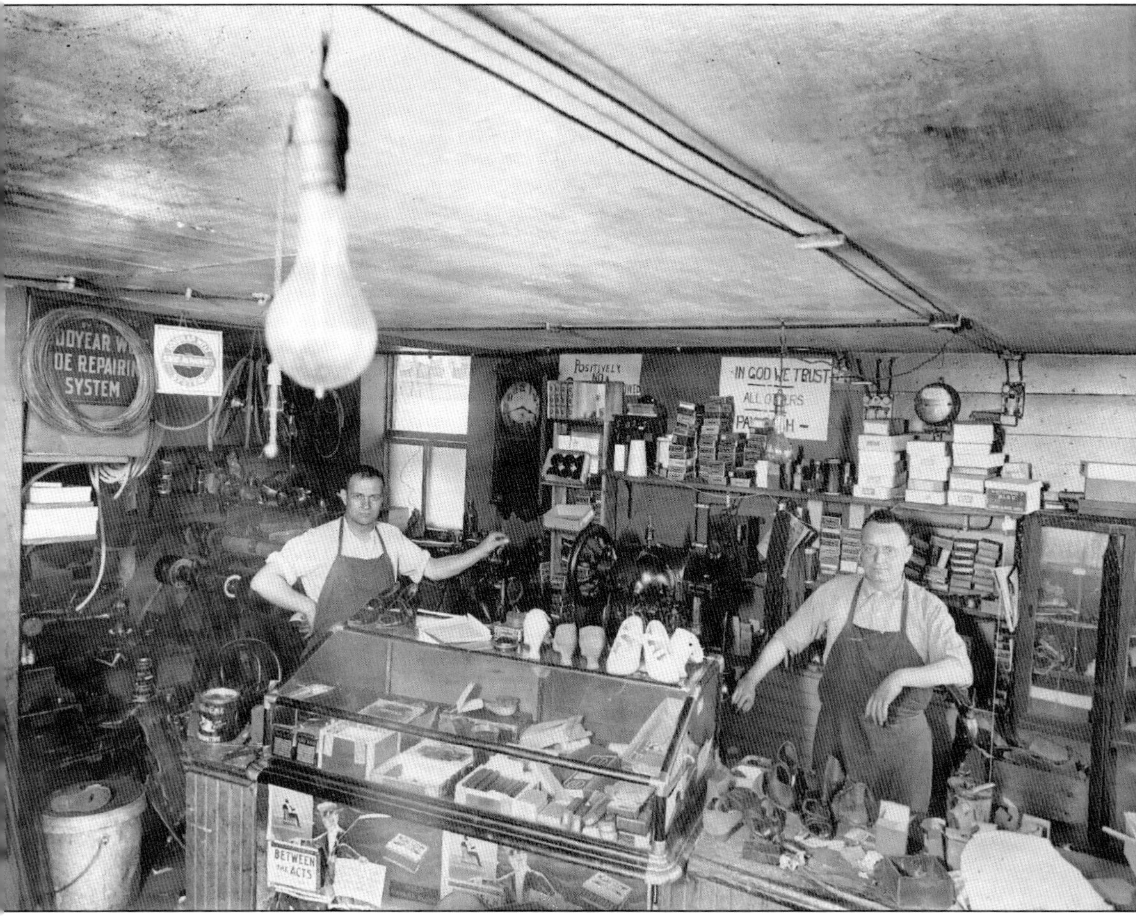

THE ADDANTE SHOE SHOP. This 1913 photograph depicts Giuseppe and Rocco Addante, old-world craftsmen who came to America from Italy. Giuseppe immigrated in 1910, and Rocco came in 1912. Giuseppe, affectionately known as Pepe (Joe), was the first shoemaker in the family. He taught his brothers, Rocco and Domenico, the business. Their first shop was at 305 Water Street.

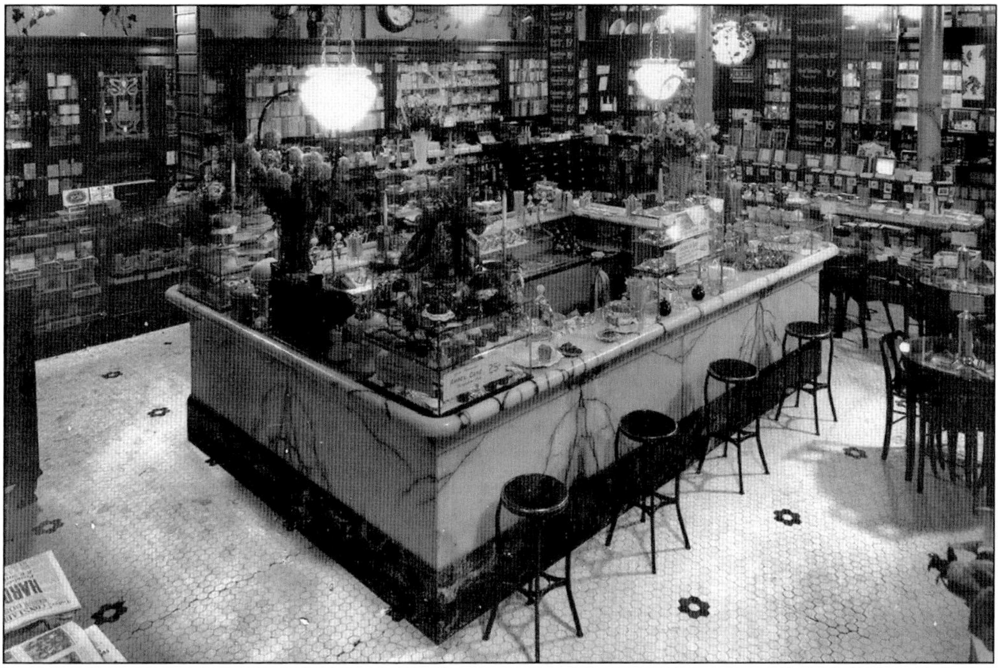

BROOKS DRUGSTORE. Harry Brooks opened his drugstore in 1906 at 465–467 Main Street. He created the saying "America's most beautiful drugstore" when he installed the most dazzling soda fountain in the city. It was an enormous square fountain in the center of the store. The business was sold to Liggett Drugstore in 1944.

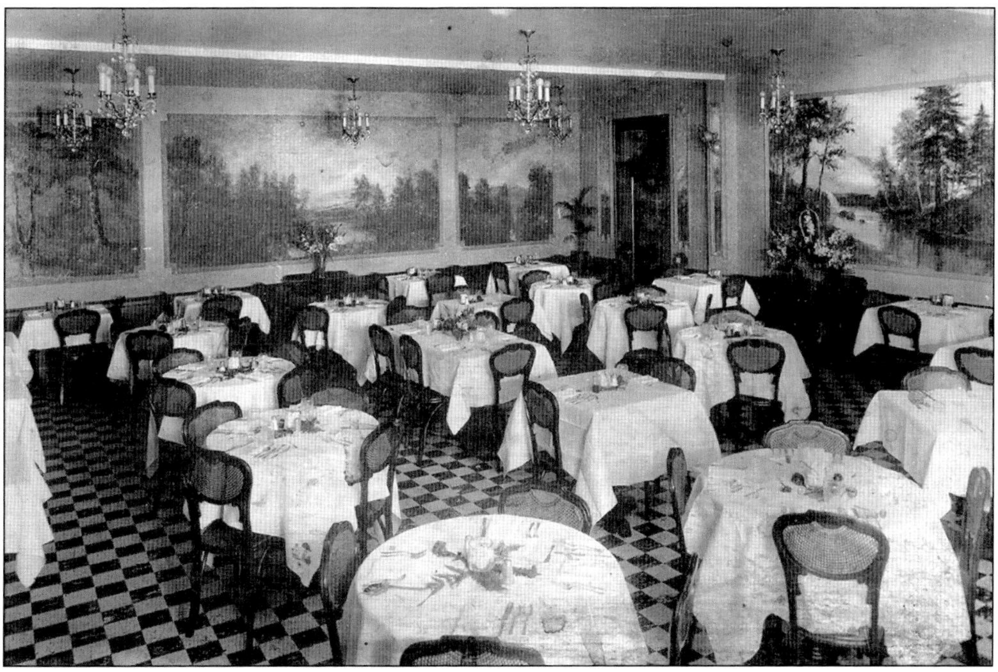

THE RESTAURANT UNUSUAL. Brooks opened a restaurant on the second floor of the building. He employed William Savery Bucklin to paint decorative murals. During the Great Depression and war years, the Restaurant Unusual was a favorite rendezvous spot for Fitchburg residents.

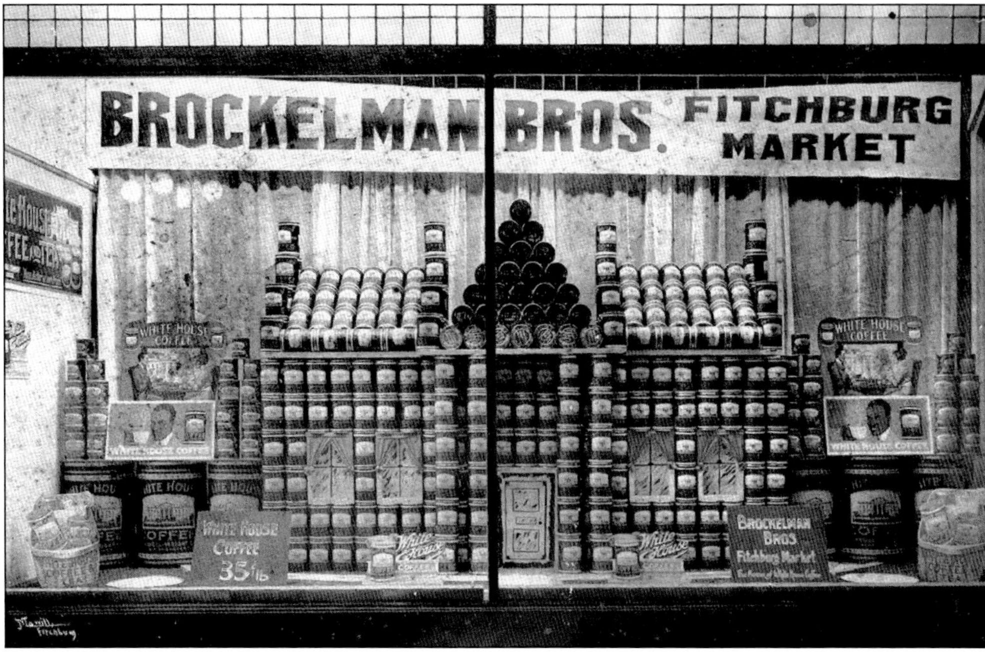

THE BROCKELMAN BROTHERS MARKET. Brockelman Brothers owned 12 other local grocery stores besides the Main Street store in Fitchburg. The stores offered a full range of meat, fowl, produce, canned goods, teas, coffee, nuts, and candy. The company also baked its own breads, pies, and cakes. The modern supermarket, with plenty of parking for cars, eventually overtook the downtown, family-owned market.

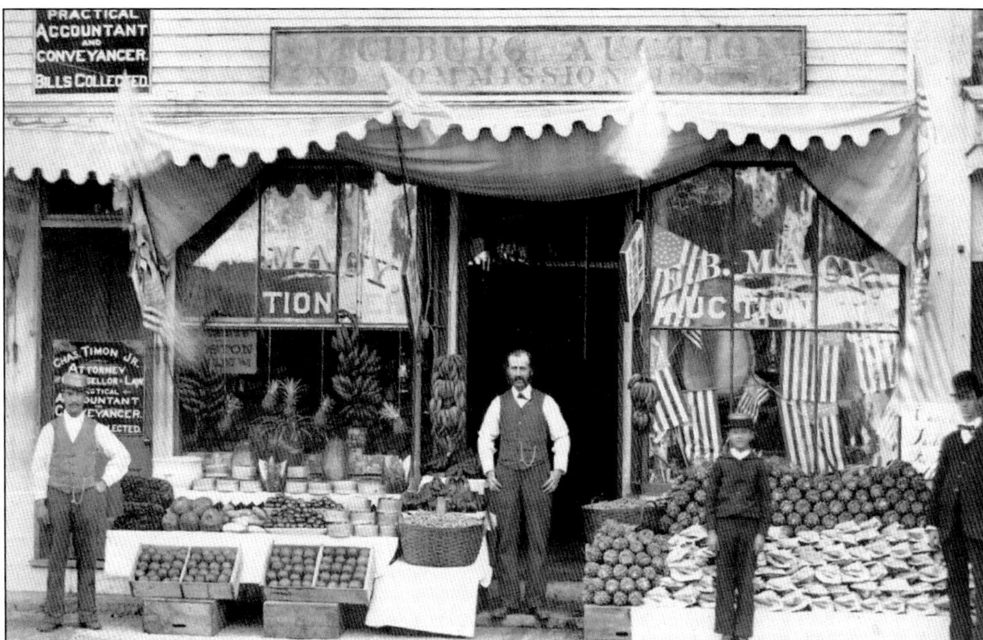

E. B. MACY AND COMPANY. Auctioneers and wholesale fruit commission merchants, E. B. Macy and Company was located at 100 Main Street.

Four

Getting Around

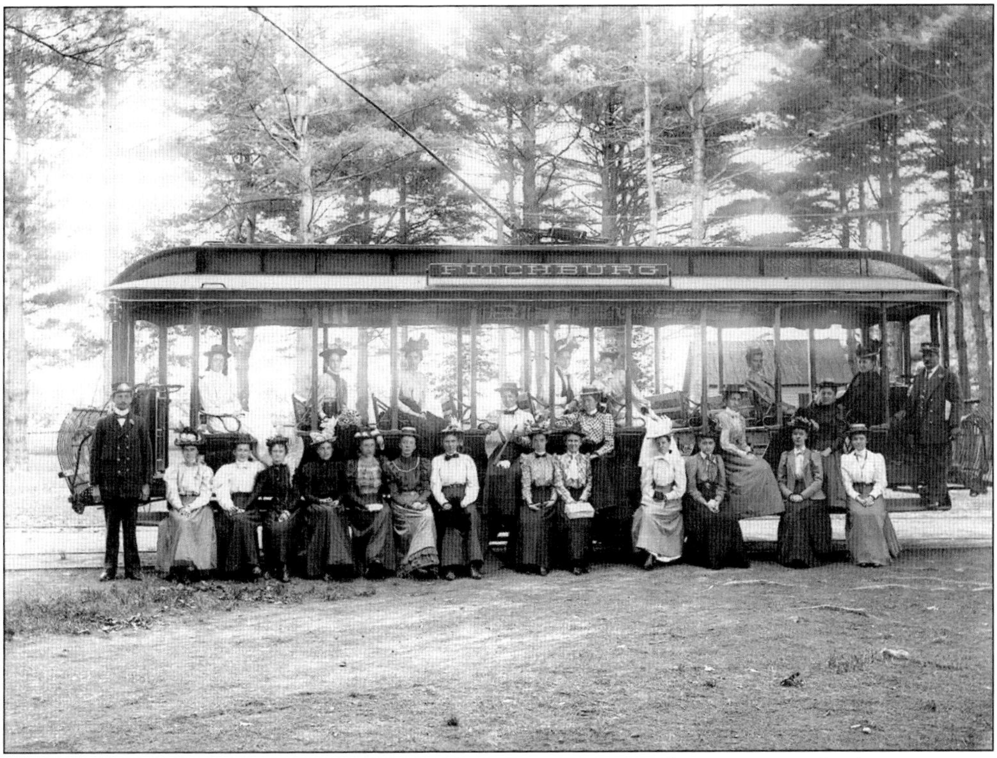

Whalom Park. In the later part of the 19th century, many trolley companies built amusement parks to increase their number of riders. The Fitchburg and Leominster Railway Company built Whalom Park for such a purpose. This group of women is about to depart the trolley at the park depot nestled among the pine trees. Park visitors could dine at Whalom Inn, feed the deer, attend a concert, or just relax at the water's edge.

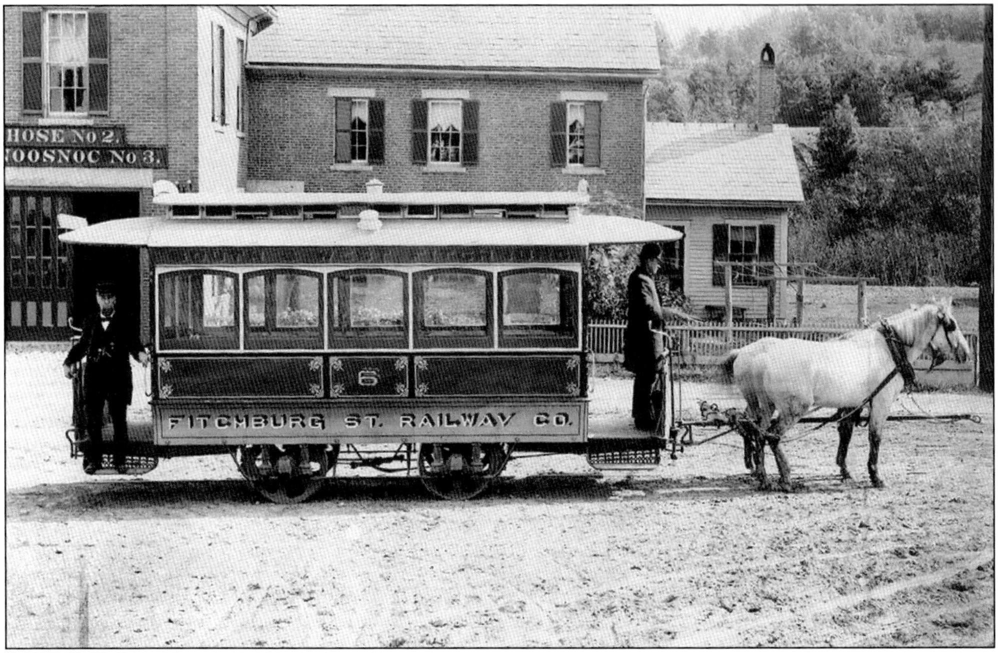

A HORSE-DRAWN STREETCAR. The Fitchburg Street Railway Company was established in 1886. The company began operation with a single three-mile horse-drawn streetcar line between Goodrich Street in Fitchburg and Westminster Street in West Fitchburg. This photograph from the late 1880s shows the horsecar in front of the West Fitchburg Steamer House.

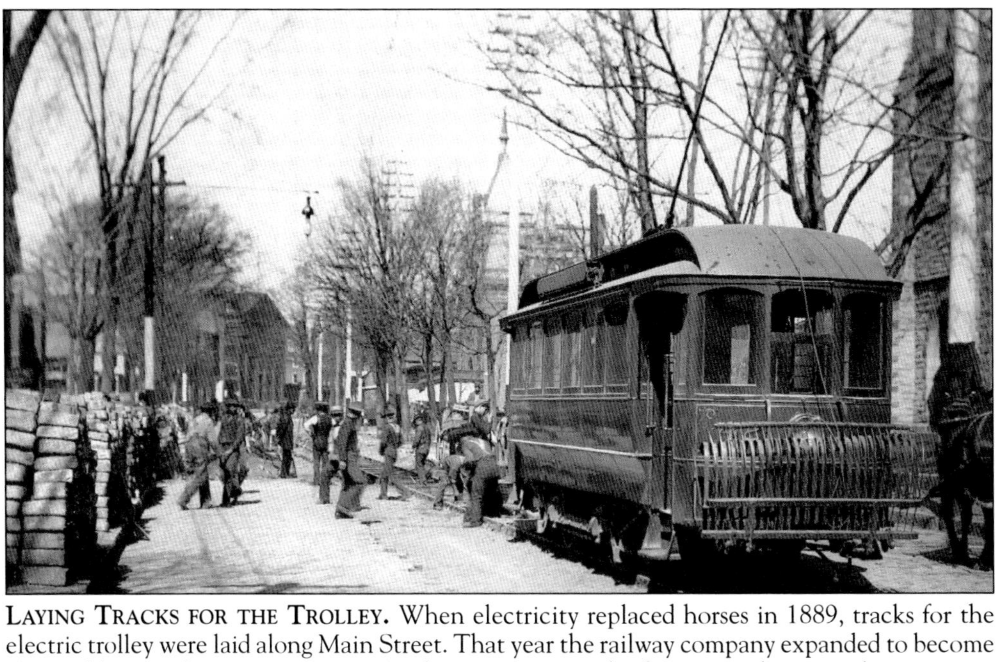

LAYING TRACKS FOR THE TROLLEY. When electricity replaced horses in 1889, tracks for the electric trolley were laid along Main Street. That year the railway company expanded to become the Fitchburg and Leominster Street Railway Company. The first transit between the two cities was made on June 23, 1892. By 1912, the streetcar company was running 62 electric trolley cars over 34 miles of track.

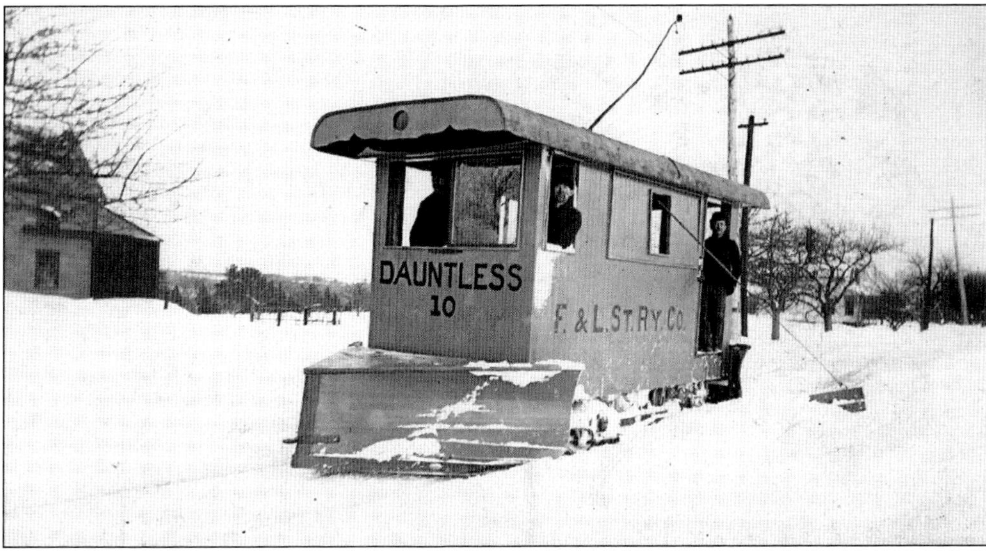

THE *DAUNTLESS*. The *Dauntless* was the Fitchburg and Leominster Street Railway Company's snowplow. Workers are shown here removing snow around 1925.

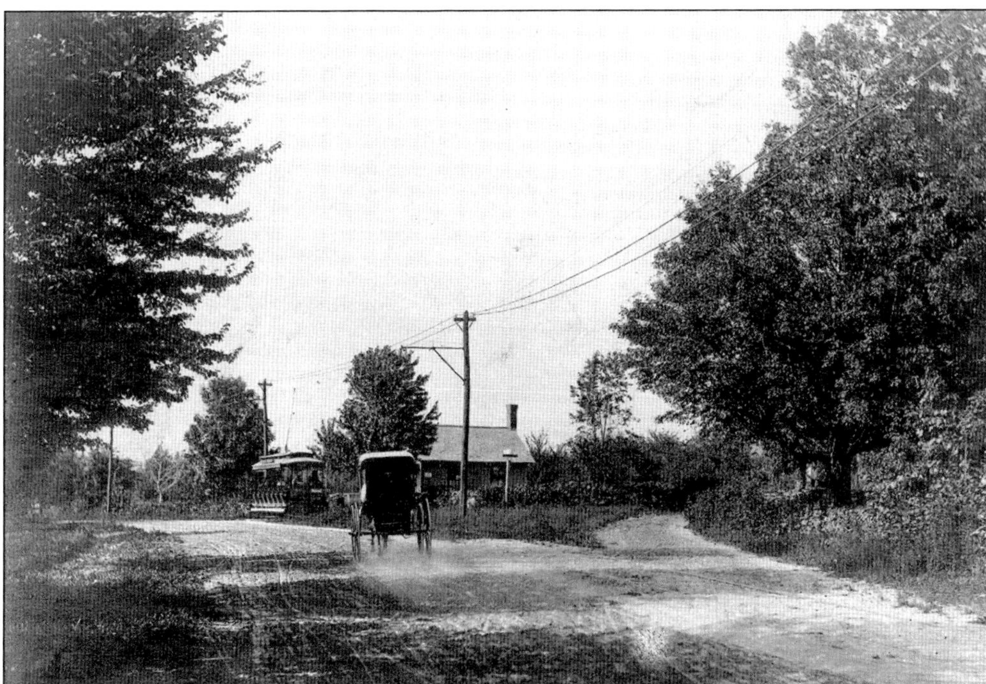

AN ELECTRIC TROLLEY AND A HORSE AND BUGGY. An electric trolley and a horse and buggy pass each other in West Fitchburg in 1896.

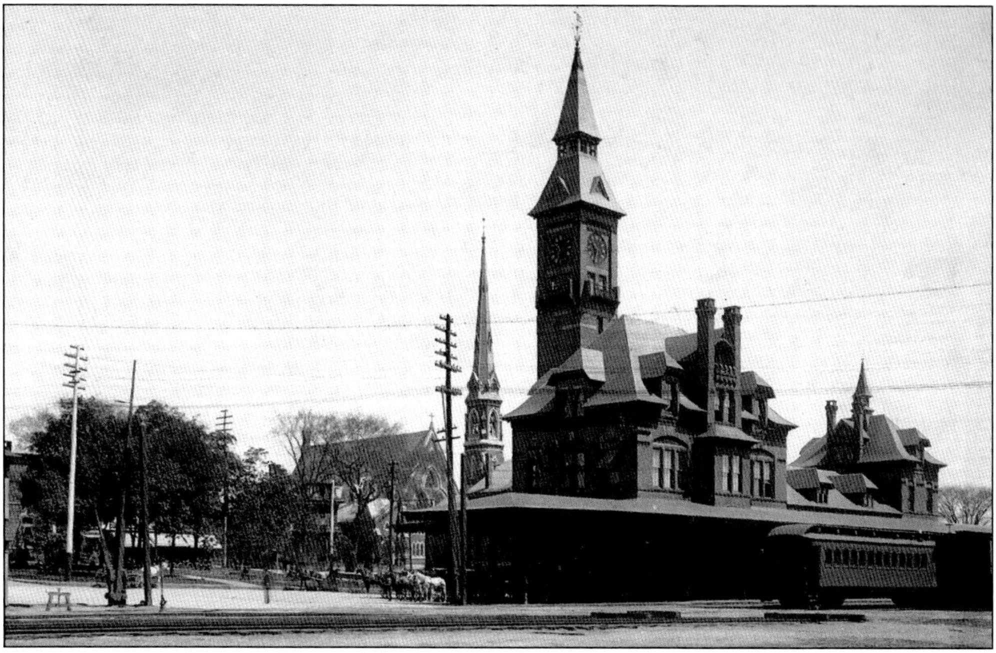

UNION DEPOT. The completion of the Hoosac Tunnel in 1874 demanded increased rail service, as did the growth of Fitchburg's industry and population. After much debate as to where to build a new depot, the decision was made to construct it in the southern part of the city, on Main Street. Union Depot, designed by H. M. Francis, was opened in 1878. It was demolished in 1961.

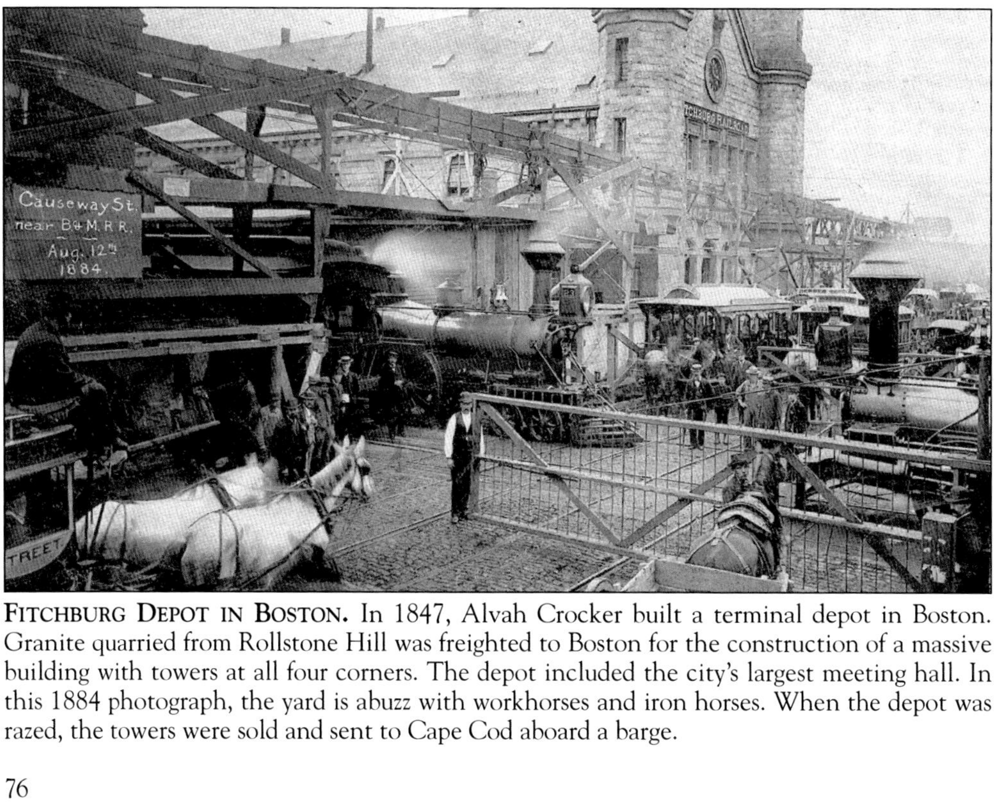

FITCHBURG DEPOT IN BOSTON. In 1847, Alvah Crocker built a terminal depot in Boston. Granite quarried from Rollstone Hill was freighted to Boston for the construction of a massive building with towers at all four corners. The depot included the city's largest meeting hall. In this 1884 photograph, the yard is abuzz with workhorses and iron horses. When the depot was razed, the towers were sold and sent to Cape Cod aboard a barge.

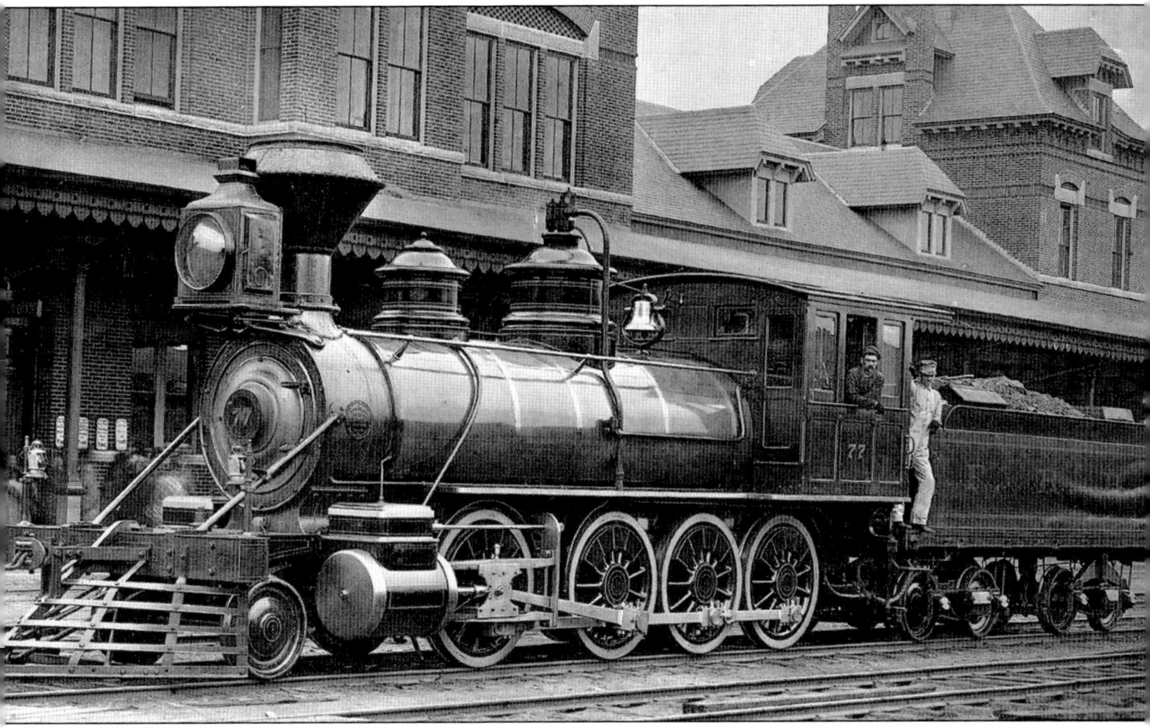

THE FITCHBURG RAILROAD. When Alvah Crocker and a group of Fitchburg citizens proposed bringing the railroad to the city, there were dissenters. But progress overcame discord. Crocker raised funds, contracted Irish labor, and purchased English steel to build a line from Boston to Fitchburg. A half-century after the line's opening in 1845, 100 engines a day traveled the tracks, bringing continued growth to Fitchburg's industry and population.

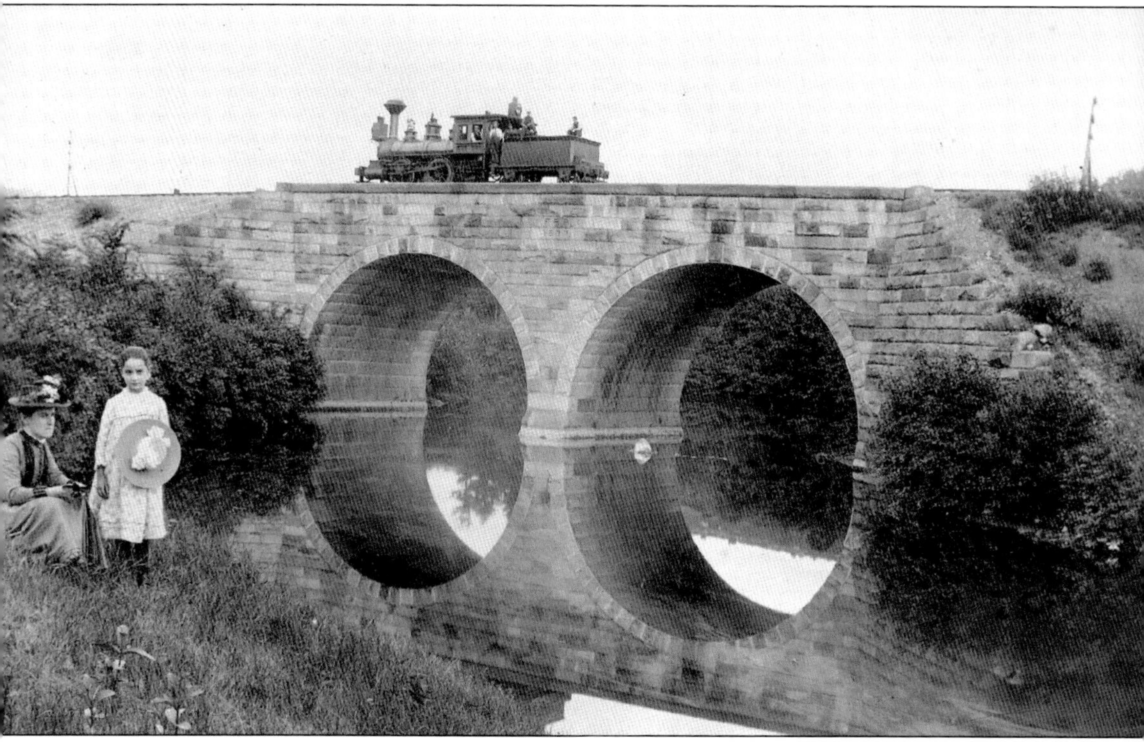

THE STONE RAILROAD BRIDGE. A beautiful stone arch bridge accommodated the railroad over the Nashua River in West Fitchburg near the corner of River Street and Wallace Road. This photograph was taken in July 1889. The bridge has not been replaced, and today trains still travel over the old stone bridge.

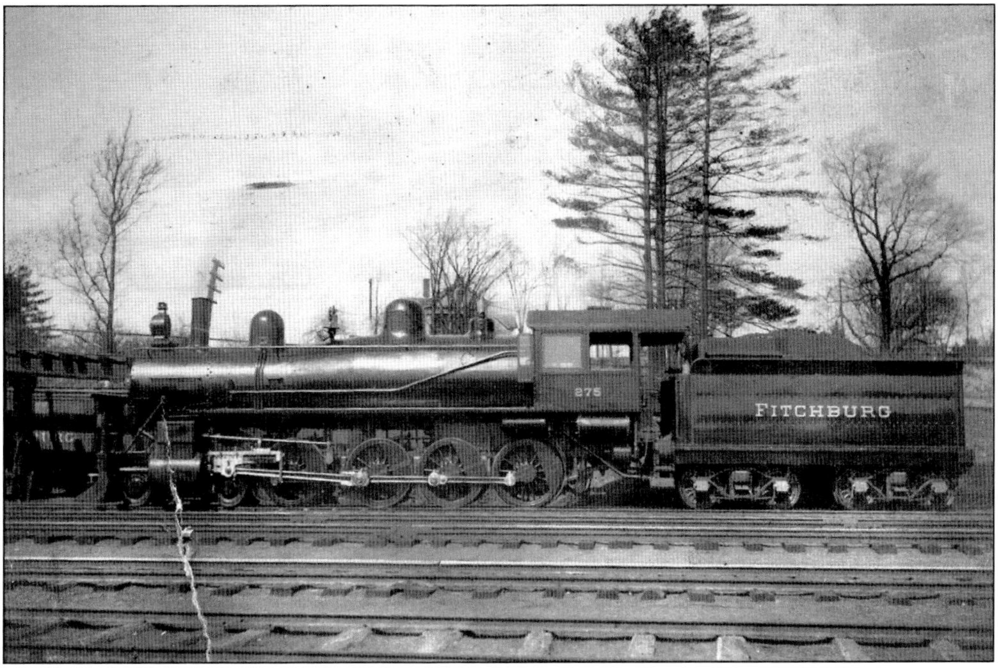

No. 275. This photograph of No. 275 was taken in 1899. The total weight of the locomotive is 175,000 pounds, and it has a steam pressure of 200 pounds. The tender holds 4,500 gallons of water and 20,000 pounds of coal.

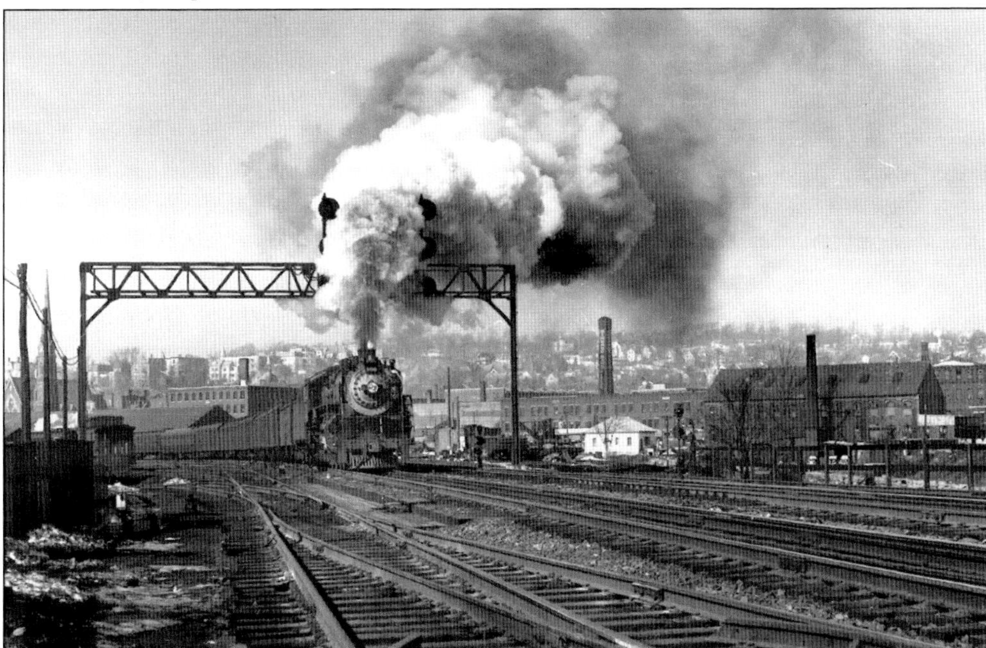

"Leaving Town," 1940s. This photograph was taken about 100 years after Alvah Crocker succeeded in bringing the railroad to Fitchburg. Landmarks visible in the image are the Simonds Saw and Steel Company factory, with its tall chimney, and the Sawyer Machine Company building (now Fitchburg Plumbing).

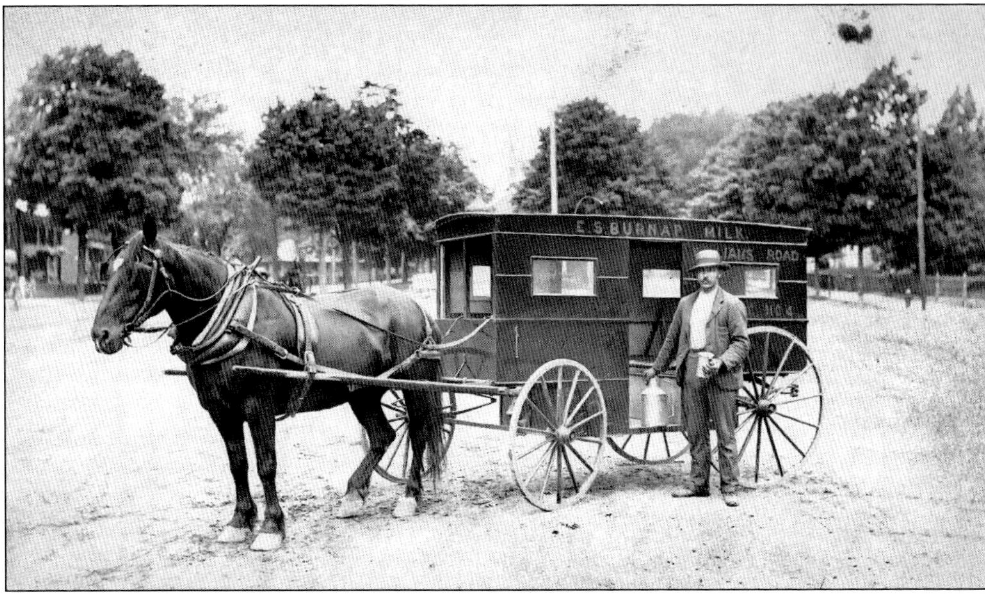

THE BURNAP DELIVERY WAGON. Delivery wagons were a common sight on the streets of Fitchburg in the 19th century. John Grubb delivered milk and farm produce for farmer Edwin S. Burnap, who had a very small farm, as a city directory advertisement explained: "Milk from one Cow supplied to those wishing daily."

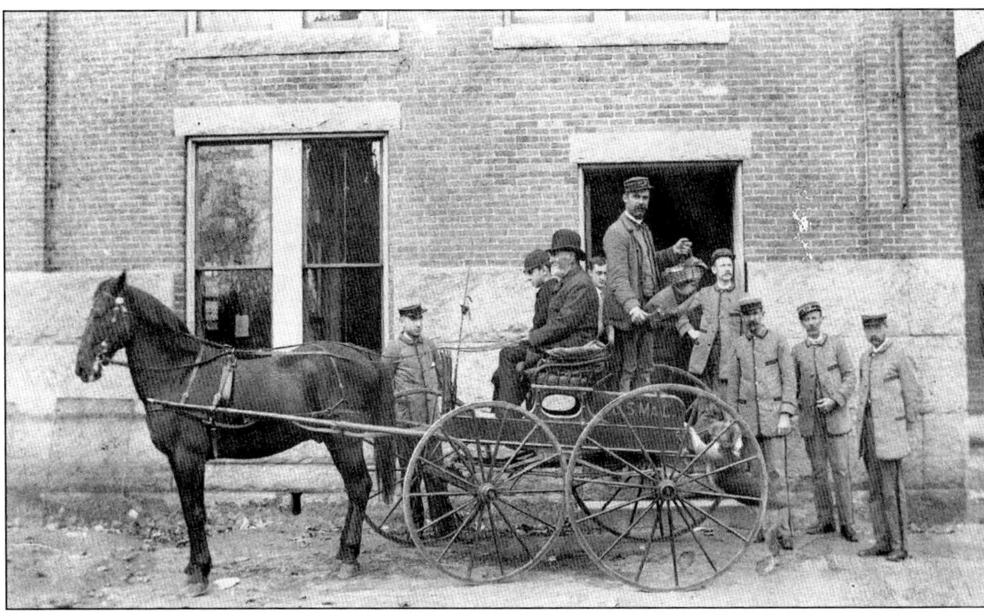

POSTAL CARRIERS AND THEIR WAGON. This *c.* 1892 photograph shows a group of postal carriers with their horse-drawn postal wagon. The letter carriers are Albert S. Pierce, P. B. Partill, Eugene Forest, F. J. Dwyer, Thomas F. McCann, F. W. Abott, Fred S. Moore, Ernest F. Schragle, and Fred Bruce.

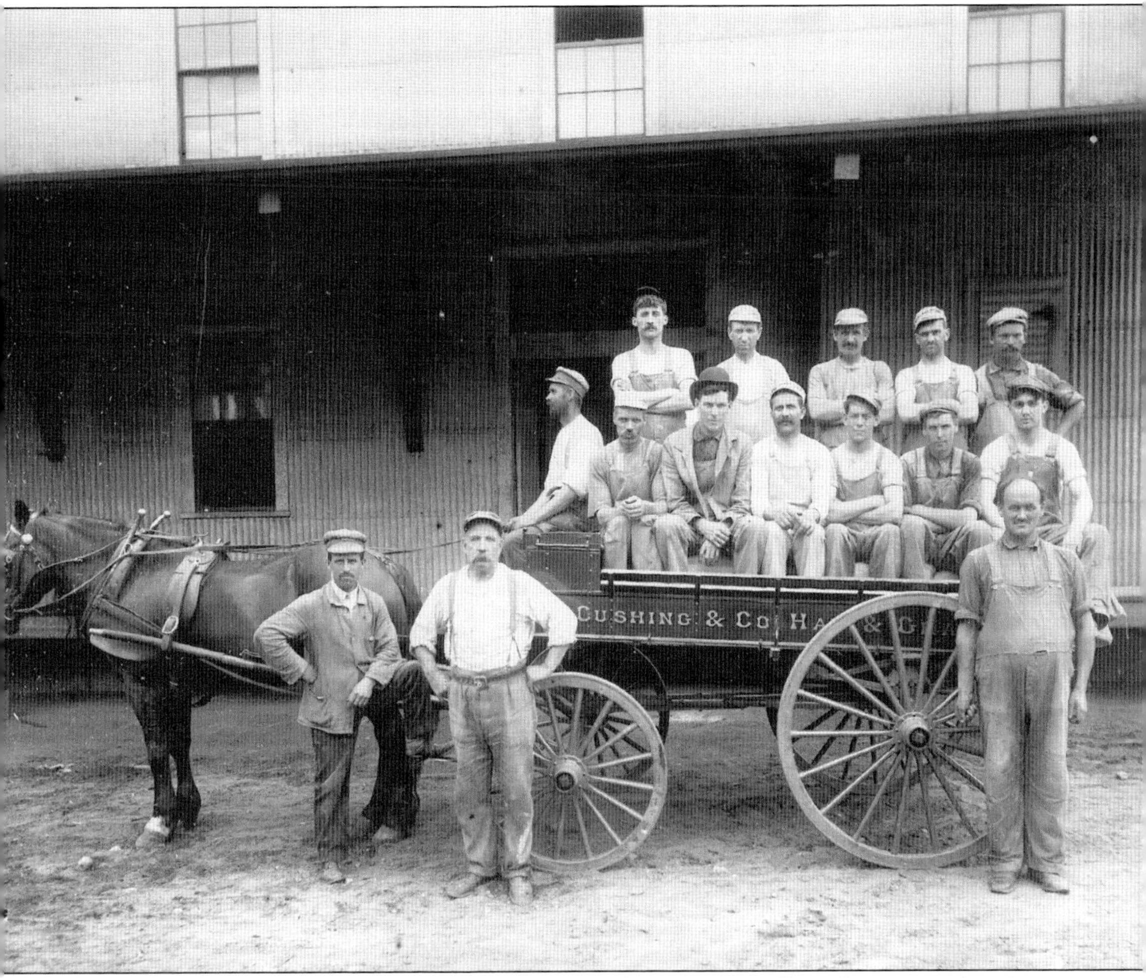

THE CUSHING GRAIN MILL WAGON. In the 1890s, Cushing Grain Mill employees posed in the company delivery wagon for this photograph. Standing are, from left to right, Ernest Russell, Mr. Amiott, and Albert Howe. The driver is Henry Burgess.

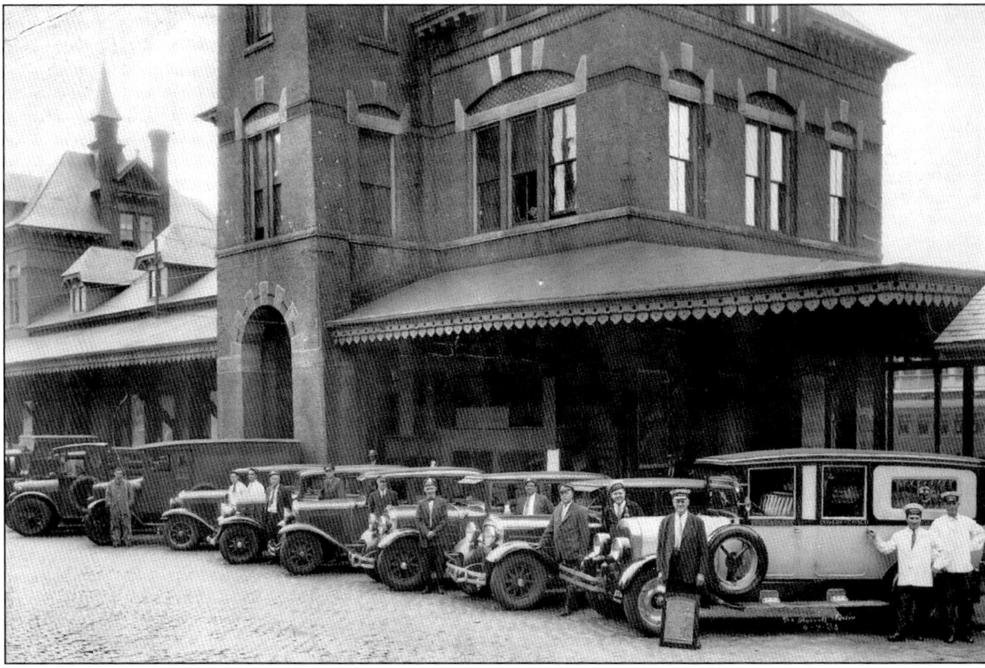

A Fleet of Taxis. During its 84-year history (1877–1961), Fitchburg's Union Depot was a central artery for immigrants, businessmen, passengers, and freight. A fleet of service people and vehicles stood sentry to the nearly 100 trains per day. The closest automobile in this image has a door sign that reads, "Invalid coach."

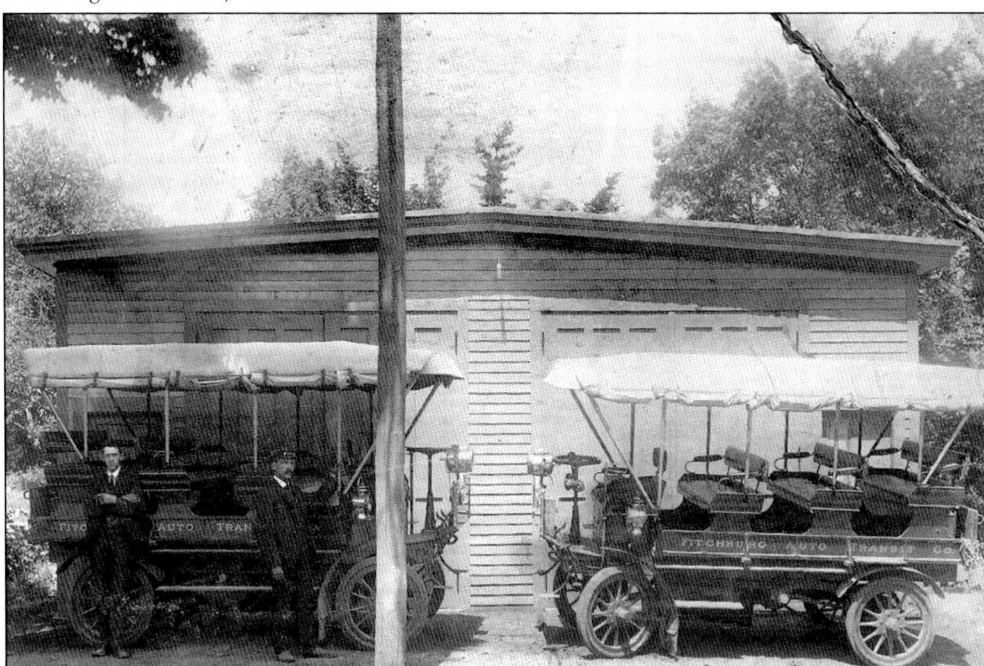

The Fitchburg Auto Transit Company. The Fitchburg Auto Transit Company was in the city directory from 1906 to 1907.

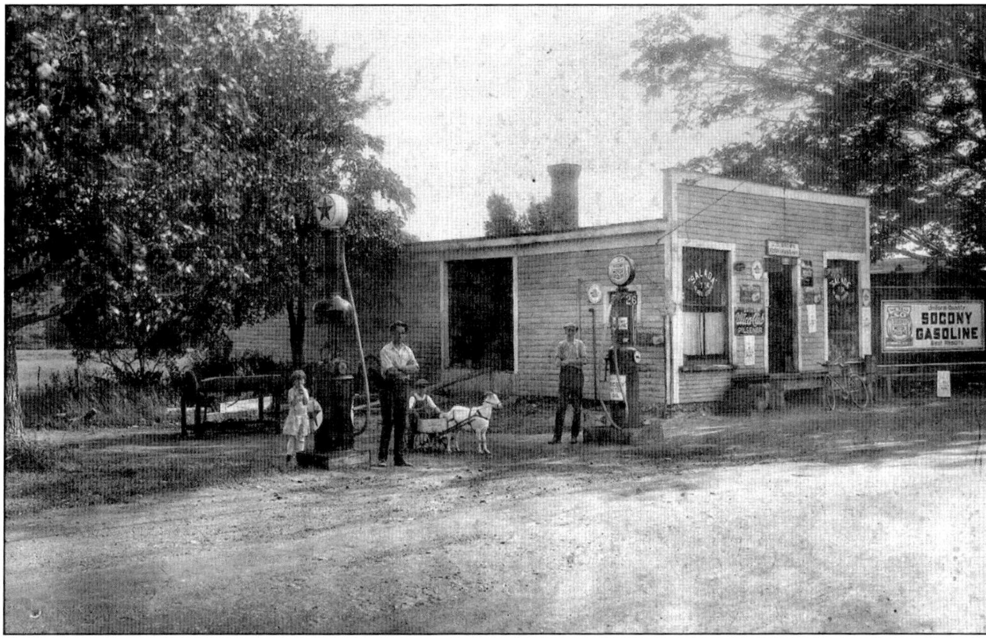

AN EARLY GAS STATION. This gas station on Lunenberg Street was owned by J. D. Brown in the early 1920s. Parked in front of the building is a truss-frame Iver Johnson's Arms and Cycle Works bicycle.

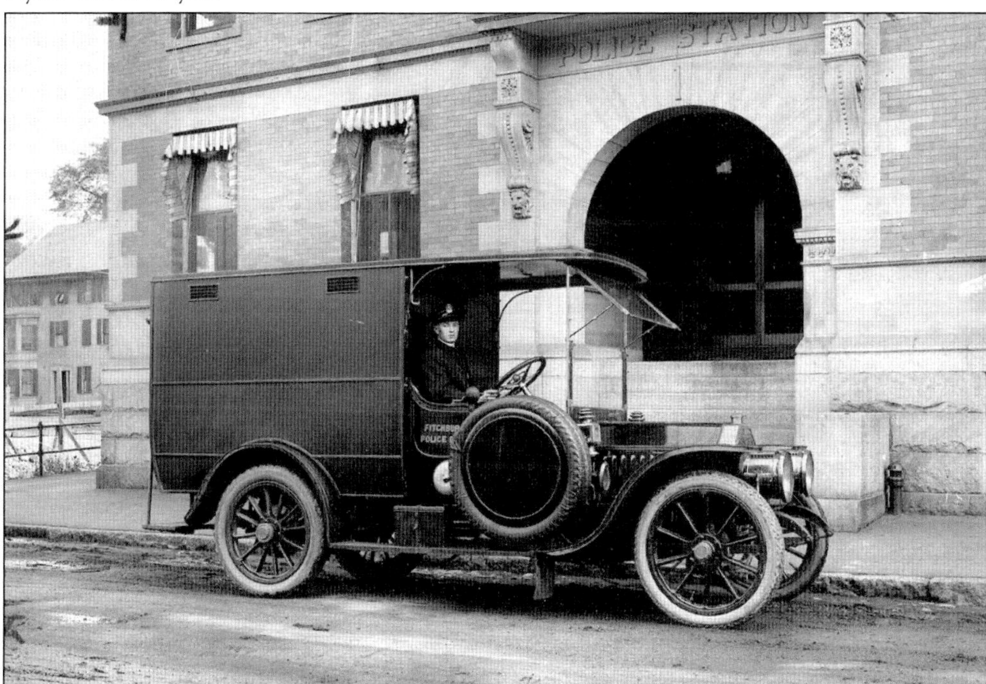

A POLICE CAR. Shown here is the first motor-driven ambulance and patrol wagon in the city, driven by E. H. Grant in 1914. Burbank Hospital first contracted with the police department for the use of its vehicle as an ambulance in 1913. During that summer, the hospital paid the police department for 83 calls at the rate of $2 per call.

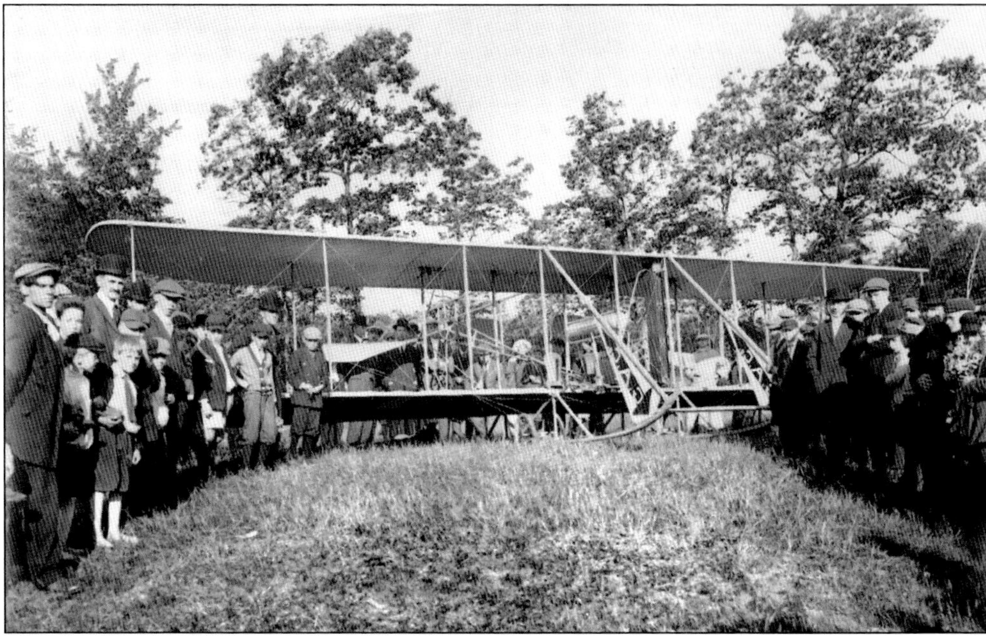

FITCHBURG'S FIRST AIRPLANE LANDING. In June 1912, Fitchburg citizens gathered to observe the first landing of an airplane in their city. The local newspaper read, "Bird-men will do stunts of the most thrilling kind." The "thrilling" part turned out to be mechanical trouble that forced the biplane to land in a swampy meadow. The aviator was unhurt, but he had to make several attempts before rising into the air again.

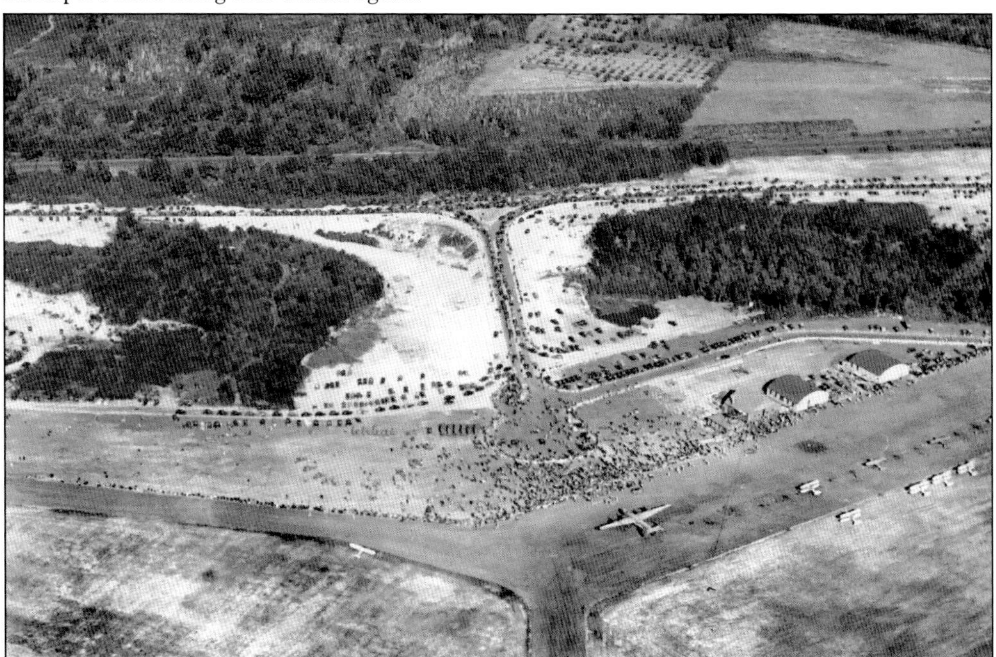

AERIAL VIEW OF THE FITCHBURG AIRPORT. During World War I, men actively took to the sky, and one pilot returned to Fitchburg with a dream of opening a city airport. He found other men with the same interest, and the airport opened for its first landing in 1929.

Five

Churches, Schools, and Other Institutions

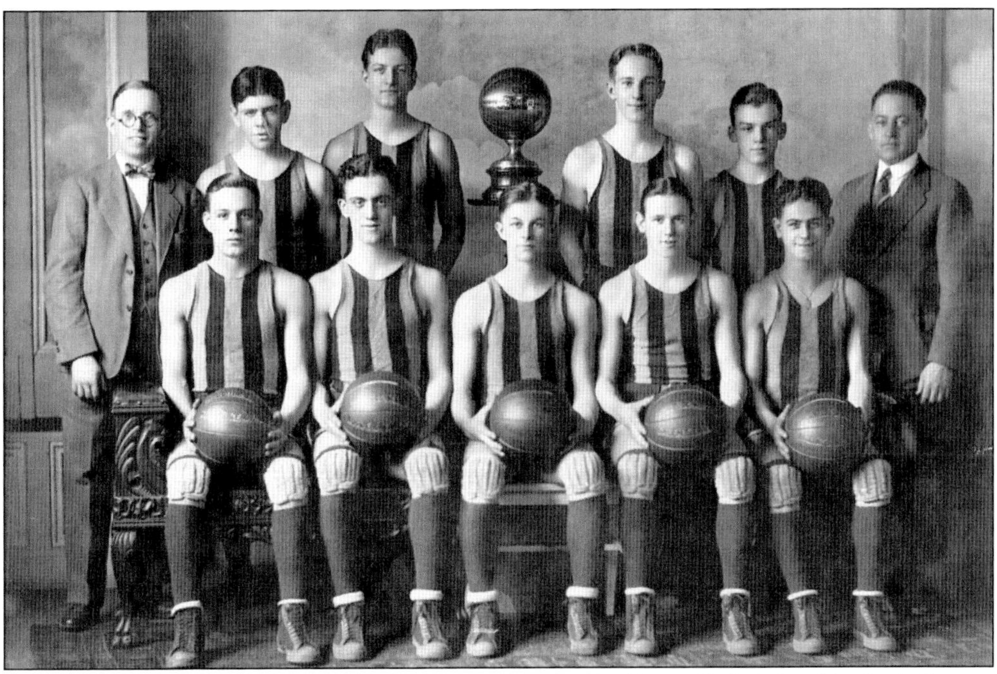

The High School Basketball Team of 1926. The Fitchburg High School basketball team went undefeated in the 1925–1926 season. The team members traveled to Chicago, where they became the first New England team to win a national championship. Today, the trophy is on display at the high school. From left to right are (seated) Alfred Maffeo, Anastos Fanos, Lauri Myllykangas, David Quinn, Tauno Puhakka, and Johnny Oliva; (standing) Ralph Howard, Daniel Quinn, Tauno Puhakka, John Marcy, Kenneth Davis, and Clarence Amiott.

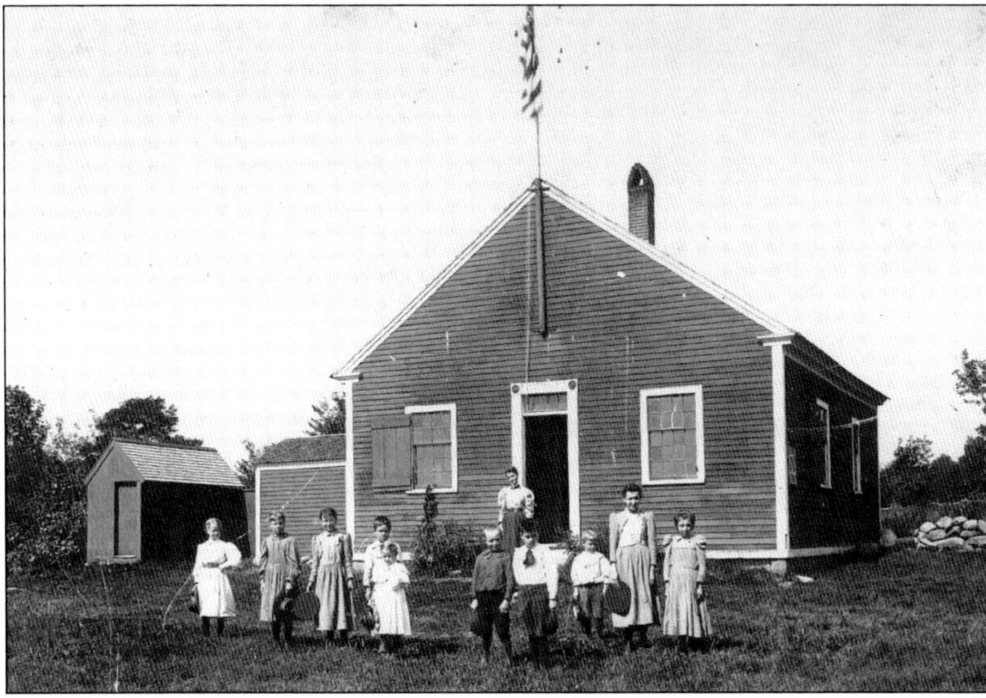

DEAN HILL SCHOOL. Dean Hill School was among the first schoolhouses built in the city. It was probably established around 1798. By 1830, there were 11 school districts within the city, with each district responsible for providing its own schoolhouse. This 1897 photograph shows that Dean Hill School had already been in use for almost 100 years.

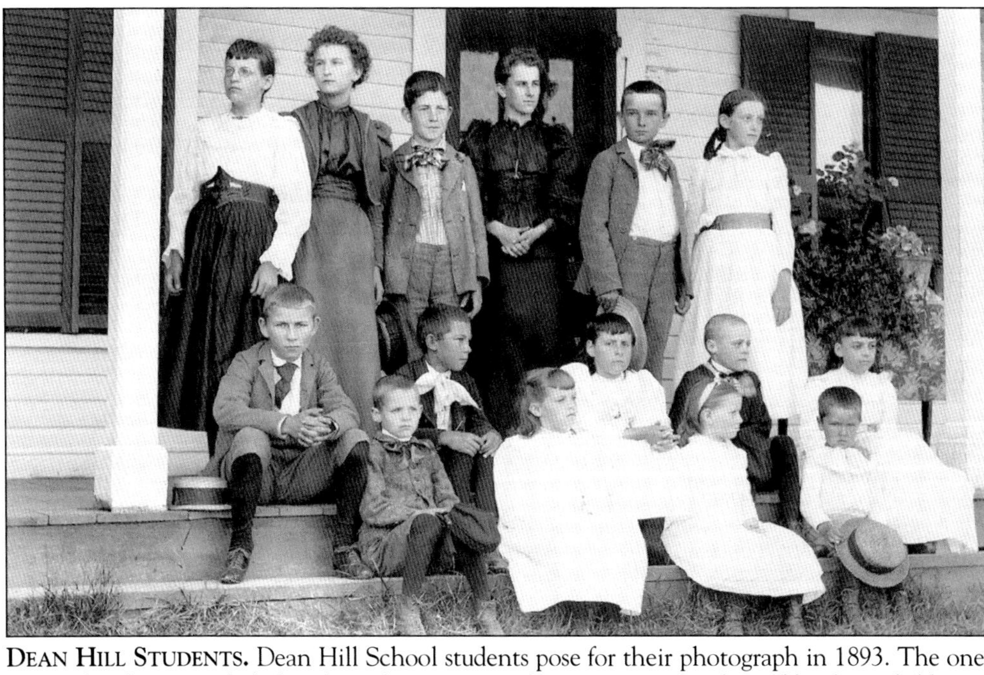

DEAN HILL STUDENTS. Dean Hill School students pose for their photograph in 1893. The one-room schoolhouse included students from a range of age groups, as evidenced by these children.

"GENERAL AND MRS. GEORGE WASHINGTON." "General and Mrs. George Washington" held a reception at the School Street School at the turn of the century. George Rodney Wallace Jr. impersonated the general, and Bessie Pierce played Mrs. Washington.

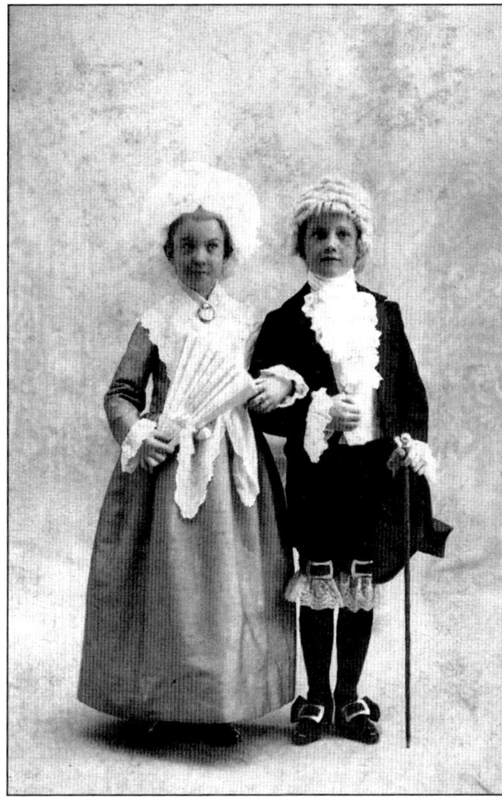

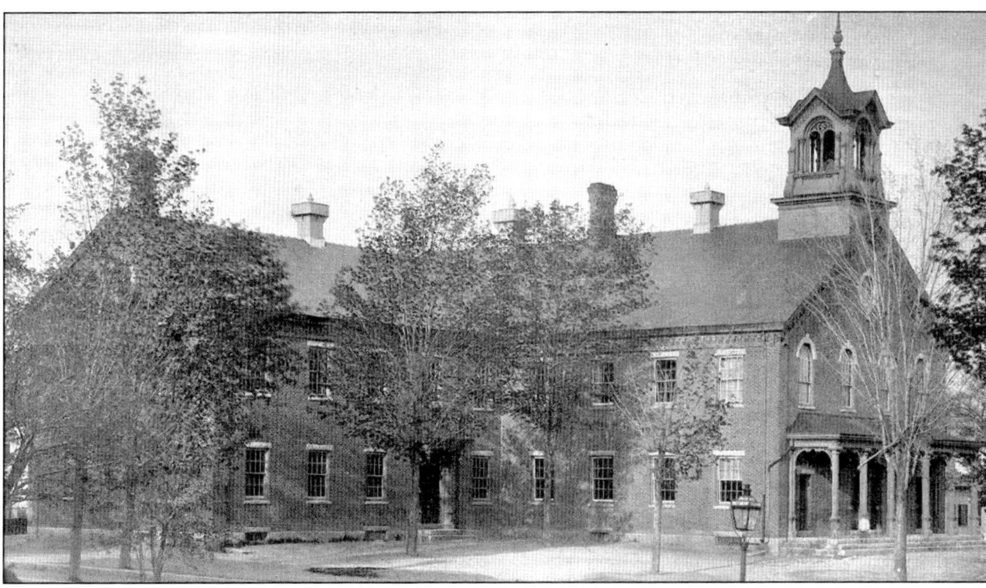

DAY STREET SCHOOL. In the mid-1800s, the Dillon School, located at 75 Day Street, was one of the largest elementary schools in Fitchburg.

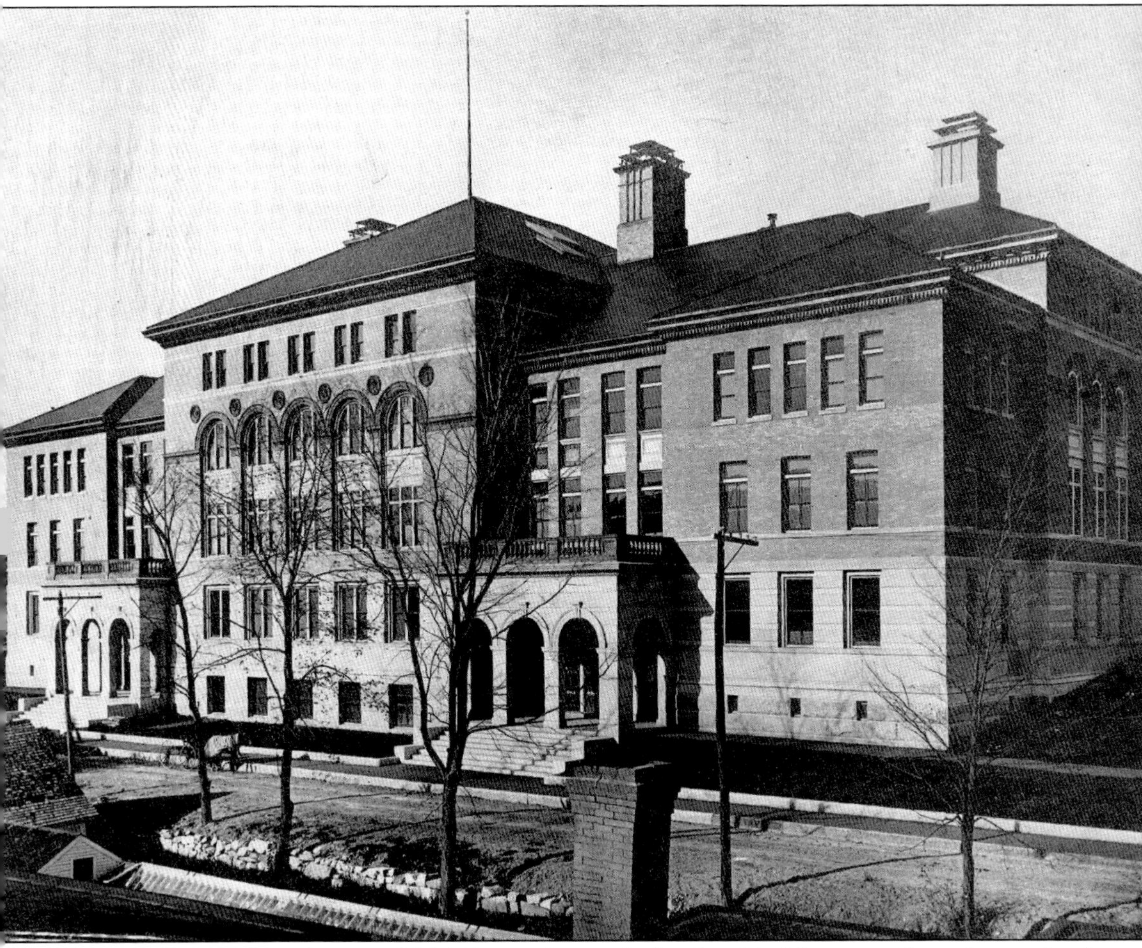

FITCHBURG HIGH SCHOOL. H. M. Francis designed schools in Fitchburg as well as a dozen schools outside the city. His first school in Fitchburg was the Academy Street High School, built in 1869. By 1893, the school committee decided to replace the older school with a larger building. Francis drew up plans for the elegant new building, and in 1895 the new school was opened.

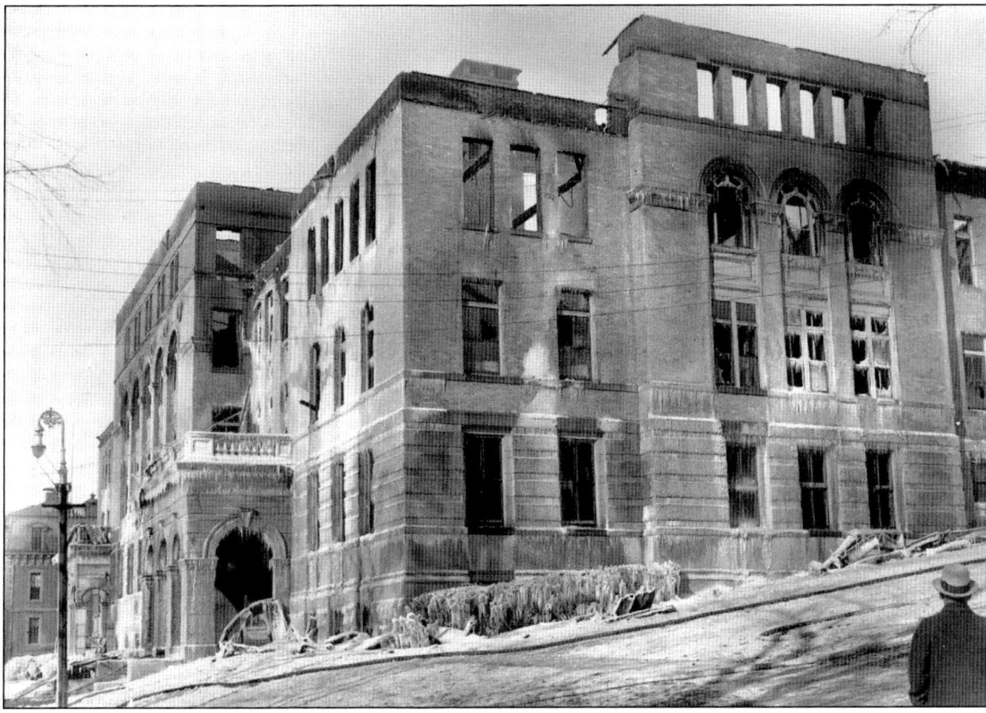

THE FITCHBURG HIGH SCHOOL FIRE. Fitchburg High School burned down in December 1934. A new high school was constructed on the same site.

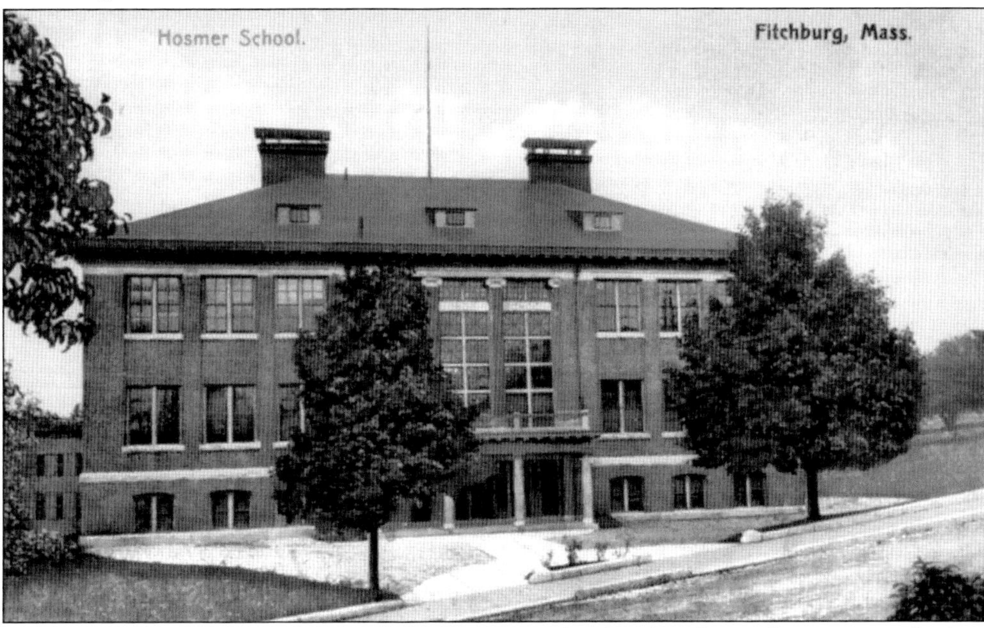

HOSMER SCHOOL. In 1907, the eight-room Hosmer School replaced a smaller, antiquated school building known as the South Street School. It was named for Clarissa D. Hosmer, who was principal of the South Street School for 30 years. Hosmer School was H. M. Francis's last school commission in the city. He died the following year, after a distinguished career in architecture that spanned 40 years.

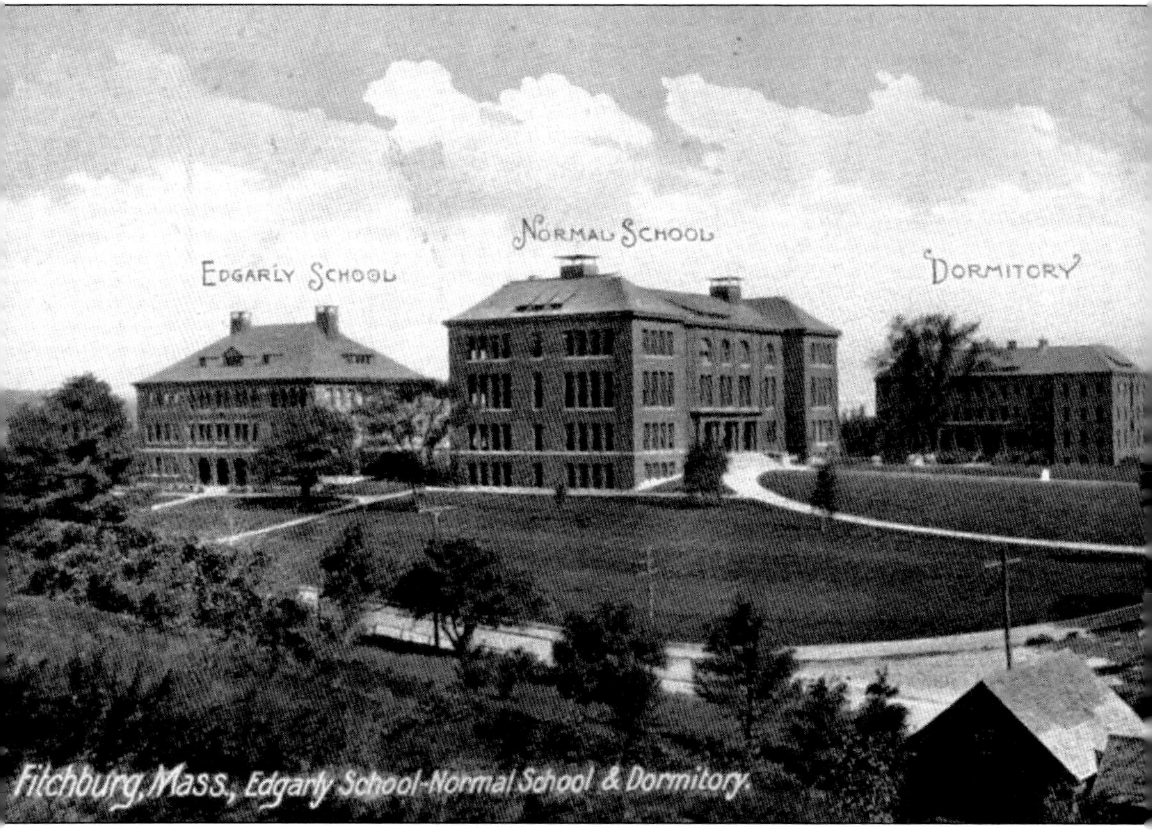

FITCHBURG NORMAL SCHOOL. Fitchburg Normal School's first president was John G. Thompson. The school started in 1894 with five faculty members. By the turn of the century, the number of teachers had grown to 12.

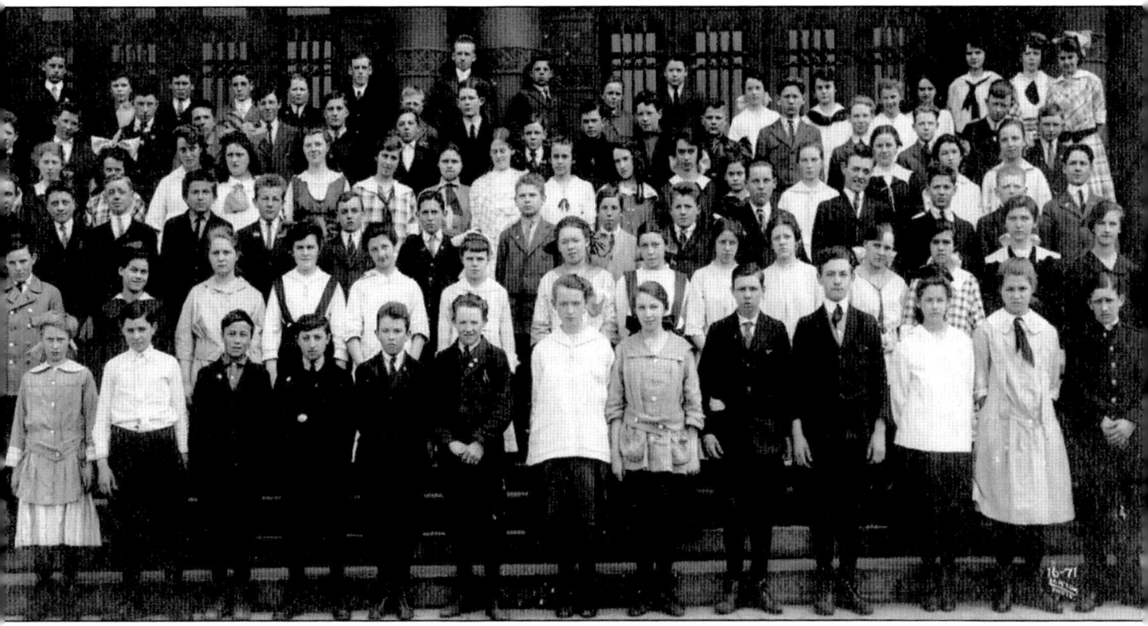

AN EIGHTH-GRADE CLASS. This 1917 group photograph was taken on the steps of Thompson Hall at Fitchburg Normal School (now Fitchburg State College). It is the eighth-grade class of Fitchburg Junior High School.

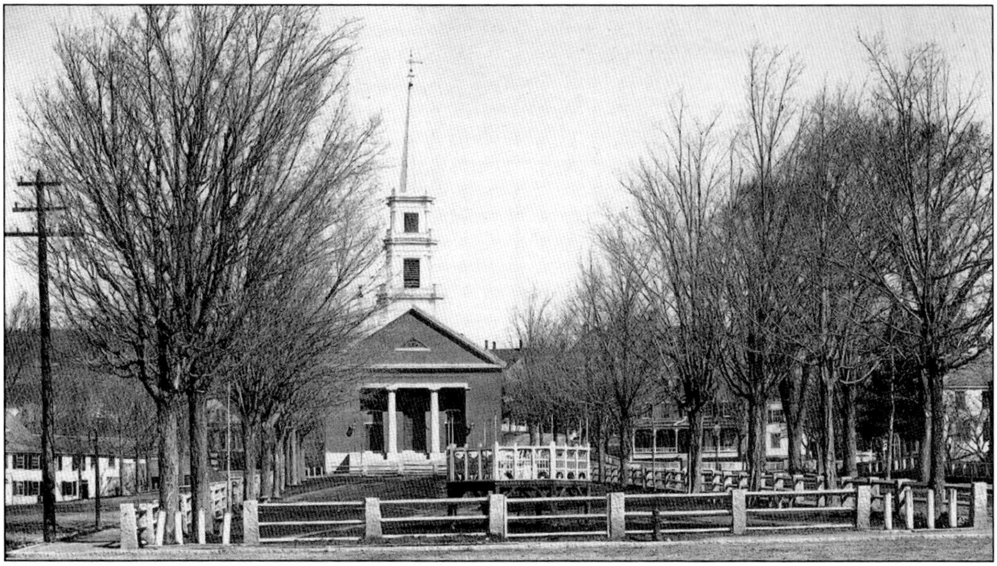

THE FIRST PARISH CHURCH. The First Parish Church, a Unitarian church, was one of the earliest congregations in the newly incorporated township of Fitchburg. Formed in 1768, the congregation built a house of worship at the head of the Upper Common in 1837. Its beautiful white steeple reflects the simplistic architecture of early New England churches.

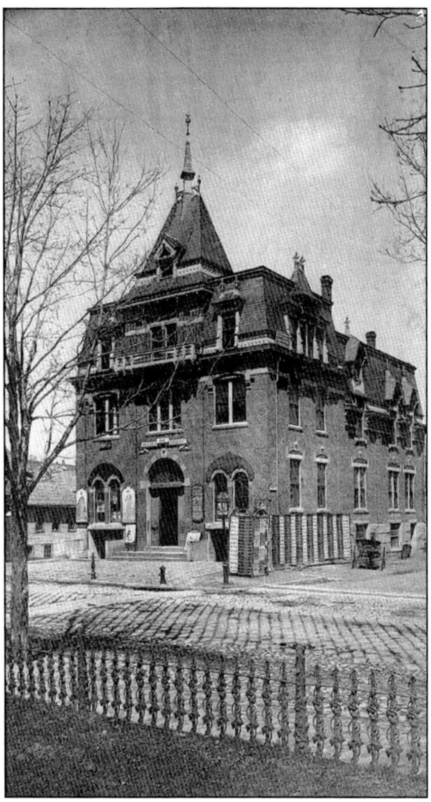

THE TRINITARIAN CHURCH. The issue of slavery was hotly debated, even in Fitchburg. In 1844, a group of antislavery sympathizers withdrew from the Calvinistic Congregational Church and founded the Trinitarian Congregational Church. The church became a stop on the Underground Railroad for runaway slaves. After the Civil War, the church's purpose diminished, and it was sold. The building served as a post office and a board of trade building before being razed.

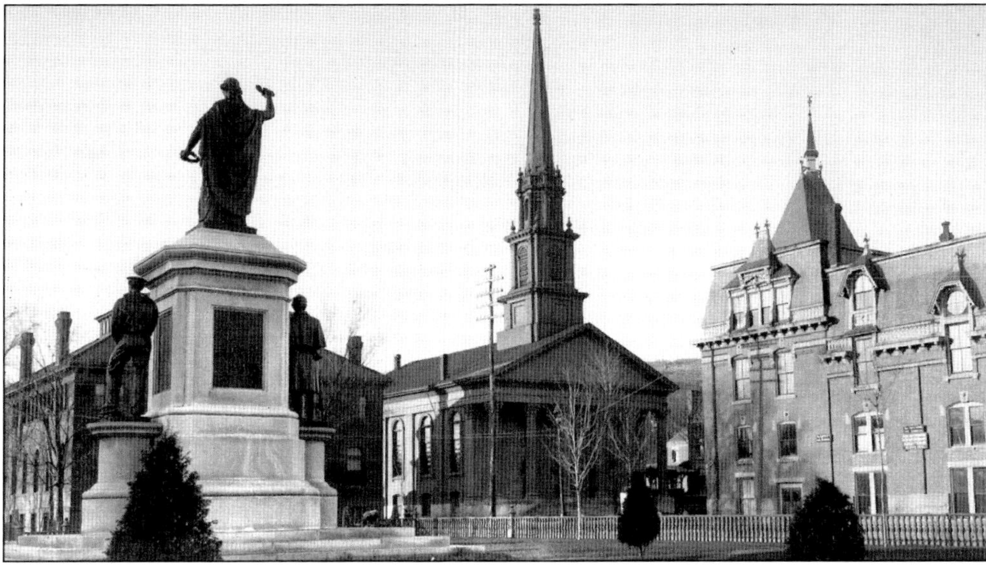

MONUMENT SQUARE. This photograph offers an unusual perspective of Monument Square. The three buildings—the Trinitarian church (right), the Baptist church (center), and the Wallace Library (partially obscured by the monument)—are now gone from Main Street. The Baptist church and the library were torn down to make way for a modern library, and the site of the Trinitarian church is now occupied by an office building.

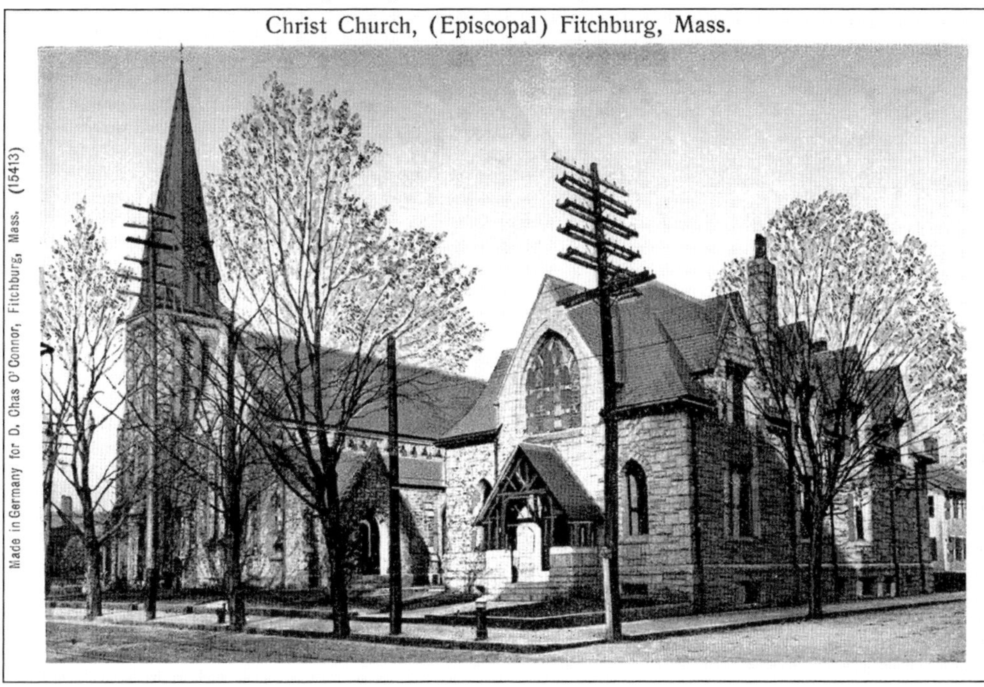

CHRIST CHURCH. Noted New York architect Richard Upjohn designed Christ Church in the Gothic Revival style. Alvah Crocker's large donation helped construction get under way, and the church was consecrated in April 1868. The parish house was added in 1893 on land donated by George Fay, whose Gothic-style house on Main Street became the Fay Club. Christ Church has nine magnificent original Tiffany Company windows that memorialize its members.

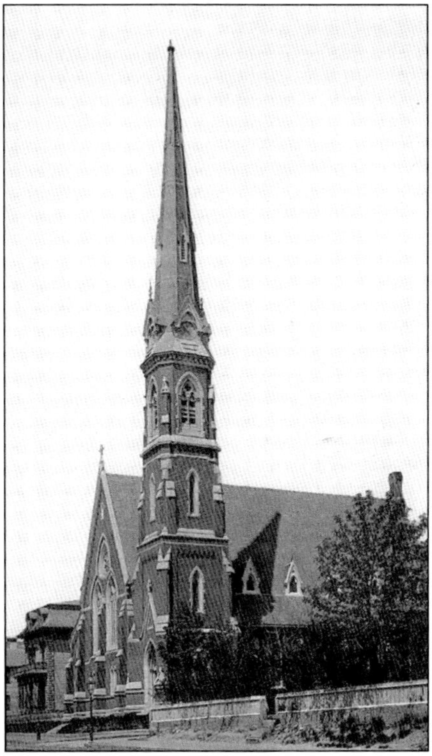

ROLLSTONE CHURCH. In 1868, some members split from the Calvinistic Congregational Church at the Upper Common to form the Rollstone Congregational Church. Dea. David Boutelle, owner of the American House, was instrumental in the establishment of the new church, contributing $28,000 toward the construction costs. A chapel bears his name, and a city street was also named after the deacon.

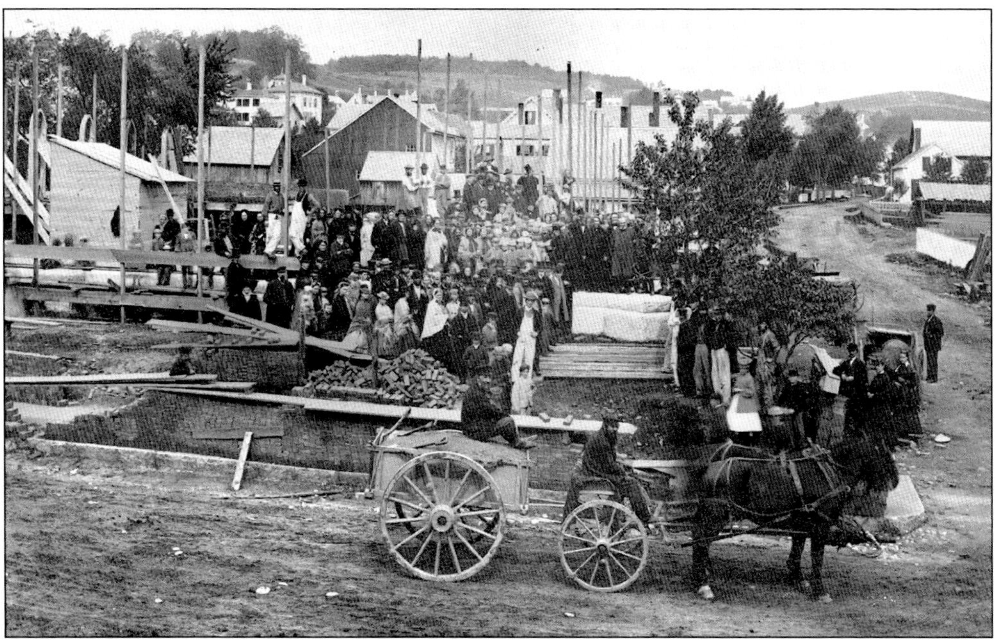

THE CORNERSTONE OF ROLLSTONE CHURCH. This very early photograph shows an interested crowd of onlookers during the laying of the cornerstone of Rollstone Congregational Church in 1868. H. M. Francis had just arrived in Fitchburg, and this was his first commission in the city. The church was dedicated in February 1870. Tiffany-style stained-glass windows replaced the original structure's windows between 1916 and 1928, many dedicated to founders of the church.

THE FIRST UNIVERSALIST CHURCH. The congregation of the First Universalist Church, organized in 1844, built its first church on Rollstone Street. Desirous of a modern church, the congregation chose land at the corner of Day and Union Streets. H. M. Francis conceived an unusual design for the new church that incorporated religious architecture from a number of faiths to create a visual message of the Universalist philosophy. The church was dedicated in 1886.

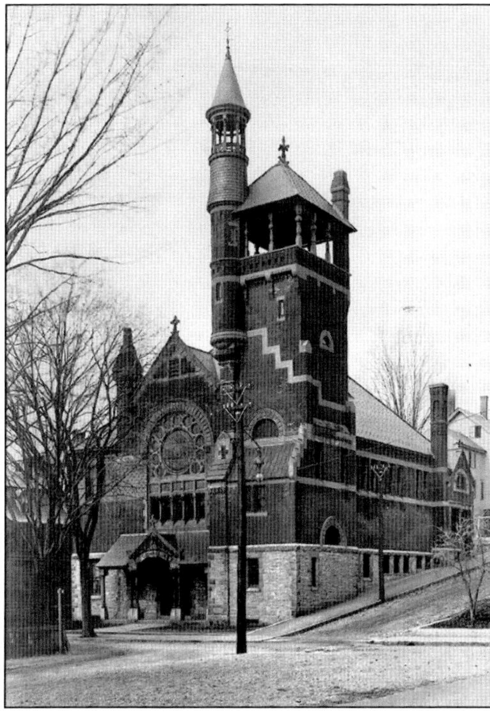

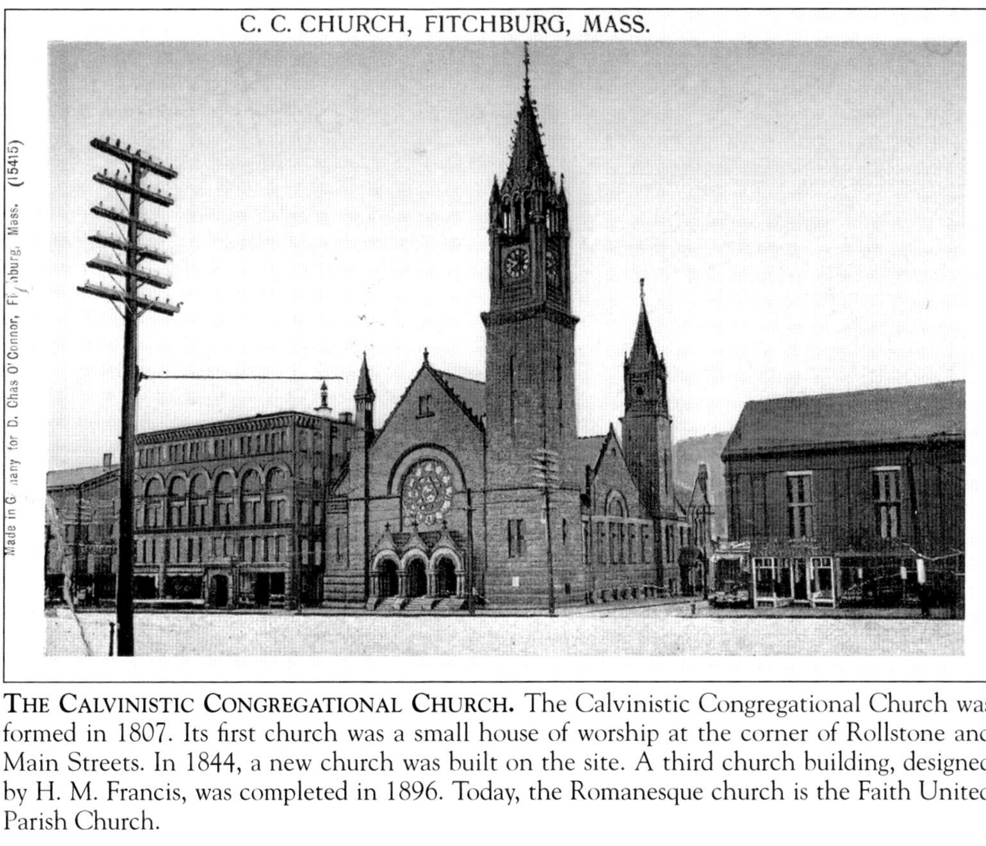

THE CALVINISTIC CONGREGATIONAL CHURCH. The Calvinistic Congregational Church was formed in 1807. Its first church was a small house of worship at the corner of Rollstone and Main Streets. In 1844, a new church was built on the site. A third church building, designed by H. M. Francis, was completed in 1896. Today, the Romanesque church is the Faith United Parish Church.

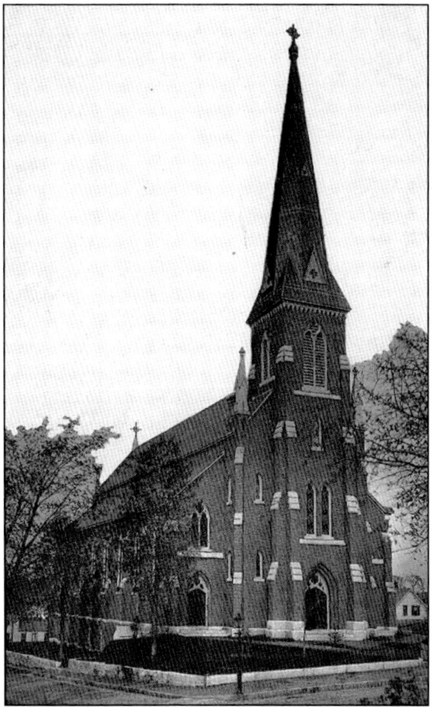

St. Bernard's Roman Catholic Parish. The Fitchburg Railroad employed Irish Catholic immigrants to build the railroad from Boston to Fitchburg. When the railroad was completed, many of the Irish workers remained in the city. The parishioners at first met in private homes for their services and then built a small church in 1848. St. Bernard's Roman Catholic Church was constructed on Water Street 21 years later.

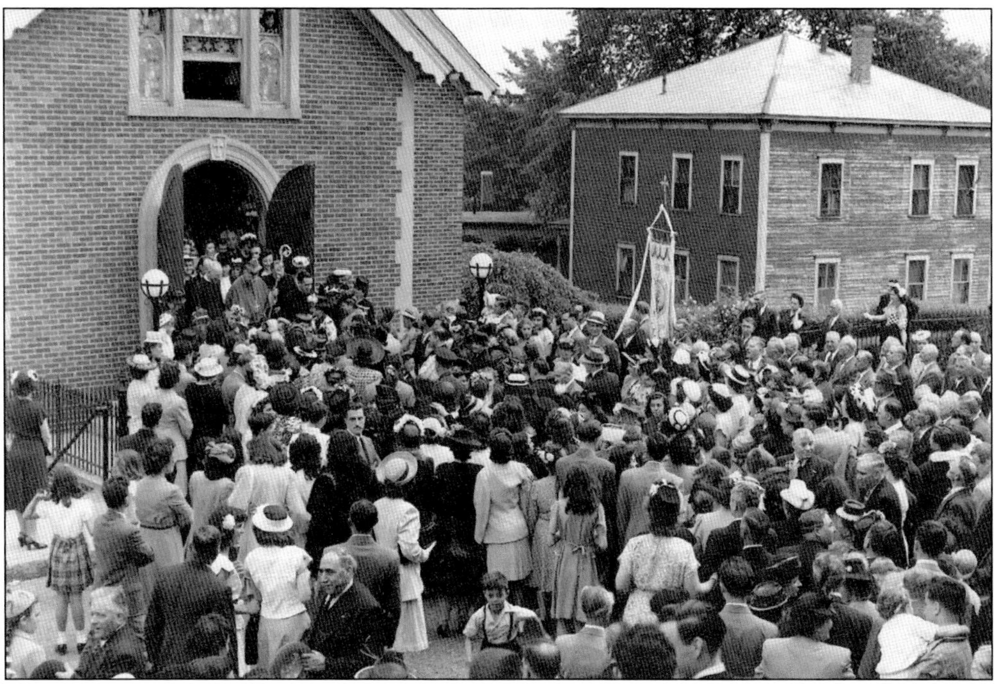

St. Anthony DiPadua Church. Parishioners of St. Anthony DiPadua Church, located at 84 Salem Street, celebrate the burning of the mortgage in the spring of 1948. Rev. Nicola Mongiello, pastor, and Thomas O'Leary, bishop of the Diocese of Worcester, are shown leaving the church. At the upper right, men of the St. Anthony Society carry their banner. (Courtesy of Betty Pagnotta.)

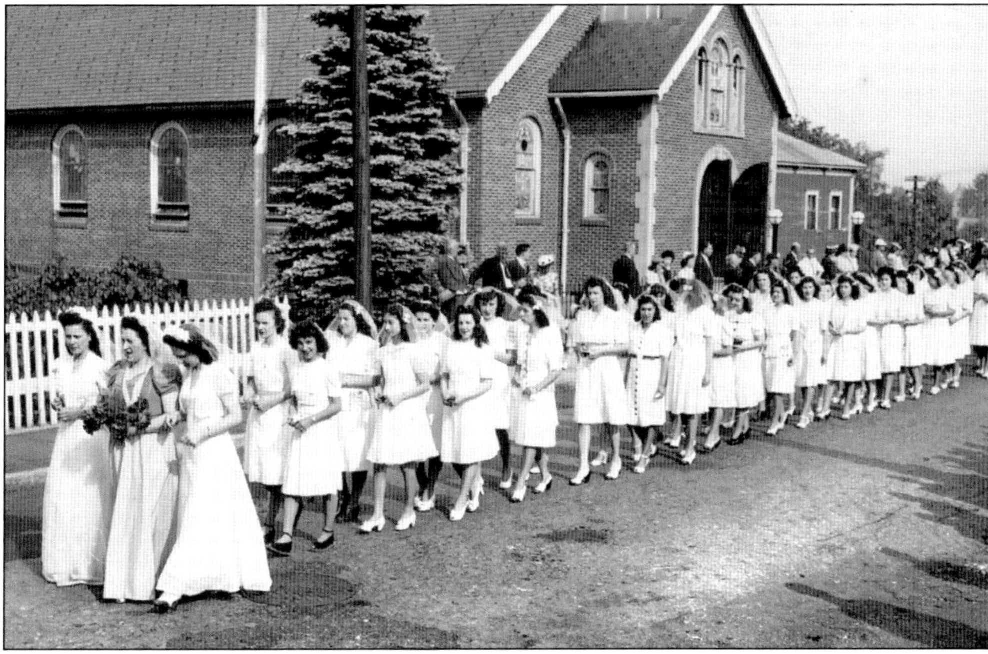

THE CHILDREN OF MARY SODALITY. The members of the Children of Mary Sodality of St. Anthony de Padua Church are shown in their white dresses and veils as they process along Salem Street in May 1948. Members of the sodality were girls and young unmarried women. (Courtesy of Betty Pagnotta.)

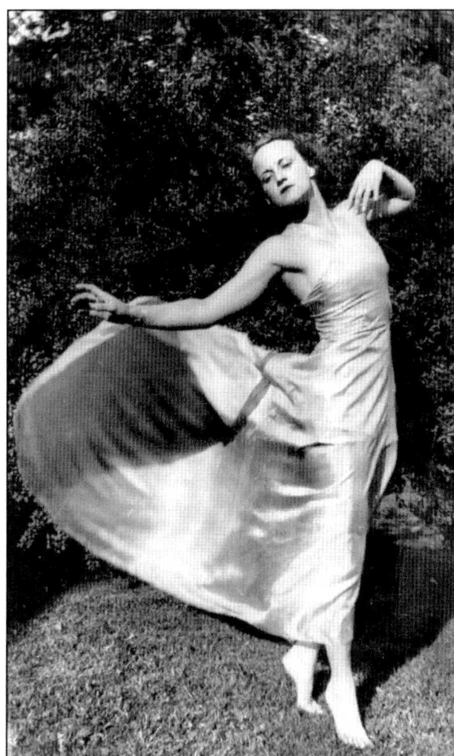

MARION RICE, C. 1930S. Legendary dancer and teacher Marion Rice always said that she was born dancing. She began her career by teaching her sisters, and she studied with Ted Shawn at the Denishawn-Braggiotti School. Rice opened her studio of dance in 1924, and she taught ballet and ballroom dancing to generations of young women (and the occasional football player). She danced in every church in Fitchburg, as well as at numerous colleges and other performance venues.

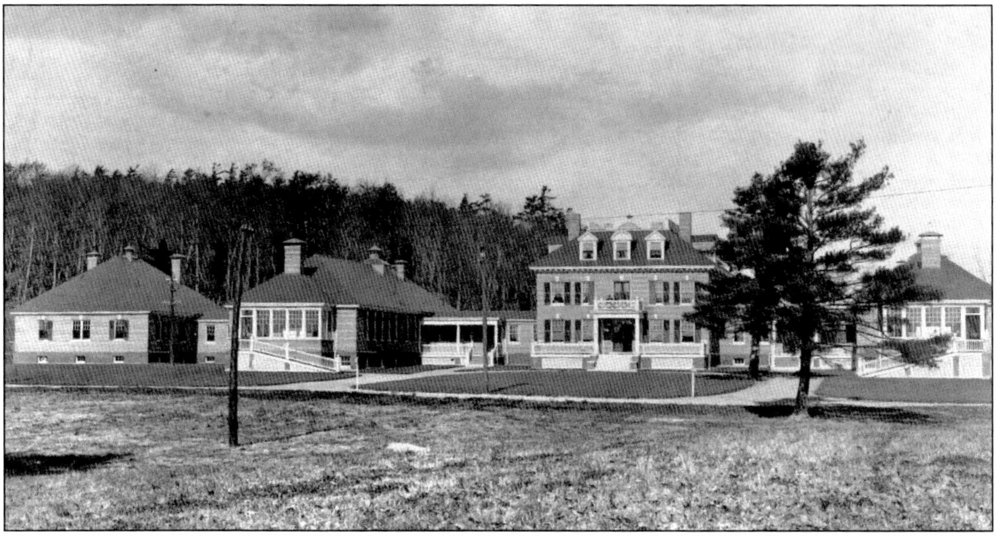

BURBANK HOSPITAL. In 1901, Burbank Hospital opened its doors with a $500,000 gift from Gardner S. Burbank and his wife, Sarah. Burbank was a partner in the Crocker Burbank Paper Company. Ill health had plagued him for much of his life, and all three of his children and his first wife had predeceased him. With no heirs for his large estate, he decided to establish a hospital that would receive the wealthy as well as the poor.

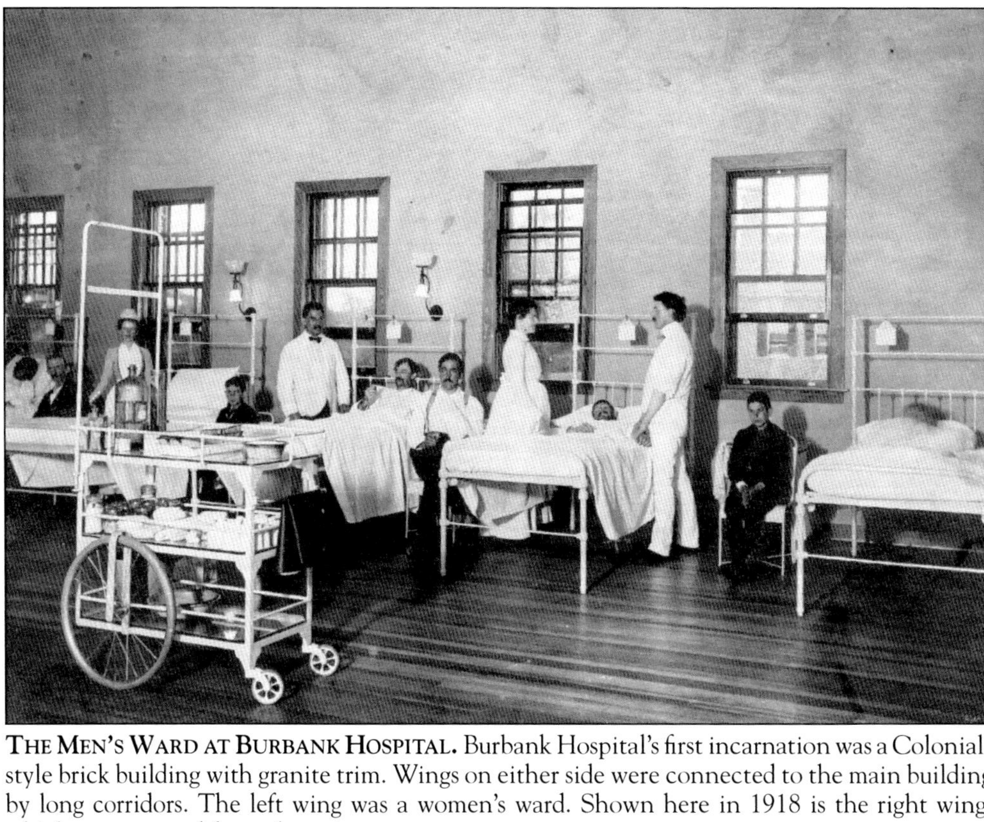

THE MEN'S WARD AT BURBANK HOSPITAL. Burbank Hospital's first incarnation was a Colonial-style brick building with granite trim. Wings on either side were connected to the main building by long corridors. The left wing was a women's ward. Shown here in 1918 is the right wing, which was reserved for male patients.

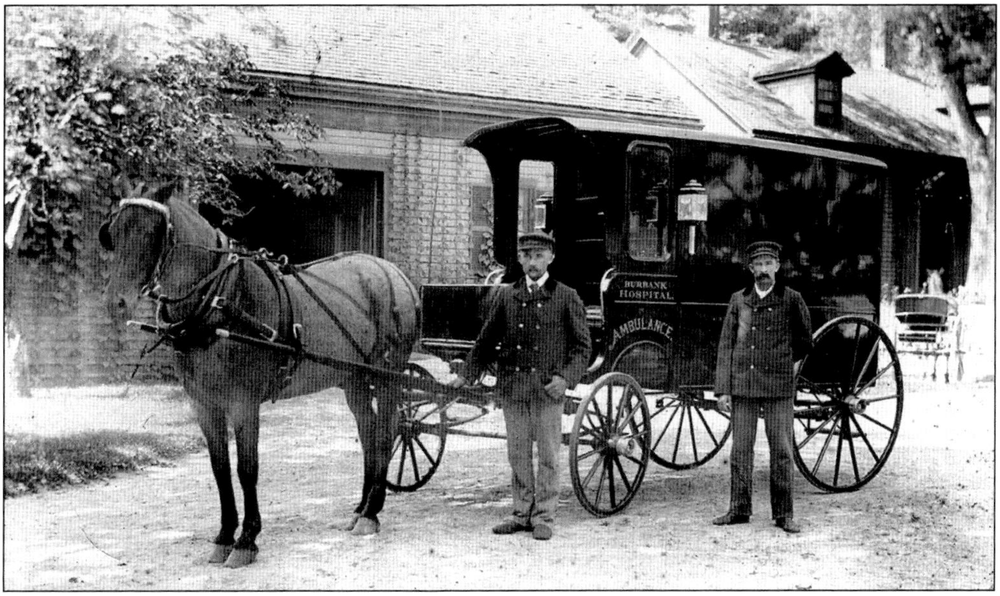

AN AMBULANCE. Burbank Hospital began treating patients in the "Mansion House" in 1894, caring for victims of accidents, typhoid fever, and other maladies. In that same year, the hospital put into service a horse-drawn ambulance. Imagine the painful journey over the dirt roads and cobbled streets of that era. When the ambulance arrived at the bottom of the hill, the driver would signal his approach by loudly ringing a hand bell.

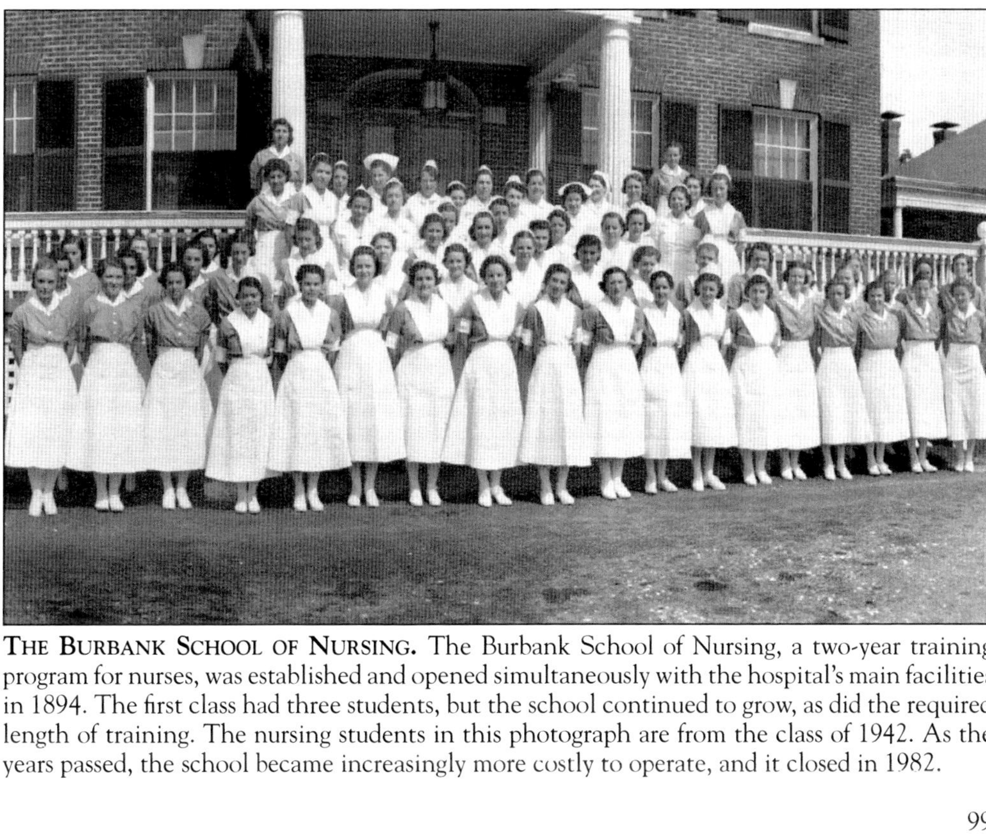

THE BURBANK SCHOOL OF NURSING. The Burbank School of Nursing, a two-year training program for nurses, was established and opened simultaneously with the hospital's main facilities in 1894. The first class had three students, but the school continued to grow, as did the required length of training. The nursing students in this photograph are from the class of 1942. As the years passed, the school became increasingly more costly to operate, and it closed in 1982.

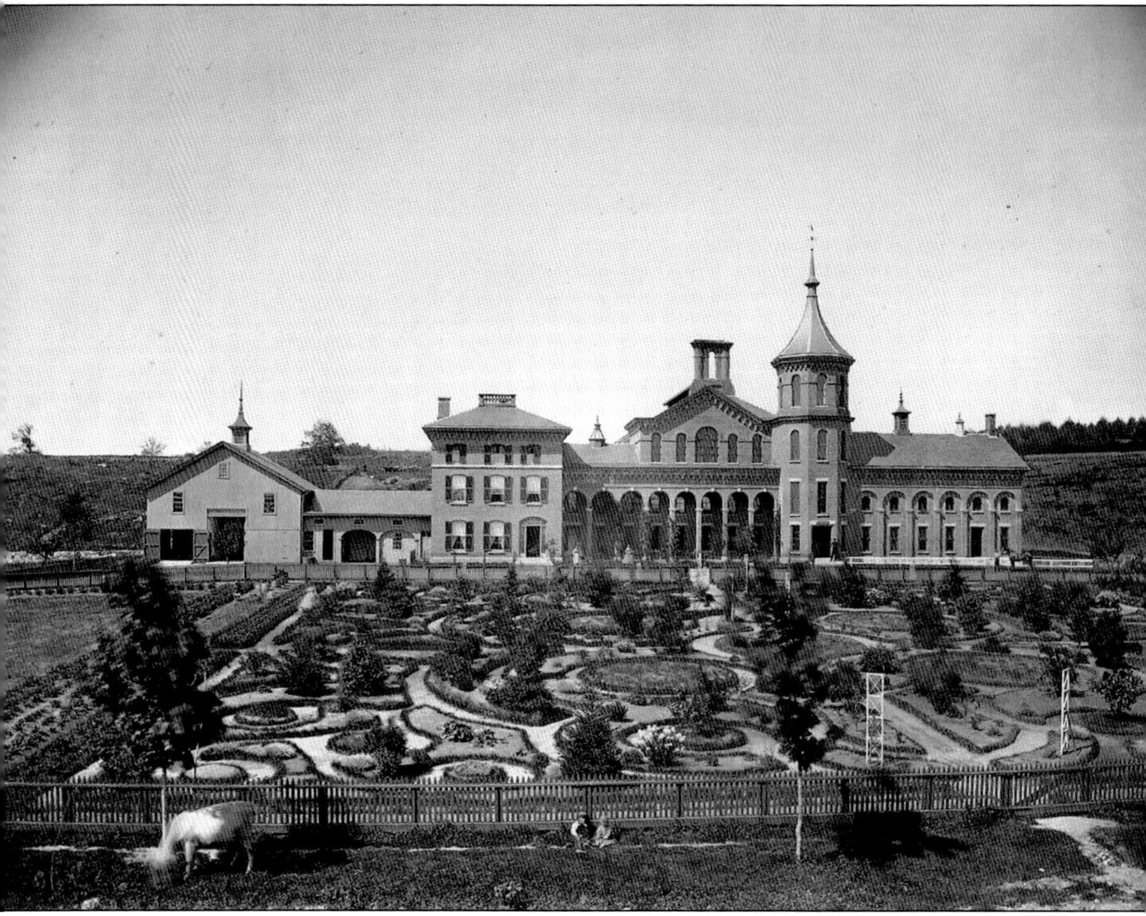

THE WORCESTER COUNTY JAIL. The Worcester County House of Corrections, with its impressive gardens, opened on Water Street in 1860. The four-story brick-and-granite building housed a hospital, a library, a chapel, and cells for over 70 inmates, some of whom were Southern women spies during the Civil War. Several local citizens were confined for such misdemeanors as not removing snow directly after a storm. Once a 10-year-old runaway boy served nine months here.

Six

Serving Our Country and Community

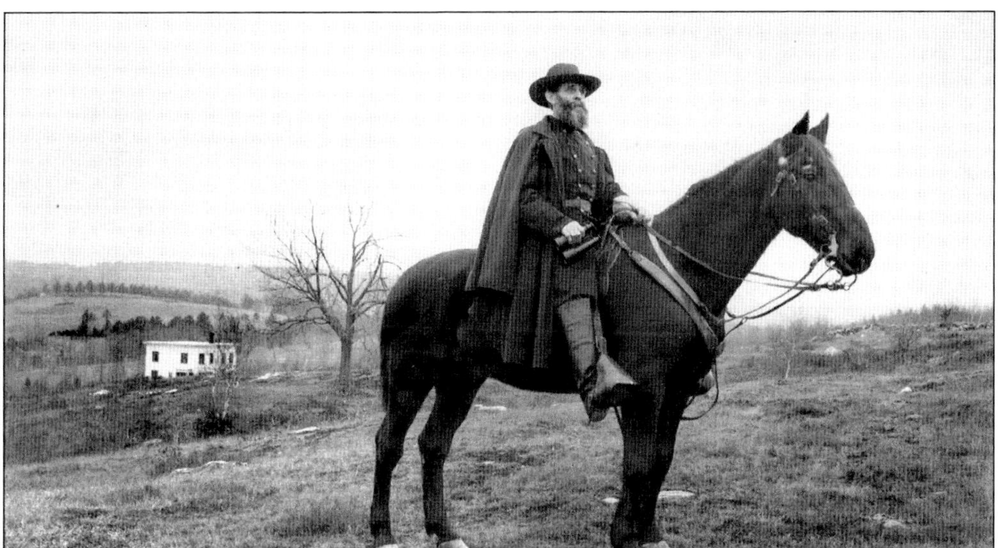

GEN. JOHN KIMBALL AND PRINCE. Upon accepting command of Company K of the 53rd Regiment in 1862, Col. John W. Kimball was given equipment and a fine four-year-old horse named Prince by 43 friends and leading citizens of Fitchburg. Colonel Kimball and Prince later saw battle in New Orleans, and Kimball was later promoted to general. In the reunion of 1887, the general mounted Prince for this photograph and had a copy made for every man in his command.

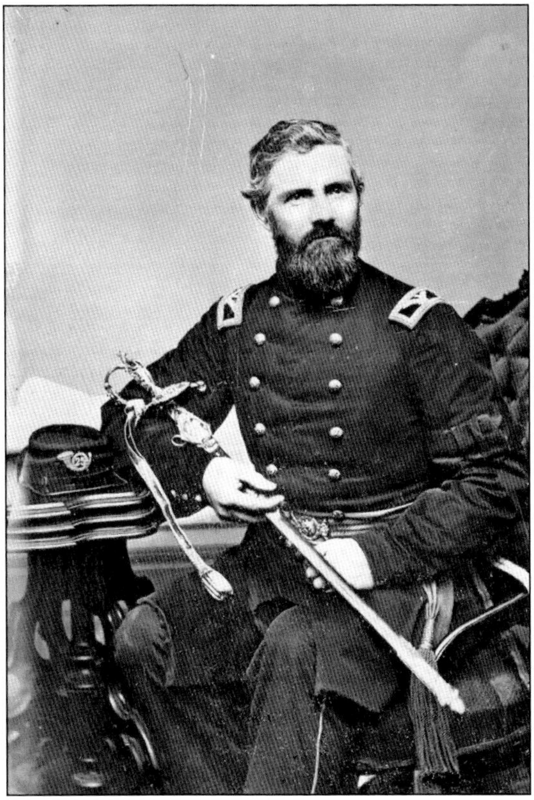

COL. EDWIN UPTON. Col. Edwin Upton, who commanded the 25th Regiment in the Civil War, was so highly regarded by his men that the noncommissioned soldiers presented him with a sword encrusted with diamonds and rubies as a token of his "noble character, for qualities of a gallant soldier and as a fearless yet considerate commander."

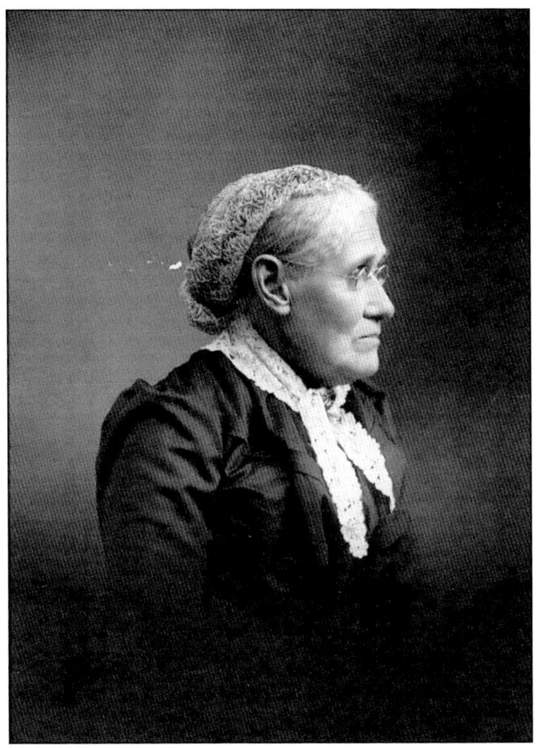

MARTHA GOODRICH. In 1862, Martha Goodrich accepted the call to become a nurse in the Union army under Dorothea Dix. She served at Mount Pleasant Hospital in Washington, D.C., at Antietam, at Point Lookout Prison Camp after Gettysburg, and lastly at Andersonville Prison until 1865. After the war, she became first matron of the House of Mercy Cottage Hospital in Pittsfield. In failing health, she returned to Fitchburg, where she died in 1910.

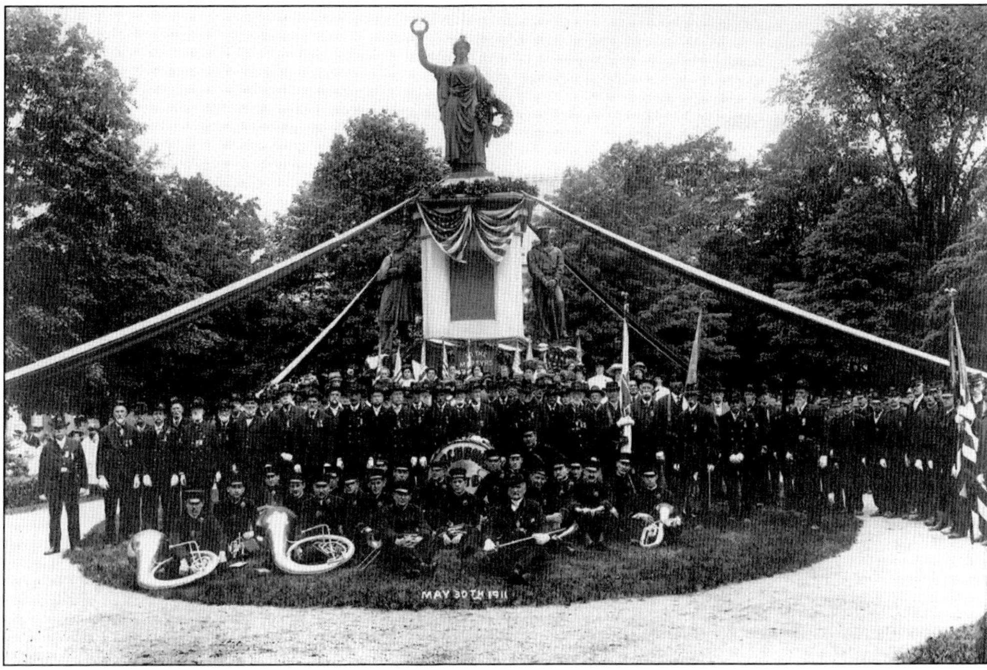

MEMORIAL DAY, 1911. On Memorial Day 1911, the Grand Army, the Women's Relief Corps, the Sons and Daughters of Veterans, and the Fitchburg Band gathered in front of the soldiers' and sailors' monument to commemorate the soldiers whose bodies were not returned to the city. Local veterans decorated 234 Fitchburg military graves that year.

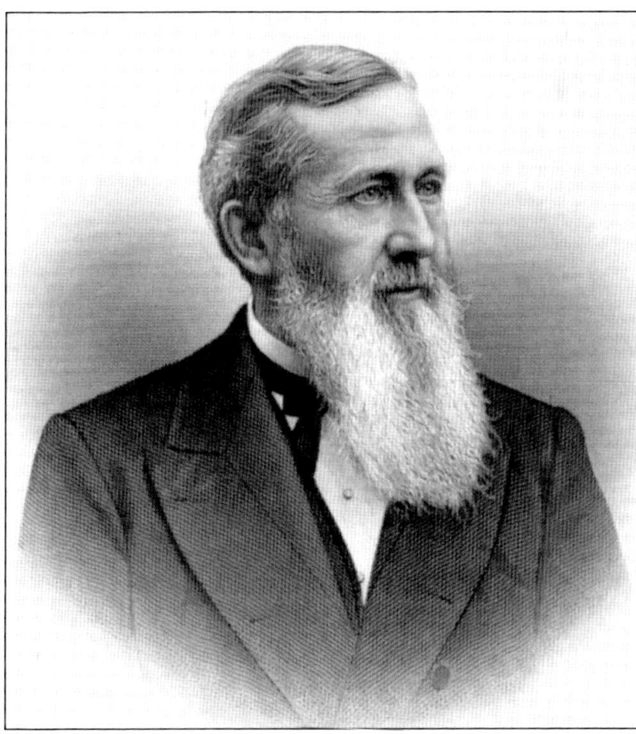

THE LAST FITCHBURG SURVIVOR OF THE CIVIL WAR. George C. Jewett, the last survivor of the Civil War from Fitchburg's roster, died in 1939. Jewett was actually from Lunenburg, but he was employed in Fitchburg when he signed up for service at the age of 18. He requested that his name be listed under Lunenburg's quota. When it was discovered that he had been entered under Fitchburg's quota, Lunenburg futilely protested to the authorities. Jewett served as a Fitchburg soldier, and Lunenburg had to find another man to fulfill its quota.

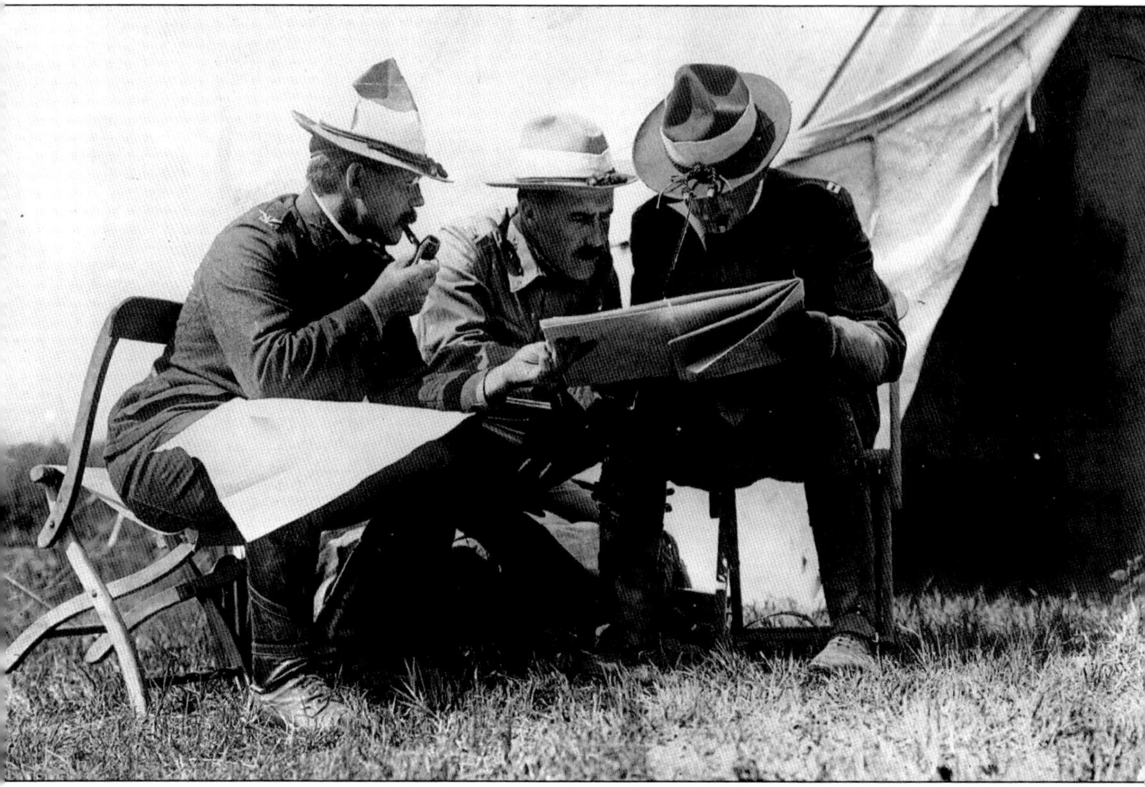

SOLDIERS OF THE SPANISH-AMERICAN WAR. George H. Priest went off to fight in the Spanish-American War in 1898, when he was 33 years old. Priest became president of the Charles A. Priest Lumber Company upon the death of his father in 1887, and he returned to the business after the war. He is among the soldiers in this 1898 photograph.

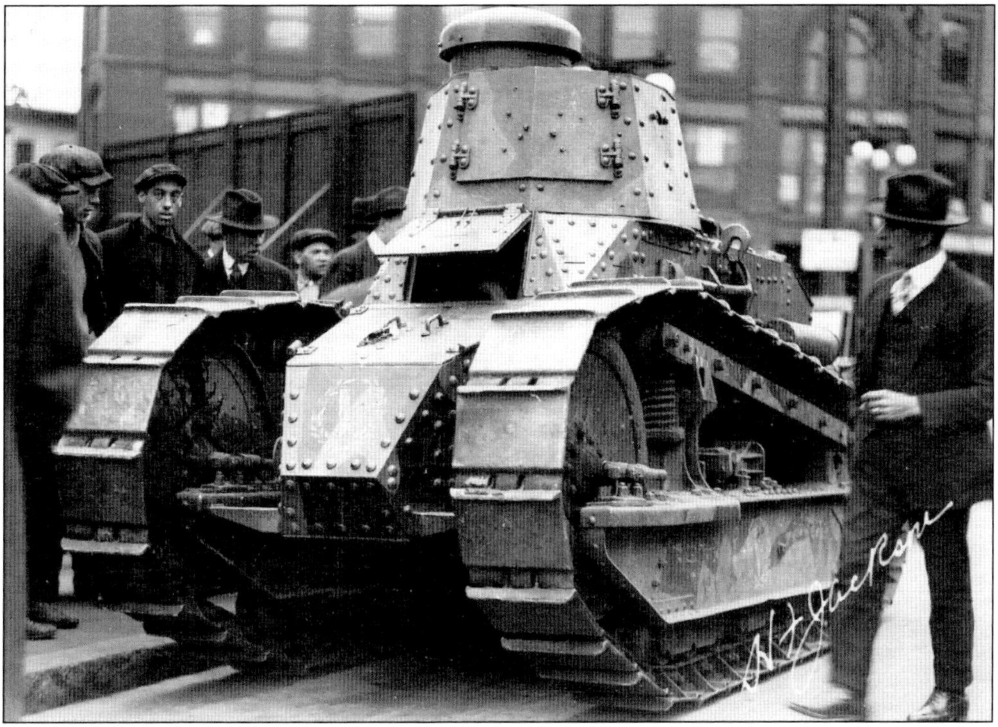

A WORLD WAR I TANK. Fitchburg men inspect a World War I tank in the American House square in 1919.

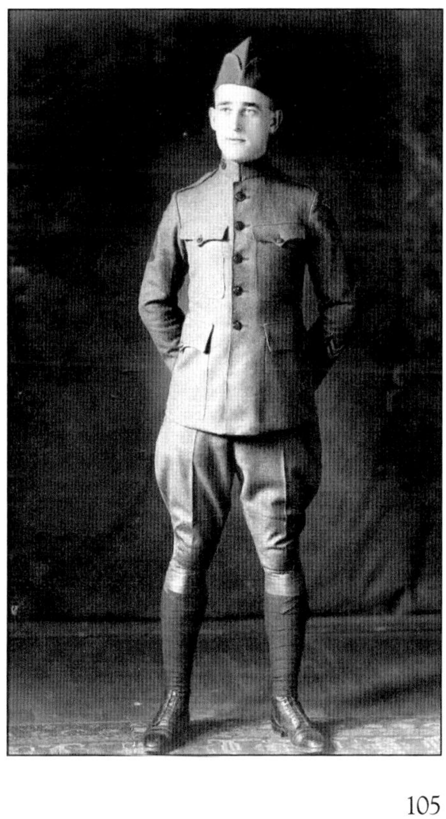

A WORLD WAR I SOLDIER. This portrait is of Ralph W. Adams, a young soldier from Fitchburg, during World War I.

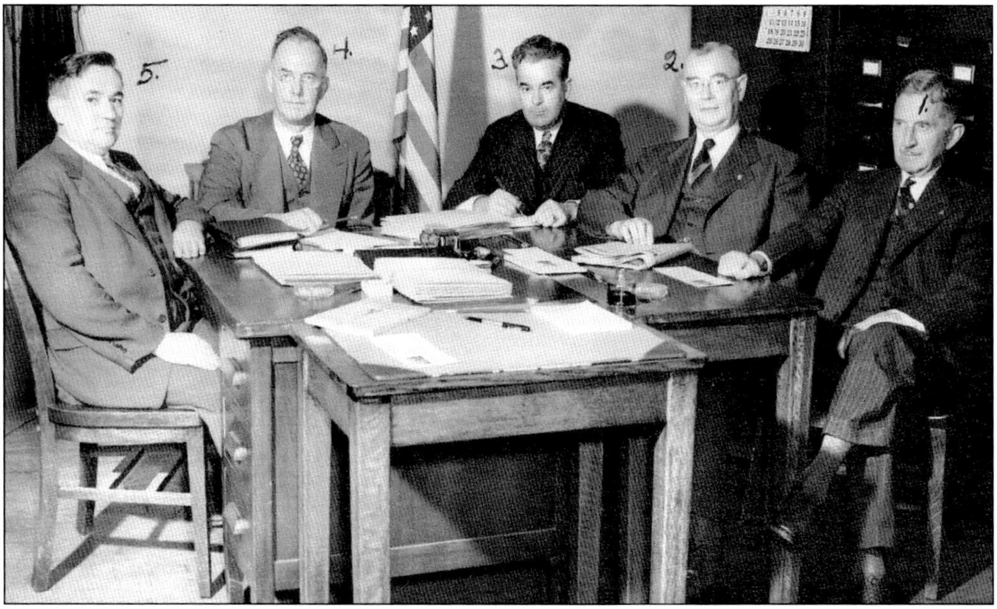

THE WORLD WAR II DRAFT BOARD. Fitchburg had two draft boards during World War II. On October 14, 1940, Area Board No. 68, which included Wards 4, 5, and 6, held a meeting. Seen here are, from left to right, chairman Charles I. Drummond, secretary W. Wellington Baumgartner, Paul G. Gearan, John Suominen, and Herbert K. Bruce. Gov. Leverett Saltonstall included Fitchburg's boards in the 173 local draft boards announced at the statehouse on October 9, 1940.

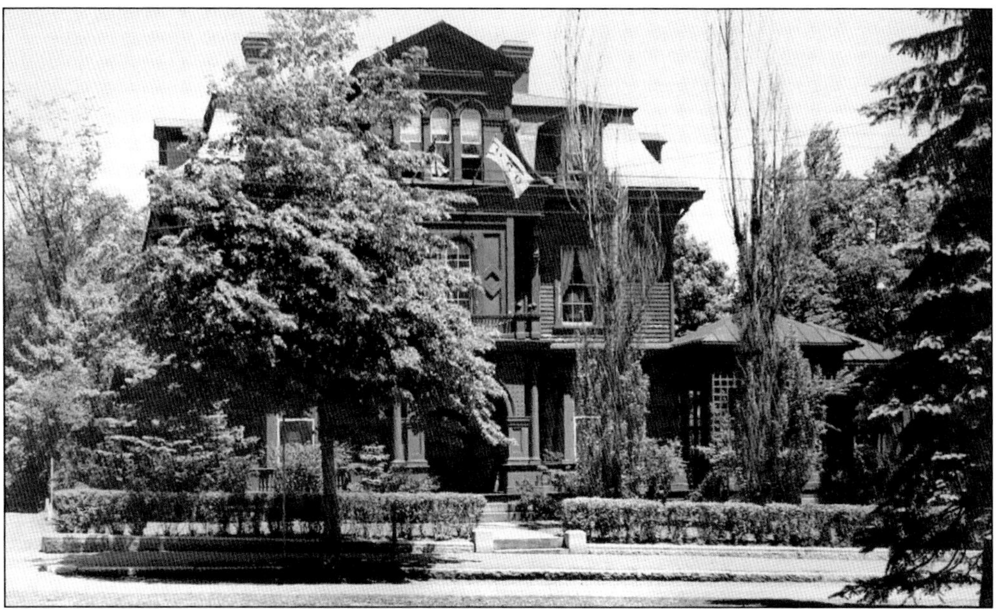

THE FITCHBURG UNITED SERVICE ORGANIZATION. This is the United Service Organization (USO) building, which was formerly the 22-room home of Arthur Lowe. Located at the Upper Common, it was built in 1870 by Leander Sprague and was purchased by Lowe in 1880. The house was vacant from the time of Lowe's death in 1932 until it was acquired by the city in 1940. In 1943, it was designated as a USO center for military personnel.

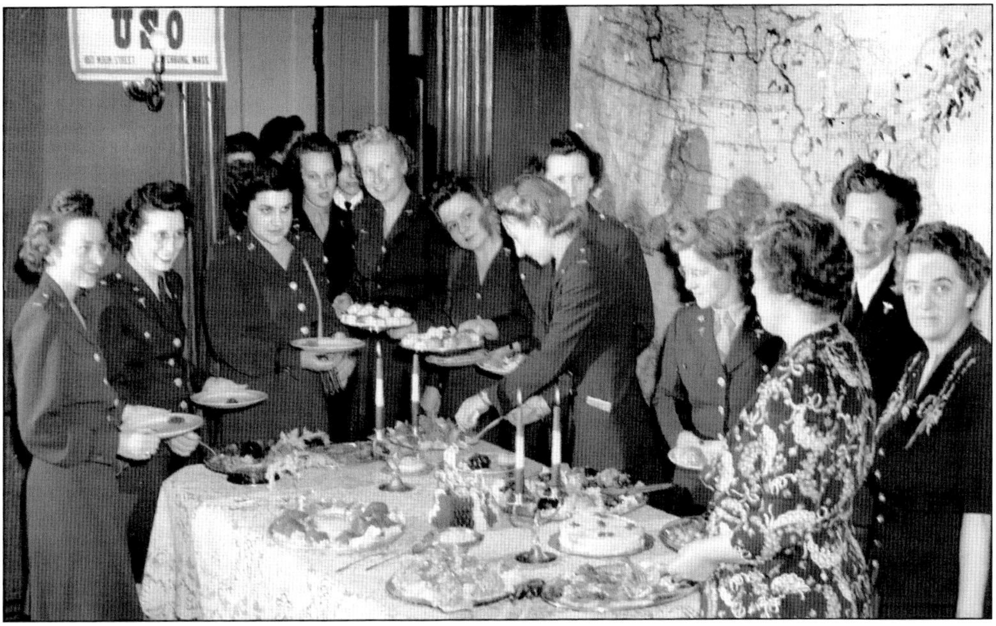

ARMY NURSES AT THE USO. The Daughters of Isabella hosted a party at the USO for the army nurses from Camp Devens. The USO became a home away from home for servicemen and women stationed in the area. It was open seven days a week for dancing, parties, and good old-fashioned hospitality.

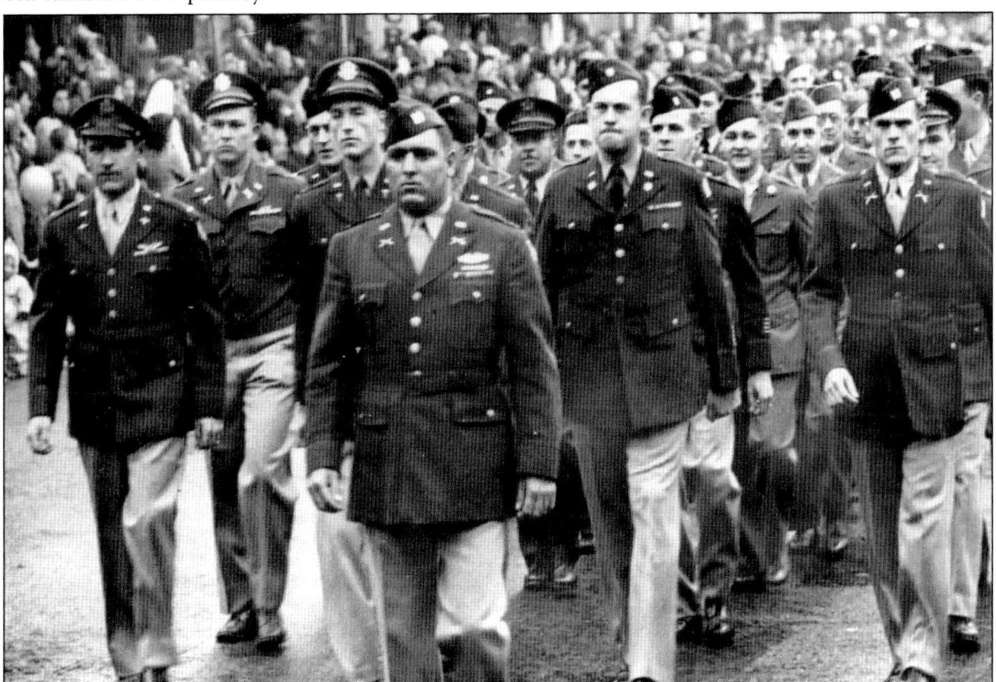

THE WORLD WAR II HOMECOMING PARADE. Returning Fitchburg soldiers march up Main Street in the 1946 homecoming parade. Raymond Roy, the most decorated Fitchburg soldier of World War II, leads them.

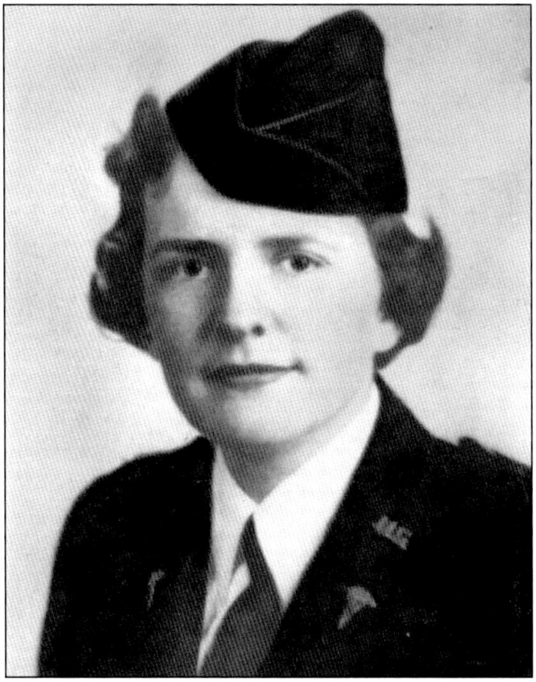

FIRST LT. ISABEL DEMMON. First Lt. Isabel Demmon of the Army Nurse Corps was born in Fitchburg. She served in India for two years, caring for military personnel who fought in China, Burma, India, and the Pacific theater. In later years, she was celebrated as a poet, and much of her work has been published.

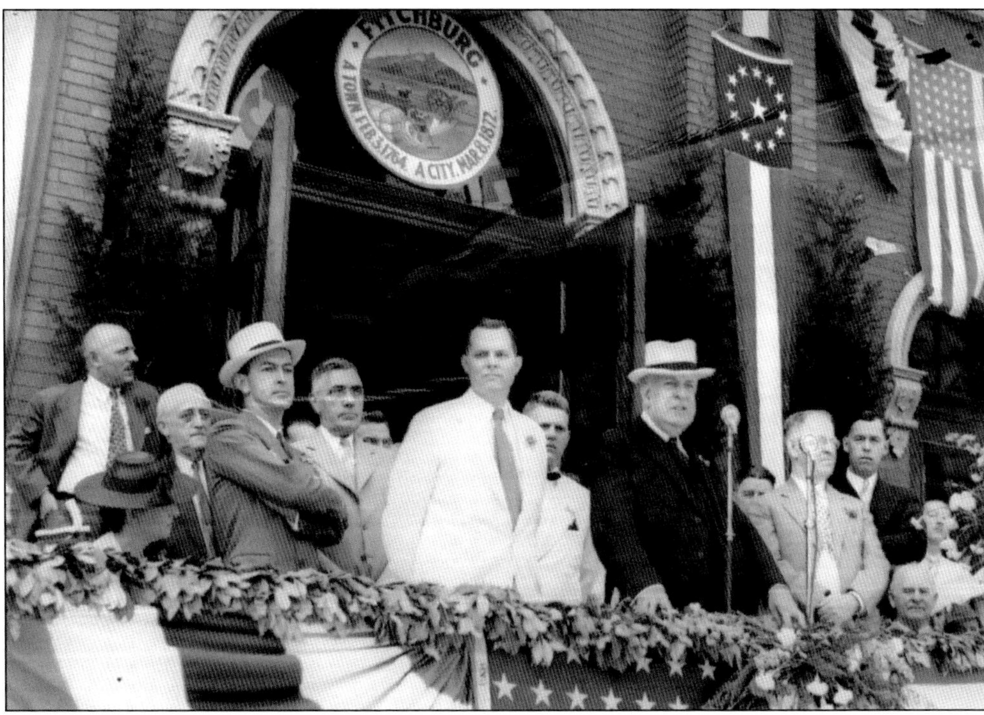

MAYOR WOLLACOTT. Alfred Wollacott (standing at the front in the white suit) was mayor of Fitchburg for five terms, from 1936 to 1946. He was a very busy man; during his active political life, he served as mayor, city councilor, acting fire chief, acting police chief, and school superintendent. He was also president of the chamber of commerce, the historical society, and Burbank Hospital, and he was a director of two banks. Wollacott died at the age of 94 in 1986.

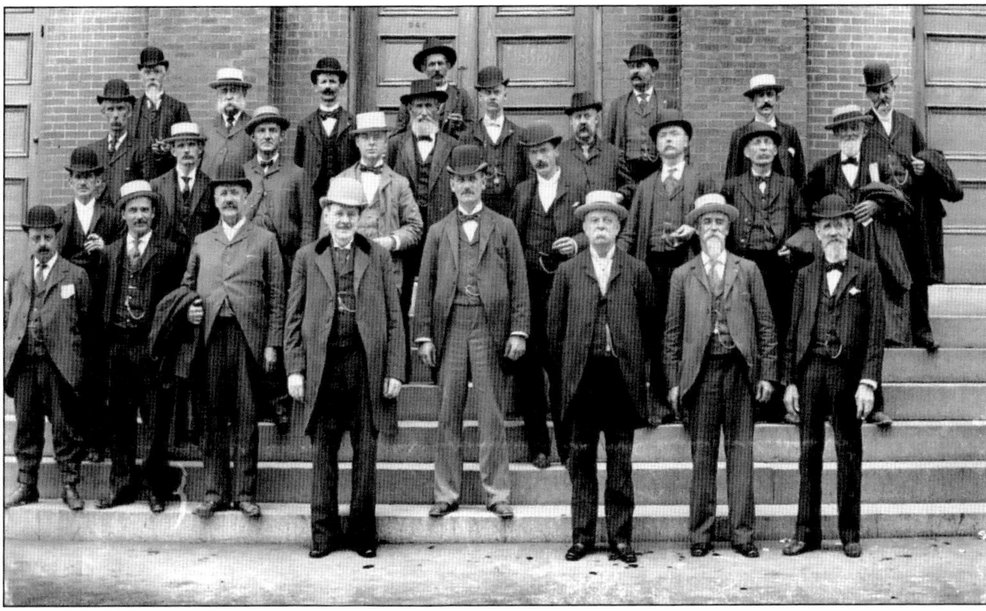

A Fitchburg City Government Outing. The attendees of an 1895 Fitchburg city government outing include Mayor Edgar S. Moulton, W. A. Davis, Harry Jackson, Albert H. Burgess, John Oldfield, Joseph W. Abbott, James A. Austin, John P. Kennedy, Joseph F. Jaseph, Frederic Rolph, John Heagney, Charles H. Doten, John Ogden, W. H. Goodwin, John Dwyer, Charles Boyle, Thomas Upton, Will Farrar, John Sheehan, and fire department chief engineer George H. Kendall.

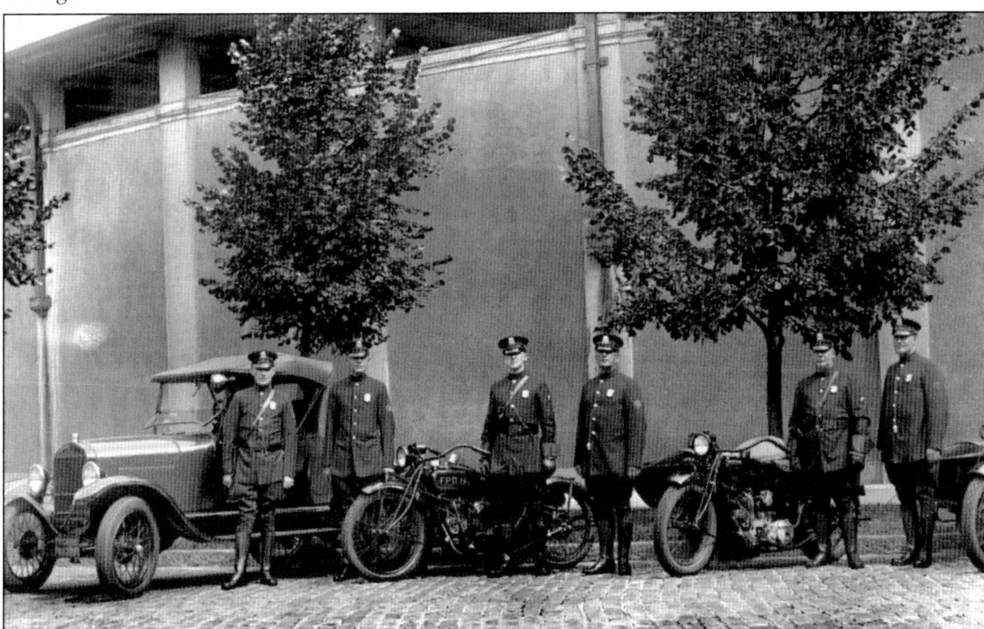

The Fitchburg Police Department Motorcycle Corps. Members of the Fitchburg Police Department Motorcycle Corps are shown standing in front of their motorcycles in this 1930s photograph. Donald Goranson, whose father, Otto G. Goranson, was a captain in the police force during the 1930s, donated this photograph to the Fitchburg Historical Society.

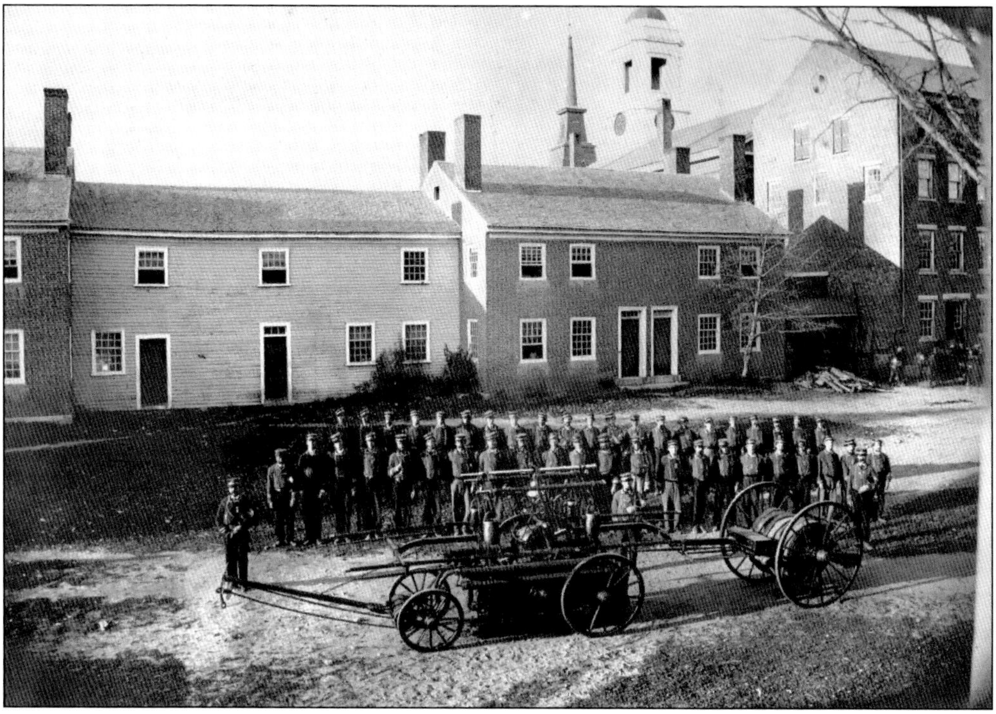

MAZEPPA NO. 3. Fitchburg's Hose No. 3 company stands in Factory Square in 1851. The birth of Hose No. 3 occurred in 1835, when the town voted to equip a two-story firehouse. Hose No. 3 was also known as Mazeppa No. 3 after Lord Byron's poem "Mazeppa." Towing the hand engine required 40 to 60 men. Sometimes a horse was needed to pull the engine up the steep hills of Fitchburg.

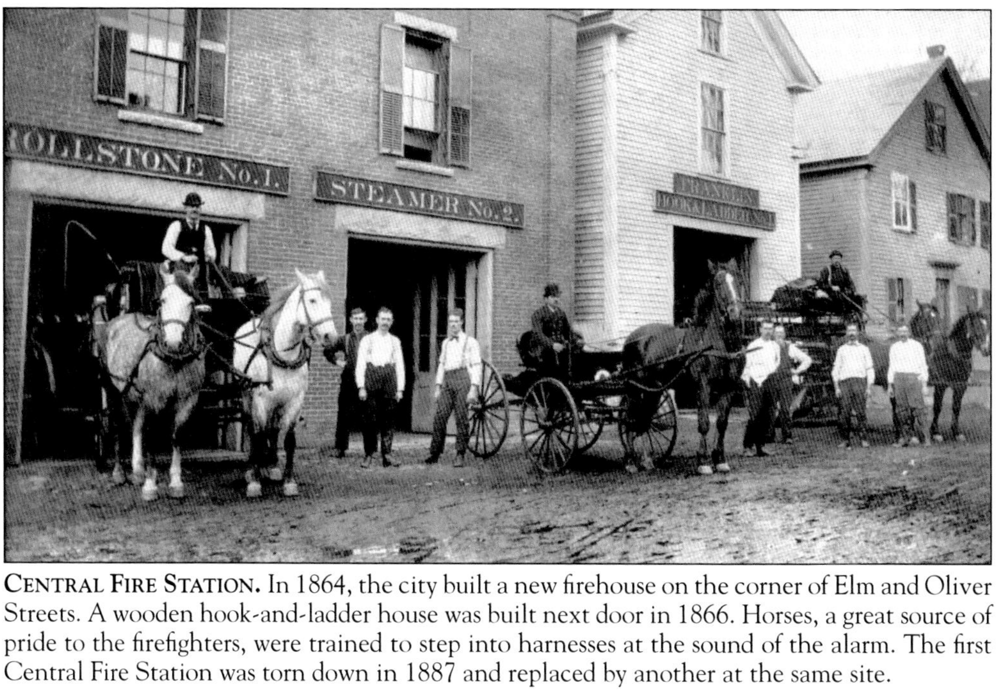

CENTRAL FIRE STATION. In 1864, the city built a new firehouse on the corner of Elm and Oliver Streets. A wooden hook-and-ladder house was built next door in 1866. Horses, a great source of pride to the firefighters, were trained to step into harnesses at the sound of the alarm. The first Central Fire Station was torn down in 1887 and replaced by another at the same site.

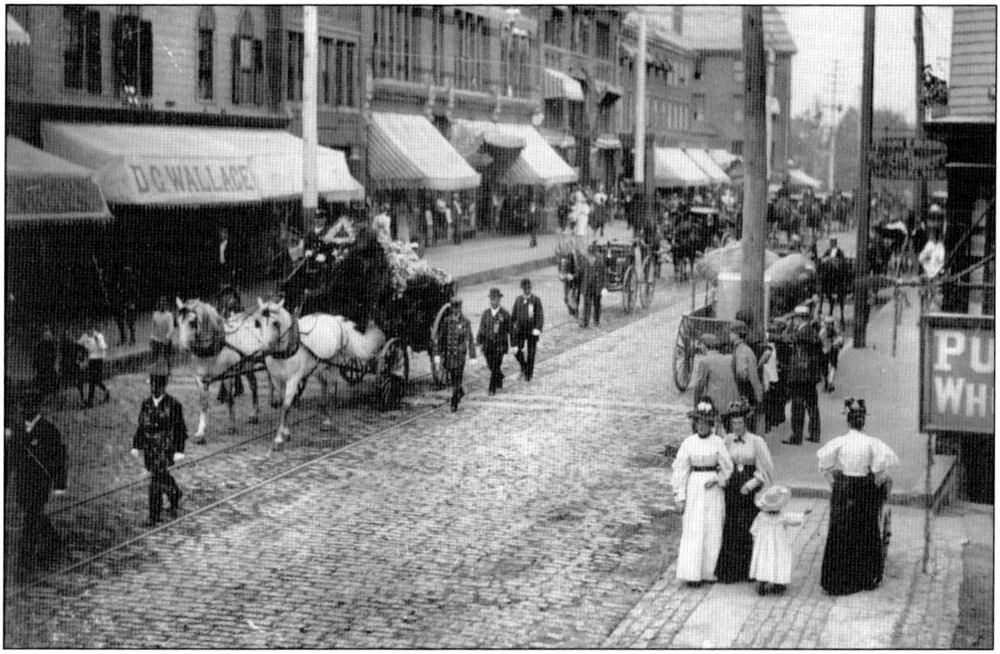

GEORGE H. KENDALL'S FUNERAL CORTEGE. Main Street was a busy place in the summer of 1896. One event that occurred that summer was the funeral cortege of George H. Kendall. The only fire chief to die in office, Kendall was highly respected, as evidenced by the flower-laden hearse pulled by two white horses and by the riderless wagon.

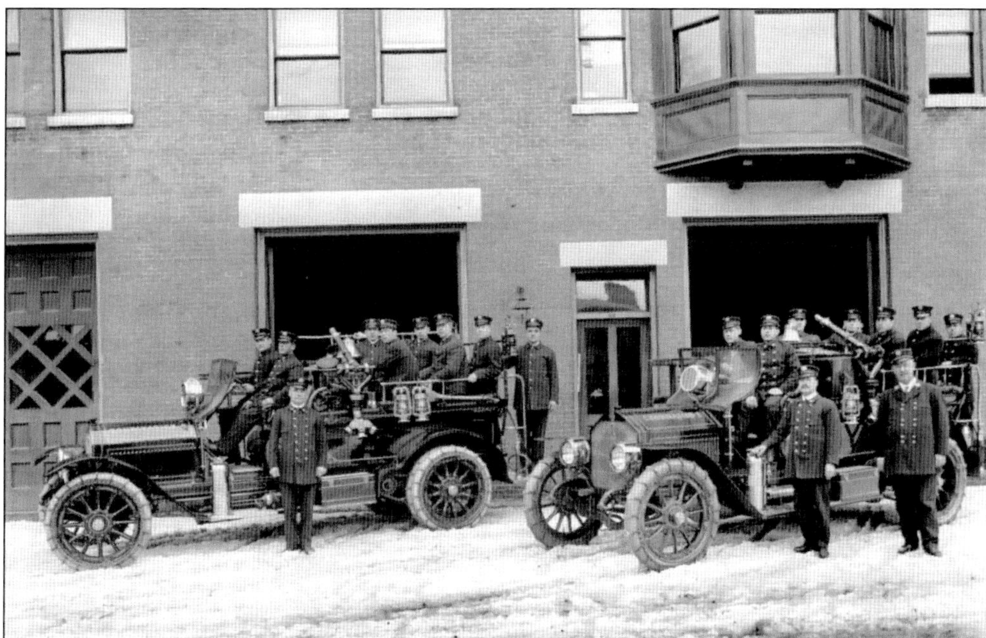

COMBINATION 1 AND 2. In 1909, the first motorized fire department vehicle, a Knox automobile to be used by the chief engineer, took its place at Central Fire Station along with the horses. This photograph, taken in 1914, shows two motorized fire engines, Combination 1 and 2. Nine Fitchburg firefighters have died in the line of duty from 1911 to 2004. (Courtesy of Phil Jordan.)

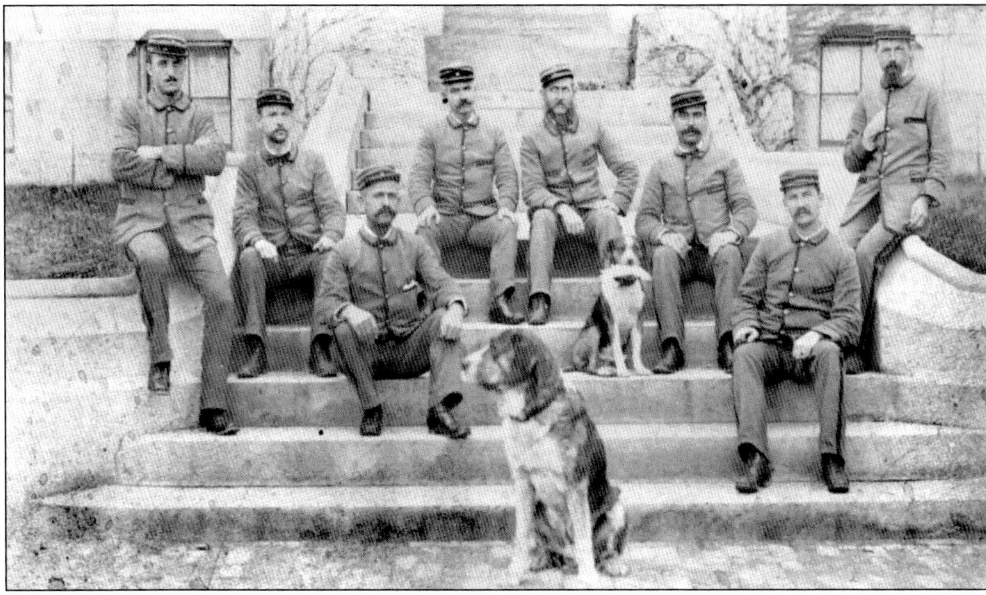

Letter Carriers. This *c.* 1890 image shows the Fitchburg postal carriers with their two dog carriers, Roger and Lion. It is ironic that while dogs once helped deliver the mail, today they are viewed as a postal carrier's worst nightmare.

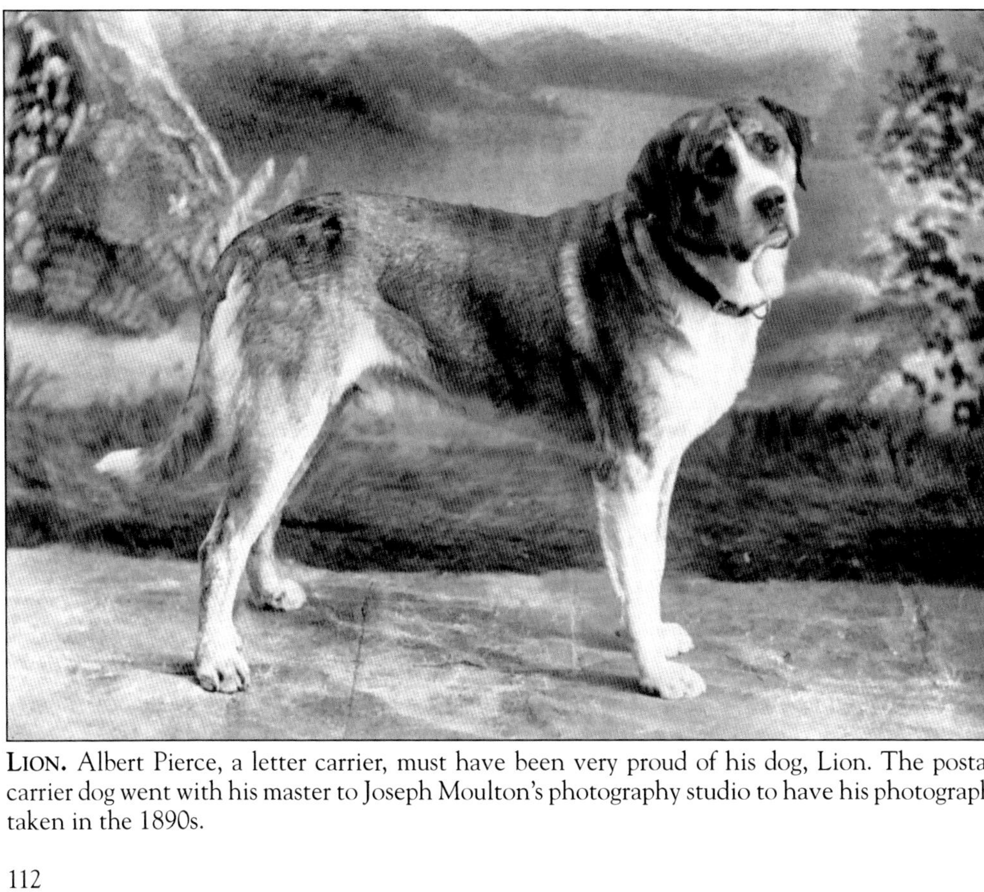

Lion. Albert Pierce, a letter carrier, must have been very proud of his dog, Lion. The postal carrier dog went with his master to Joseph Moulton's photography studio to have his photograph taken in the 1890s.

Seven

Pastimes and Fitchburg Events

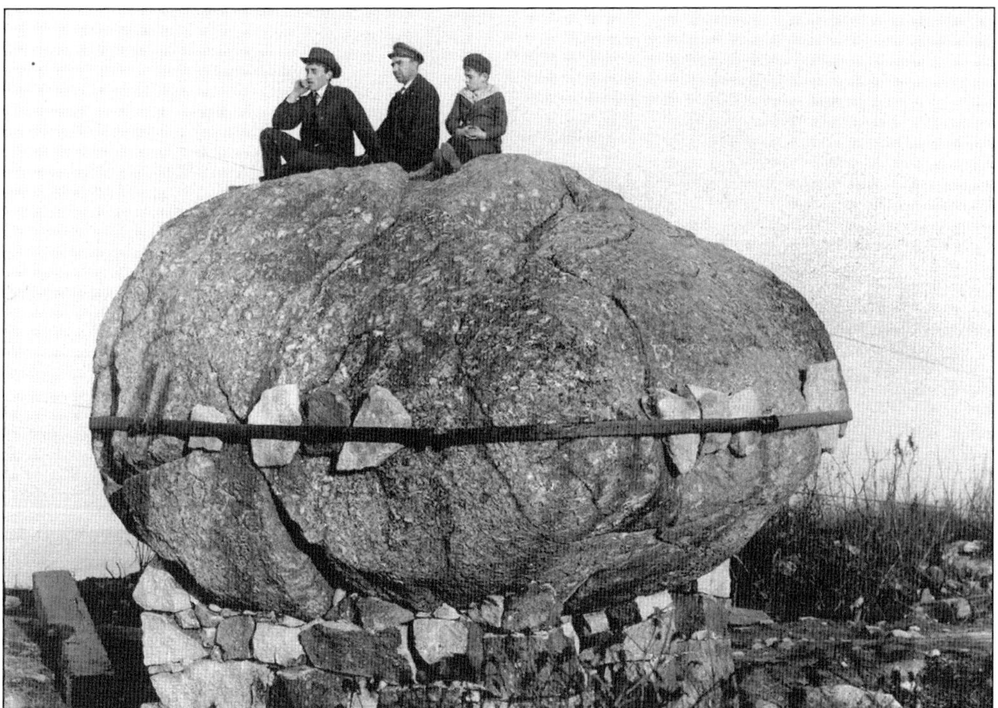

The Rollstone Boulder. Thousands of years ago, during the ice age, a large boulder was deposited on Rollstone Hill. The famous landmark, which became known as the Rollstone Boulder, was a popular destination for hikers and picnickers during Fitchburg's heyday. Citizens loved the boulder so much that it was blown apart and reassembled on a small park near the Upper Common in 1929.

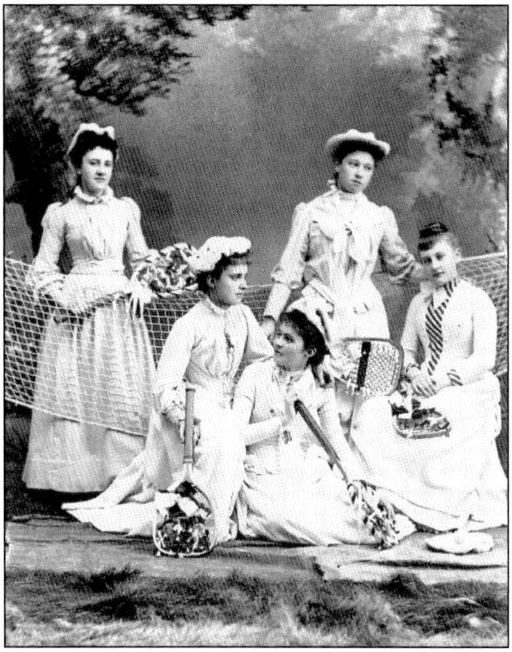

THE LAWN TENNIS CLUB, 1889. Five precocious ladies of the lawn tennis club, Susie Sprague, Alice Moulton, Josie Grant, Catherine Smith, and Carrie Goodwin, posed for this photograph in 1889. Women of the 1880s cast off the Victorian attitude that athletics were unfeminine.

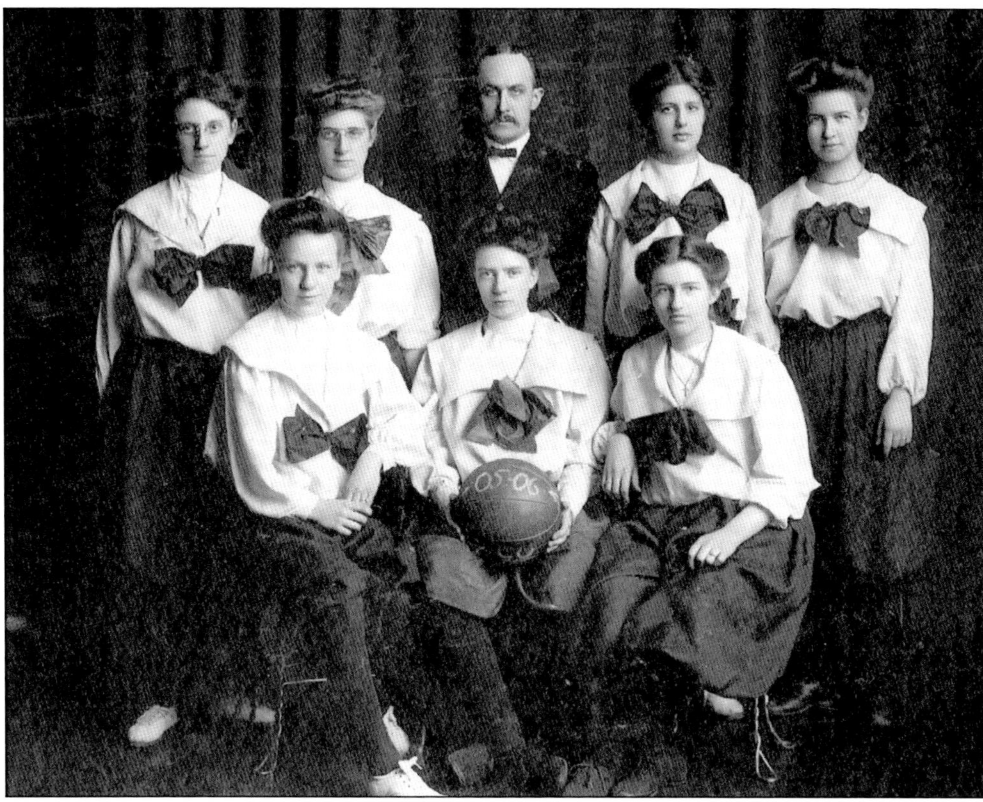

YMCA GIRL'S BASKETBALL TEAM. The YMCA girl's basketball team is shown in 1906. From left to right are (first row) Elizabeth Symonds, Marion Ewen, and Barbara Bullard; (second row) Ethel Farwell, Ruth Wheeler, John Waters, Alice Stockwell, and Anne Goodspeed.

THE ROLLSTONES. The Rollstones were one of several Fitchburg baseball teams that played squads from outside of the city beginning as early as 1866. The number of teams, including the Fitchburg Rovers, Boulders, Parkhills, and the Magics of West Fitchburg, tell just how popular local baseball was in the last part of the 19th century and early 20th century. Several Fitchburg players went on to play with national teams.

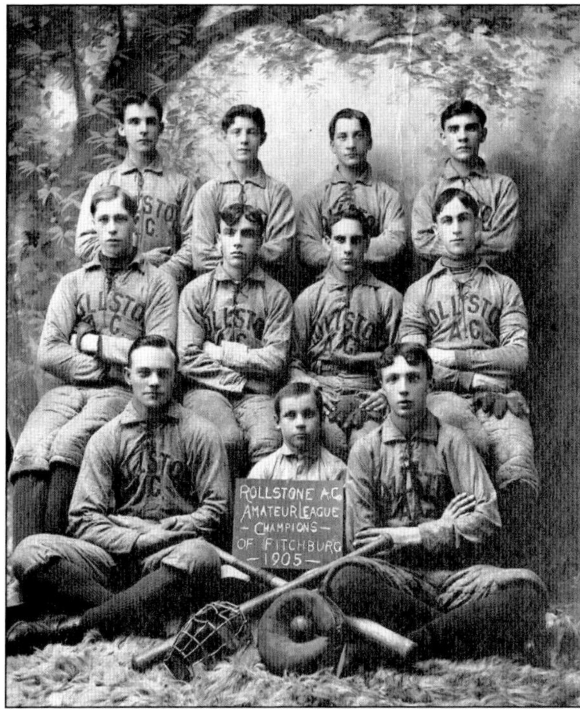

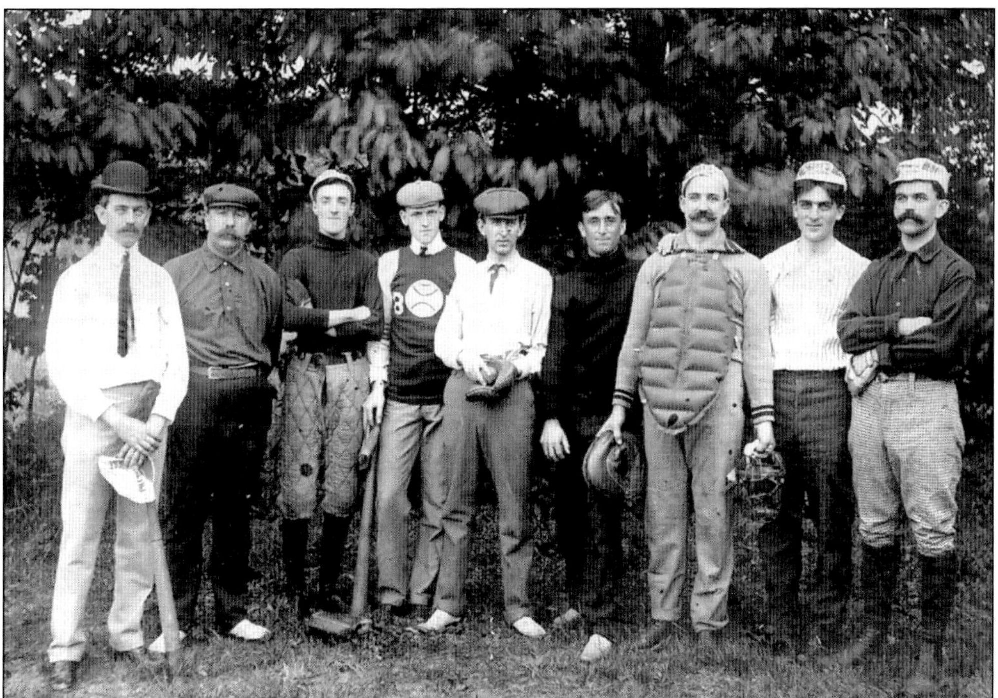

IMPROVED ORDER OF RED MEN. The Improved Order of Red Men, originally the Sons of Liberty, is a native fraternal order that was founded in the United States in 1765. A local group of Red Men is called a tribe. Whether a team or just out for a day of baseball, the Wanoosnoc Tribe of Red Men from Fitchburg pose with their equipment.

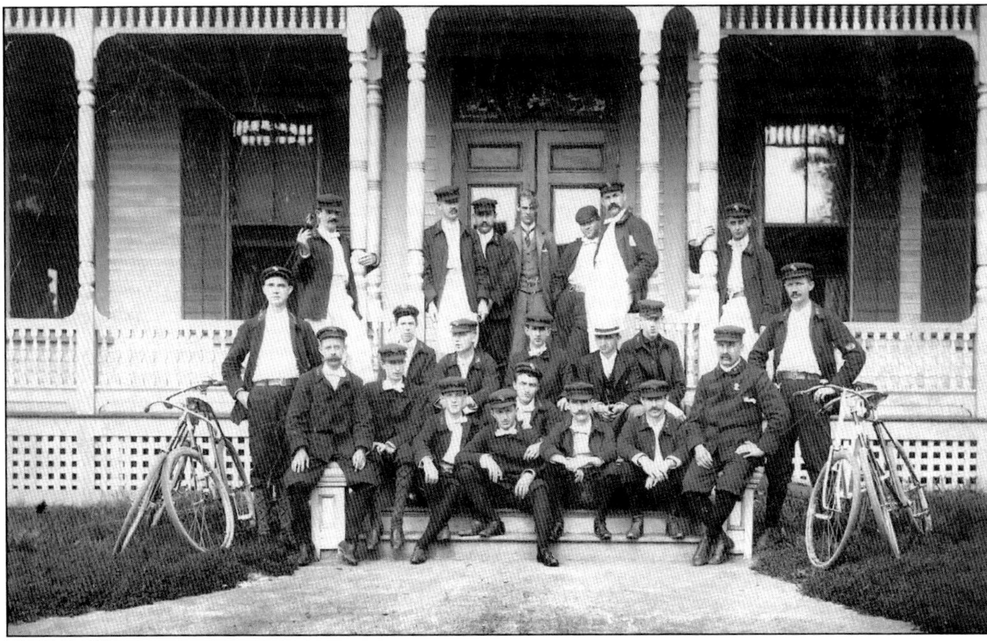

ROLLSTONE CYCLE CLUB, C. 1895. The bicycle craze of the 1890s precipitated the formation of bicycle clubs all over America. Fitchburg supported two clubs, the Rollstone Cycle Club (established in 1892) and the Fitchburg Cycle Club (founded a year later). Dressed in the Rollstone uniform with the club's insignia, members pose for their photograph taken on Mount Wachusett.

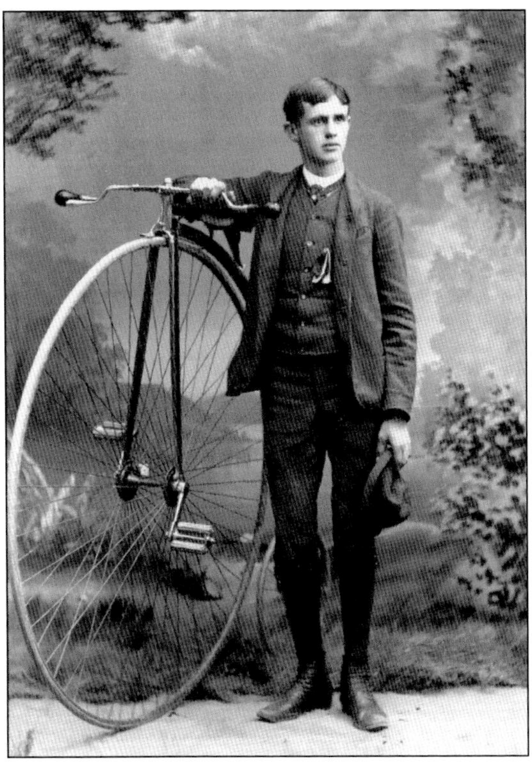

HIGH-WHEELS. The high-wheel was popular from 1876 until the late 1880s. Proud young men flocked to photographers to have their photographs taken with the costly wheels. J. C. Moulton, who took this photograph, was the best and most experienced photographer in the city. He came to Fitchburg in 1848, when photography was in its infancy, and recorded the city and its inhabitants for the next 65 years. (Courtesy of Barbara Edsall.)

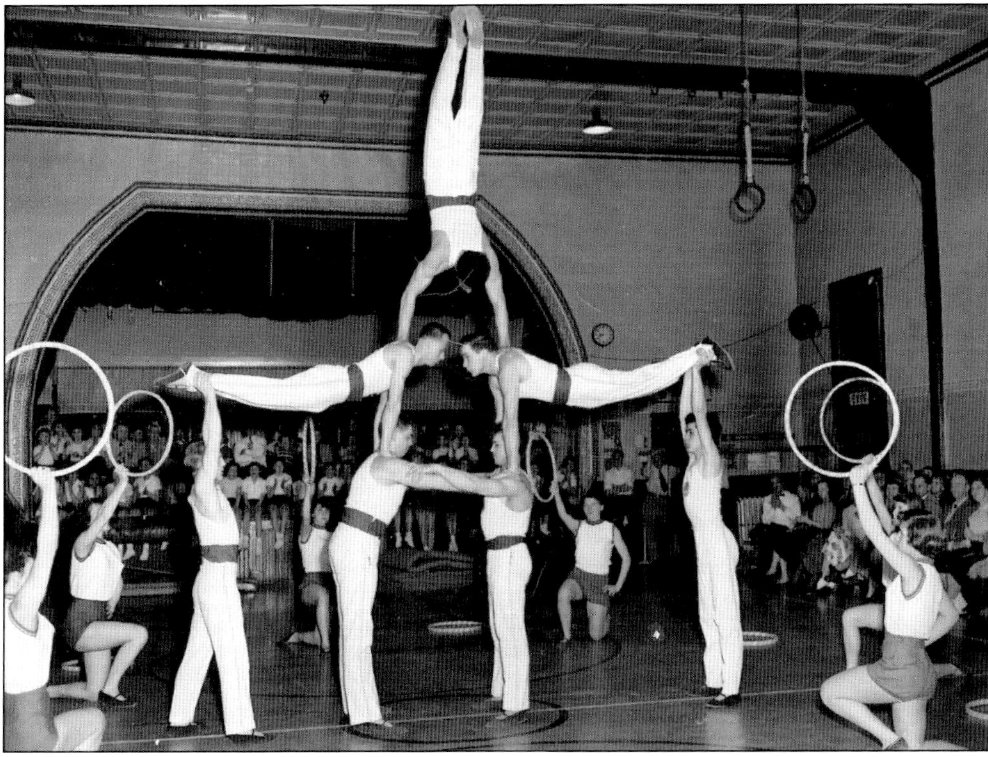

REIPAS GYMNASTS. The Reipas Athletic Club was formed in 1903, when some of Fitchburg's newly arrived Finnish immigrants organized a calisthenics and gymnastics club to enhance their physical condition and well-being. They named the club Reipas, which is Finnish for "brisk and healthy." As the club grew, its activity expanded to include many other sports. Competitions were held between other clubs and leagues for both men and women.

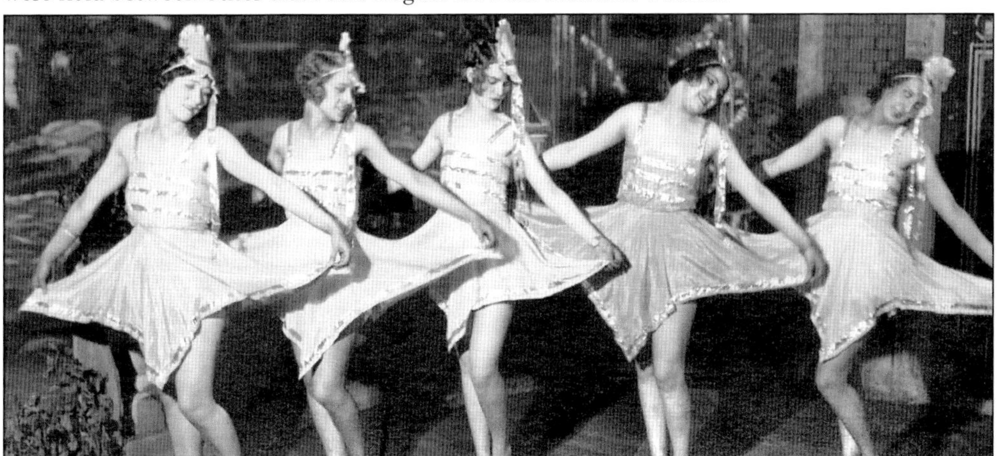

THE AAMUNKOITTO TEMPERANCE SOCIETY. The Aamunkoitto Temperance Society staged an operetta, *Oletteko naimisissa?* (meaning "Are you married?"), in the Grove Street Theater's Temperance Hall in 1928. The hall was located in what is now the Fidelity Bank parking lot. The operetta, in three acts, was presented in Finnish translation. The director of the production was Urho Heisson. The dancers seen here are, from left to right, Saimi Nivel, Aili Niemi, Signe Tastula, Irene Johnson, and Lillian Storm.

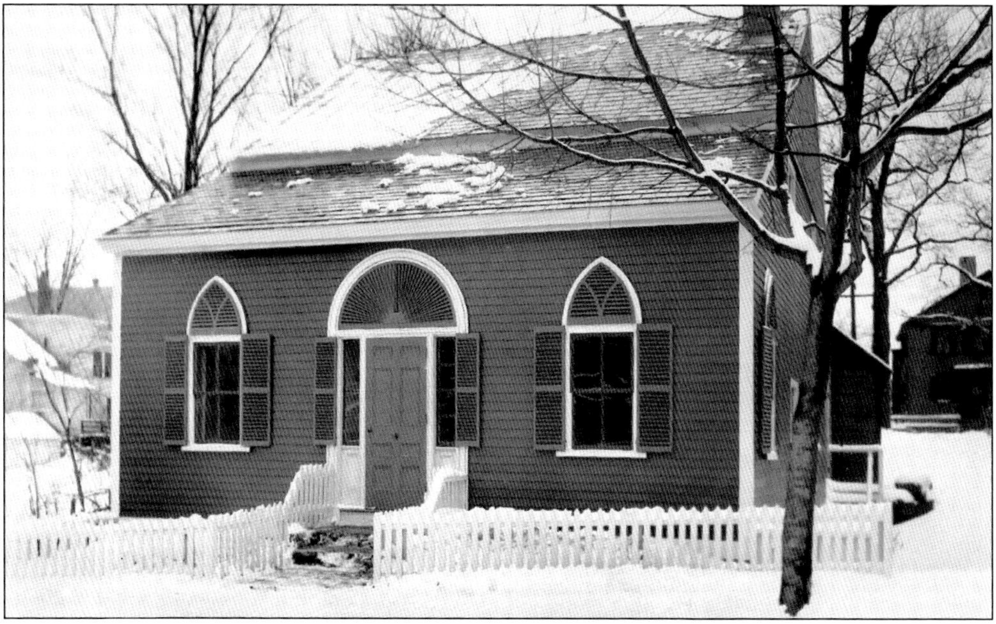

The Stratton Playhouse. The Stratton Playhouse on Wallace Avenue is one of the oldest community theaters in the United States. It was founded in 1925 by Helen F. Stratton and Mrs. Charles T. Crocker. A barn was the original home of its predecessor, the Amateur Workshop. Adding a façade from a home on Upper Main Street to the barn created the playhouse that is in active use today. In 1939, the Amateur Workshop was renamed the Stratton Playhouse.

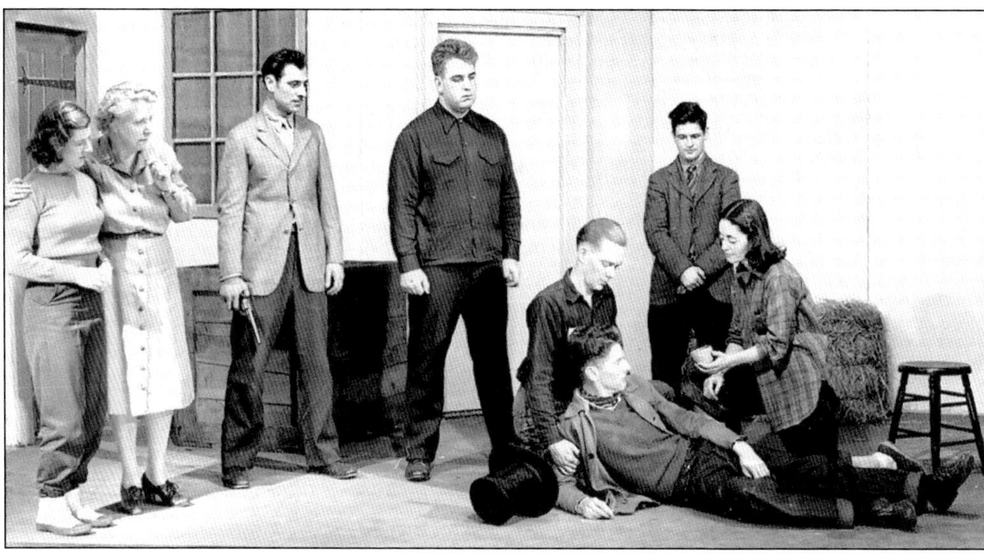

Actors at the Stratton Playhouse. Pictured here is the cast of the romantic melodrama *Silas the Choreboy* rehearsing at the Stratton Playhouse in December 1945. The cast members are, from left to right, Wanda Cyr, Isabel Dennett, Paul Petalas, Jacques Aubuchon, Albert Stone, Emerson Foster, Timothy Mylott, and Anne Beauchemin. One of the players, Jacques Aubuchon, later went on to Hollywood and Broadway, where he appeared on the stage, in movies, and in television shows as a character actor. (Courtesy of Anne Beauchemin.)

THE DRAMA CLUB. The Fitchburg Athletic Club's membership of 200 men formed many interest groups, including a drama club. The group staged yearly productions with all the trappings: costumes, staging, lights, and music. The city of Fitchburg eagerly awaited these productions and generously supported them.

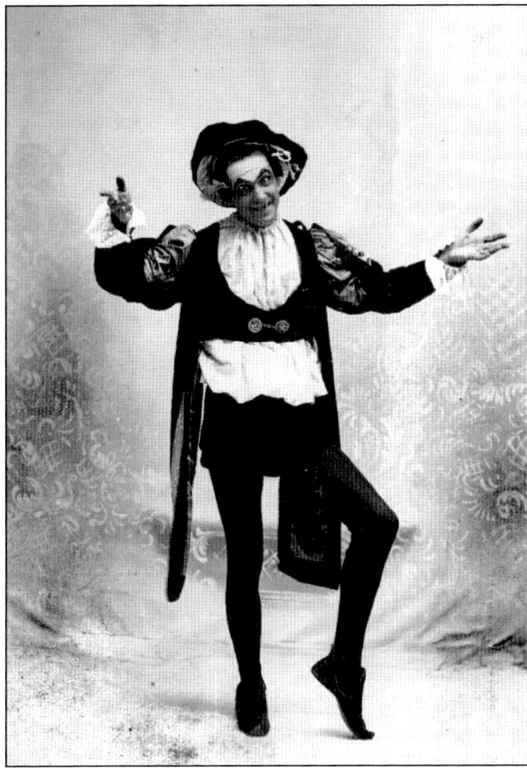

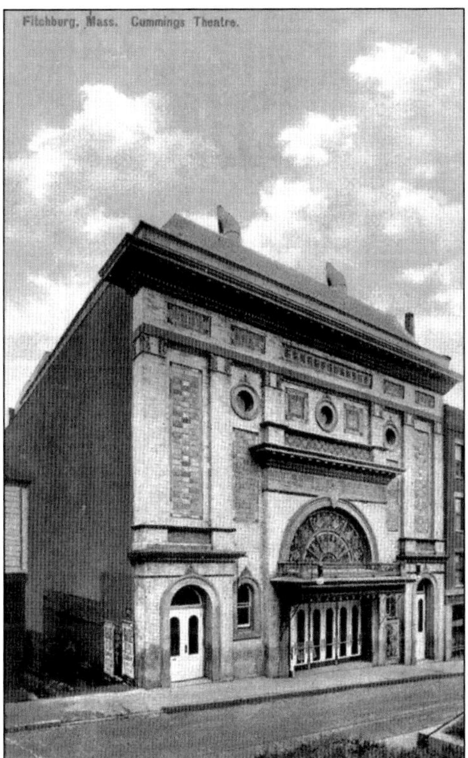

THE CUMMINGS THEATER. The Cummings Theater was built in 1899 for vaudeville shows and for plays. When movies became popular, the theater discontinued live entertainment. By 1940, the theater had seen better days, and it began showing reruns of movies that had played at the uptown Fitchburg Theater. As an added attraction, the Cummings gave out dishes on Wednesday evenings. The theater was demolished in 1955, and the area became a parking lot.

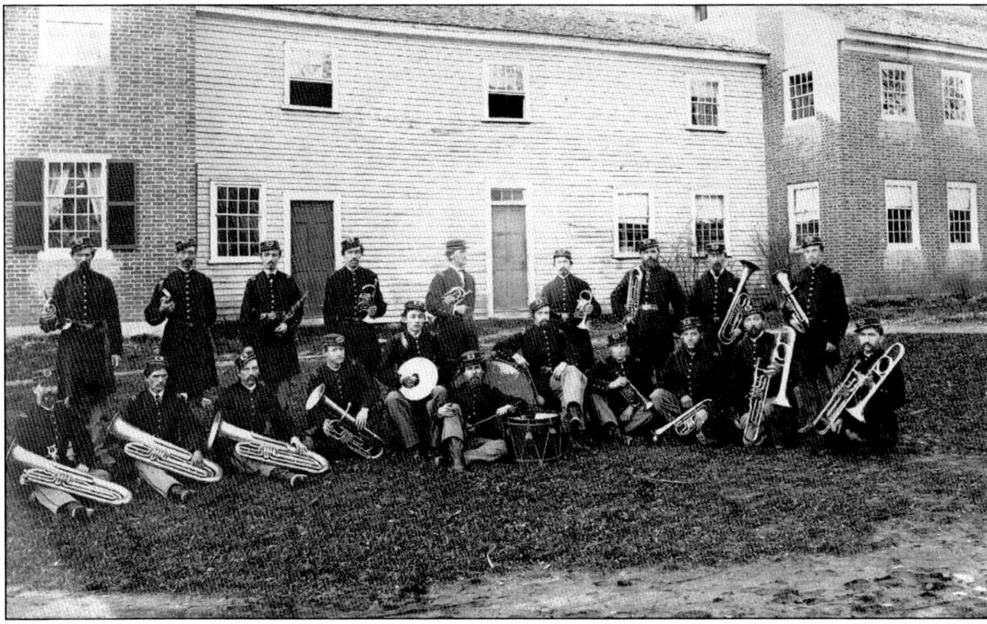

THE FITCHBURG CORNET BAND. Fitchburg has a long history of military bands that served the city. The Fitchburg Brass Band escorted the Fitchburg Fusiliers to the train station when the soldiers departed for the Civil War in 1861. The brass band later disbanded, but the Fitchburg Cornet Band was organized in its stead in 1868.

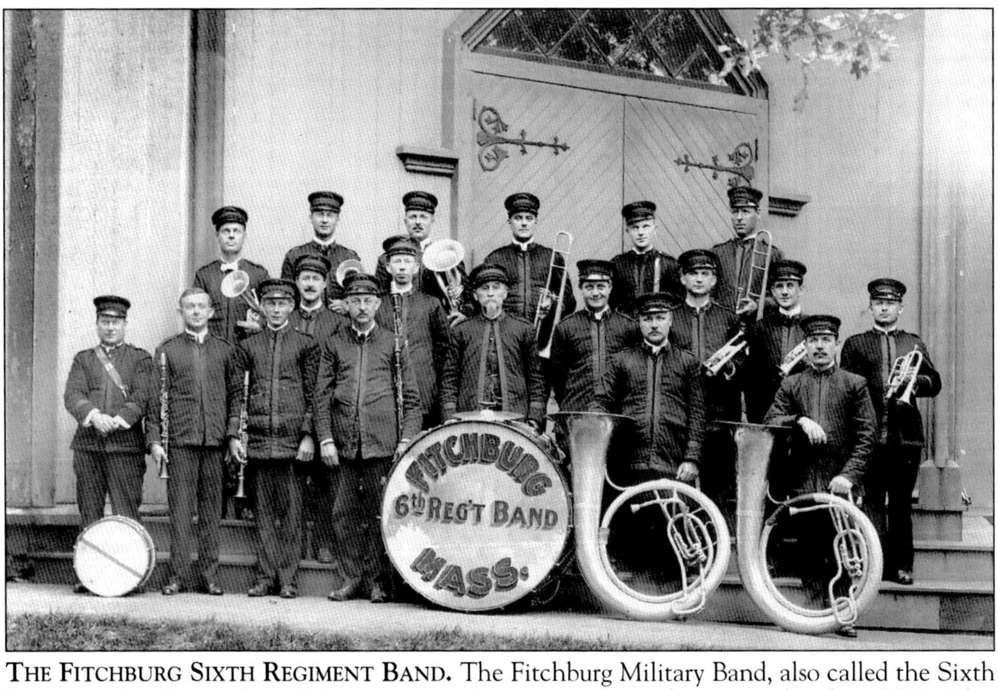

THE FITCHBURG SIXTH REGIMENT BAND. The Fitchburg Military Band, also called the Sixth Regiment Band, was formed from a core of musicians from the cornet band in 1871. This photograph was taken on Martha's Vineyard, where the band played summer engagements from the 1880s until 1910. Just behind the drum is George Patz, who arranged great masterpieces of music for bands and gave the band its distinct reputation.

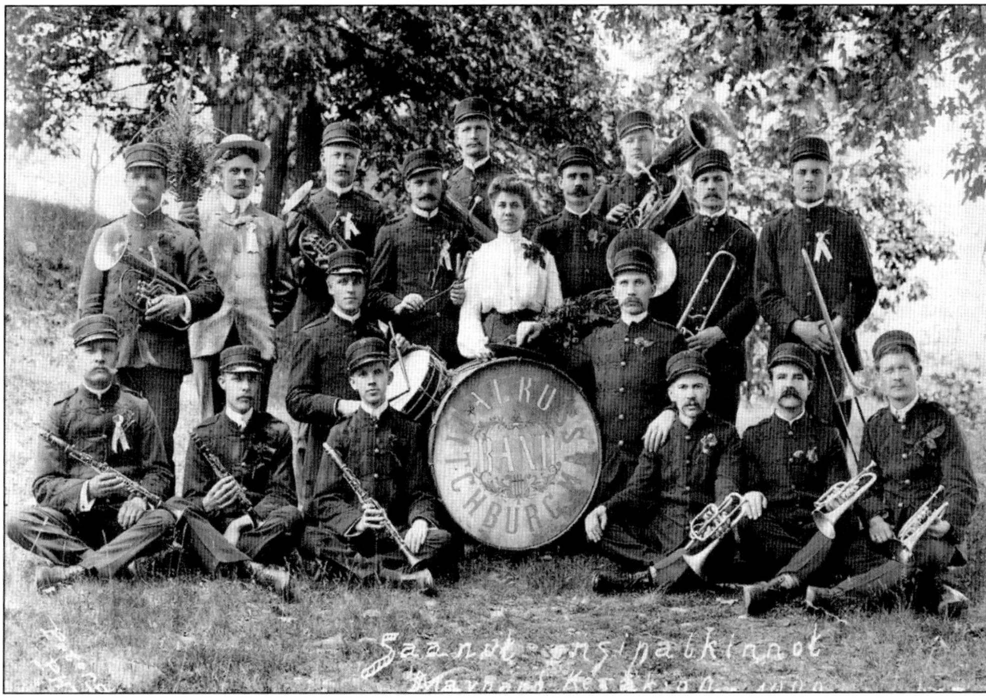

THE ALKUSS BAND. In the summer of 1903, the Alkuss Band, a group of young Finnish musicians from Fitchburg, competed against bands from Maynard, Worcester, and Gardner. Fitchburg took first prize. The man in the back row, second from the left, is holding the prize bouquet.

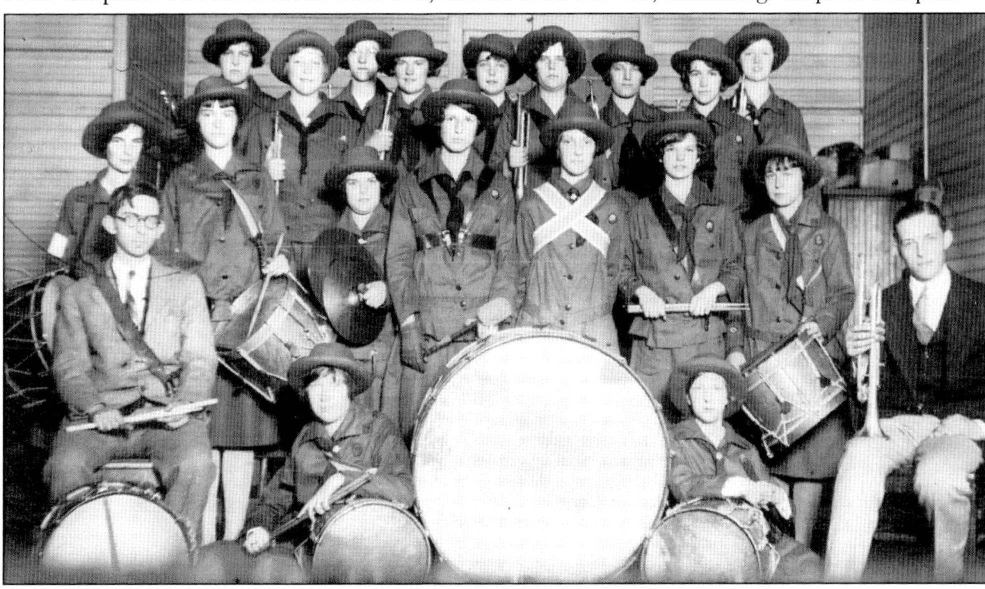

THE GIRL SCOUT DRUM AND BUGLE CORPS. Members of the 1928 Girl Scout Drum and Bugle Corps are, from left to right, as follows: (first row) director George Talcott, Claramal Cady, Marietta Marshall, and Ray Thomas; (second row) Jane McMurray, Peggy Greenwood, Thelma Newton, Elsie Lowe, Ruth Benere, Dorothy Bosk, and Marjorie Kenney; (third row) Myra Bull, Frances Angevene, Beverly Spaudling, and Margaret Slattery; (forth row) Irene Fogarty, Jean Lowell, Marjorie Hildreth, Edith Keyes, and Louise Benere.

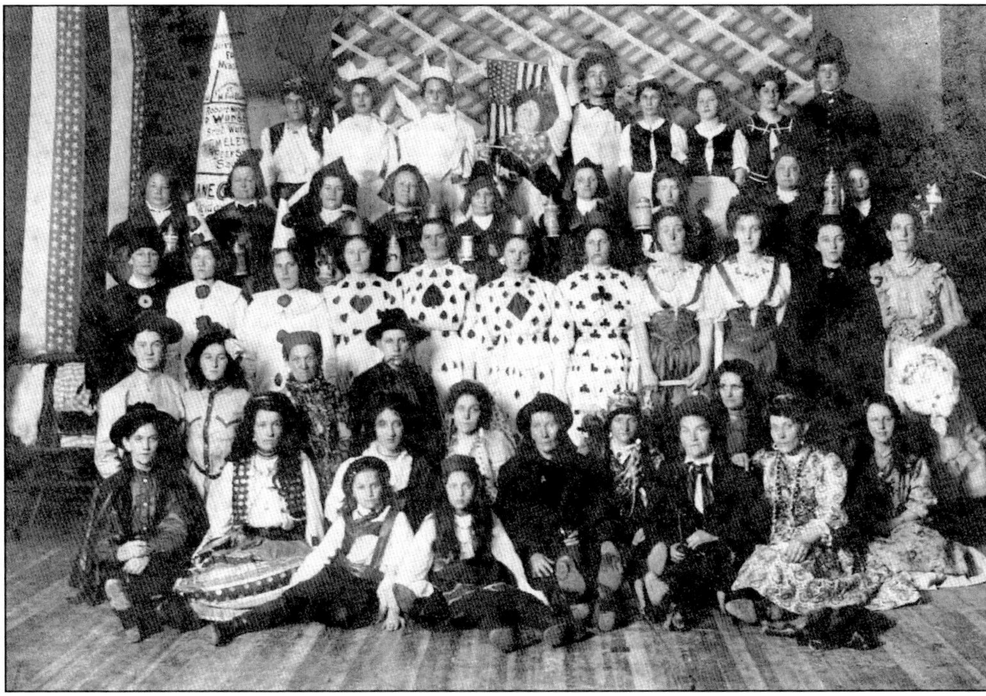

A GERMAN "SONGFEST." In 1890, German families built Saenger Hall on Leighton Street in Fitchburg to hold "songfests." The weekly masquerades and dances for children and adults were always well attended. Pictured is a group of people in costume around 1905. Note the cone in the upper left-hand corner, where Robert Wagner, owner of a sausage shop on Kimball Street, has an ad for his "Wurst."

THE DAUGHTERS OF ISABELLA. Fitchburg residents, ever mindful of elevating the intellect and enjoying pleasurable social affairs, joined various clubs in droves. In the early 1900s, there were hundreds of clubs dedicated to varying purposes, such as athletics, politics, and heritage. Every occasion had its song, and music was everywhere. The Daughters of Isabella, in this 1940s minstrel show, carried on an old tradition of blackface entertainment.

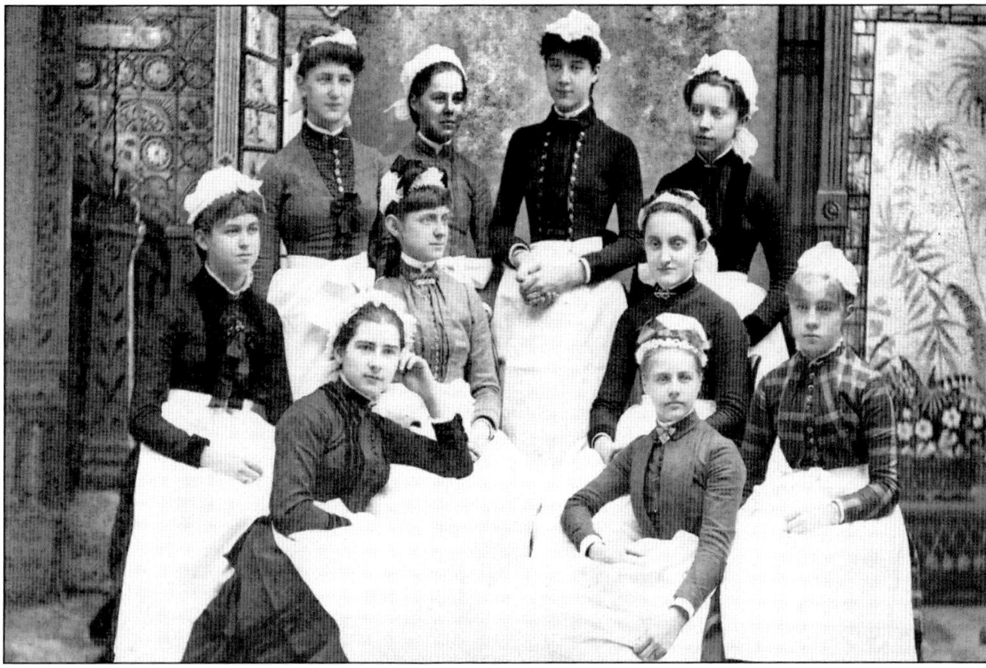

COOKING CLUB. By the 1890s, young Fitchburg women were eager to start or join clubs, be they musical, literary, or athletic. Here, Cooking Club members are dressed in their aprons and caps. They are, from left to right, as follows: (first row) Susie Upton and Mary Spencer; (second row) Sophie Hitchcock, Florence Simonds, Elizabeth Merriam, and Margaret Miller; (third row) Ruth Pierson, Helen Spencer, Genevora Storie, and Cora Blanchard.

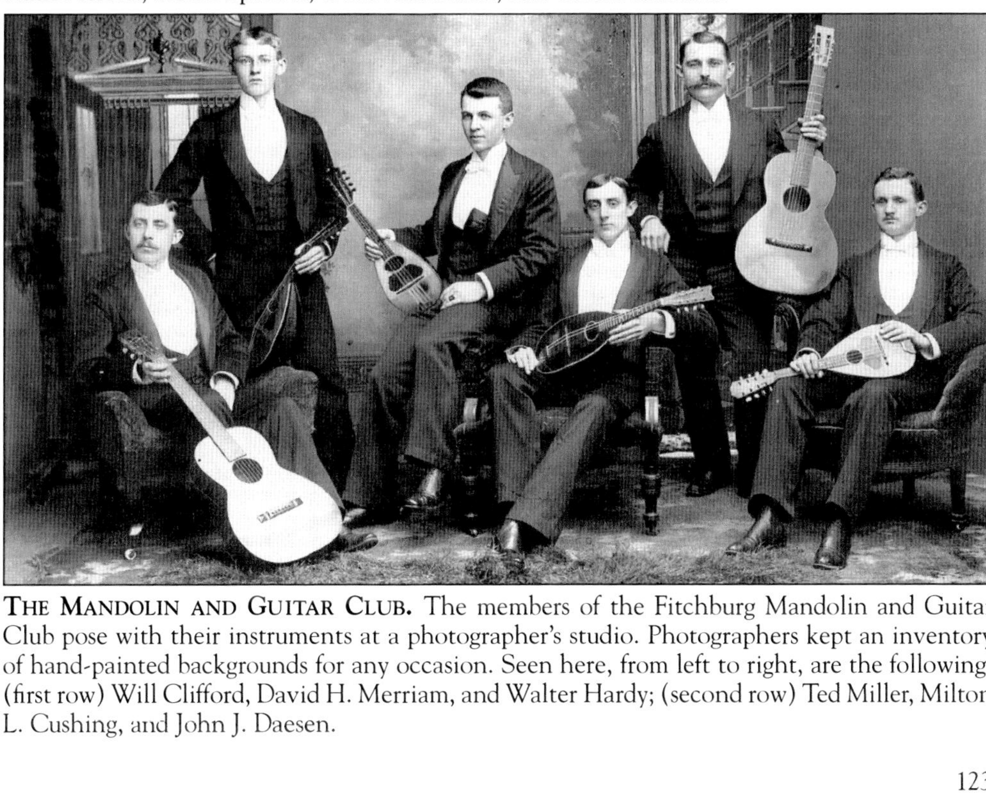

THE MANDOLIN AND GUITAR CLUB. The members of the Fitchburg Mandolin and Guitar Club pose with their instruments at a photographer's studio. Photographers kept an inventory of hand-painted backgrounds for any occasion. Seen here, from left to right, are the following: (first row) Will Clifford, David H. Merriam, and Walter Hardy; (second row) Ted Miller, Milton L. Cushing, and John J. Daesen.

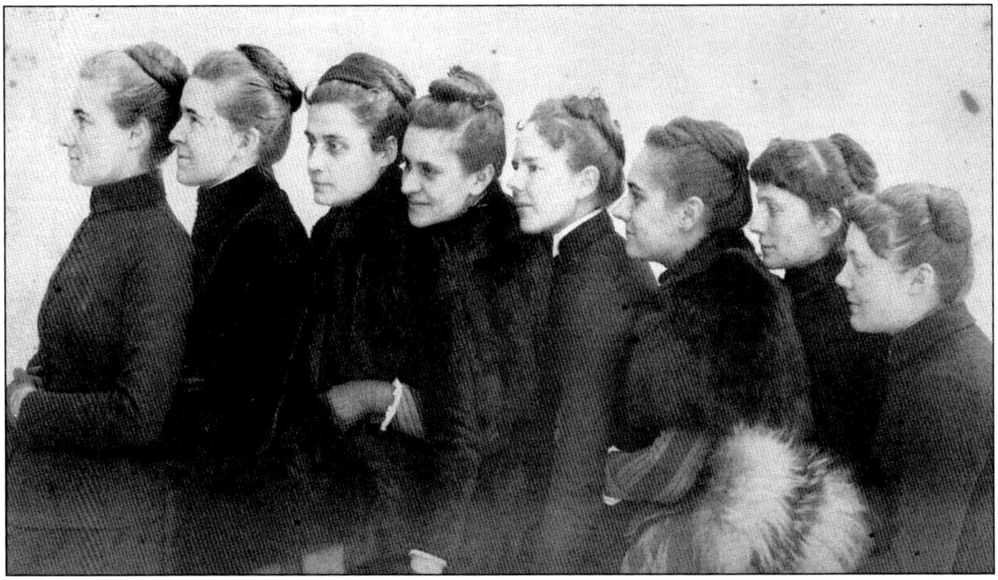

THE SPLINTERS CLUB. In July 1889, the eight members of the Splinters Club, a literary club comprised of young Fitchburg women, posed for this photograph. The club's motto was "To Light the Way." Seen here, from left to right, are Florence Dwinnell, Flora Ripley Bullock, Marie Sieboth, Mary Snow, Mary Garfield, Ellen Snow, Marion Works Priest, and Alice Porter Reed.

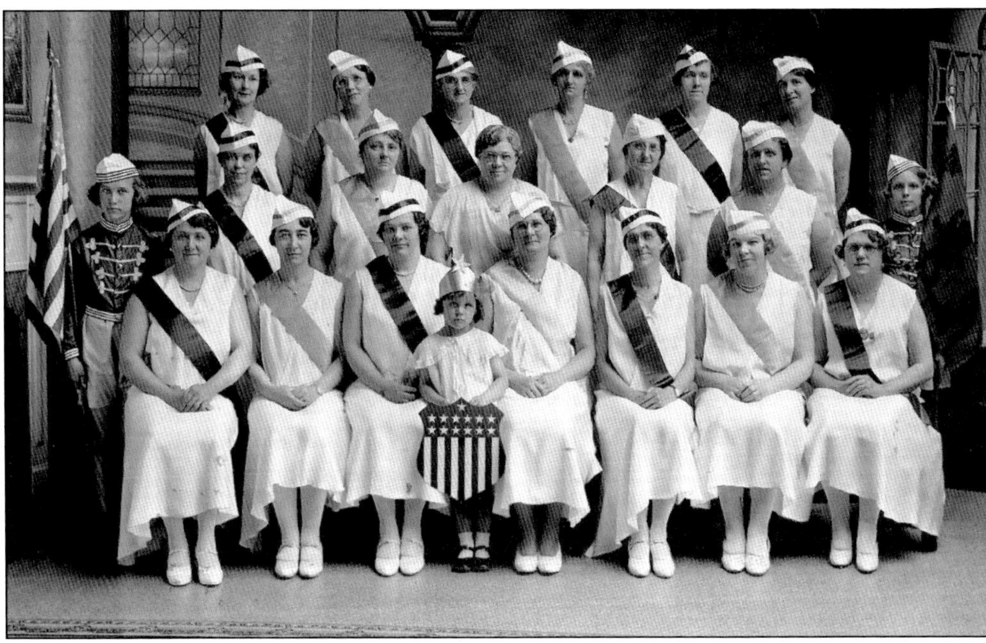

CLAN LESLIE. On July 14, 1933, the Degree Team of the Ladies Auxiliary, Clan Leslie of the Order of Scottish Clans, sat for this photograph. The women always wore white gowns for their parties. Pictured are, from left to right, Agnes McGregor, Agnes Tracquair, Jean Hay, Katherine Burton, Mary Stark, Dorothy Parker, Katherine Murray, Viola Crosby, Nellie Meldrum, Isabella Illingsworth, Adeline Crotch, Isabelle Newsholme, Mary Sharpe, Leta Louden, Florence Parkhurst, Harriet Logan, and Grace Reynolds.

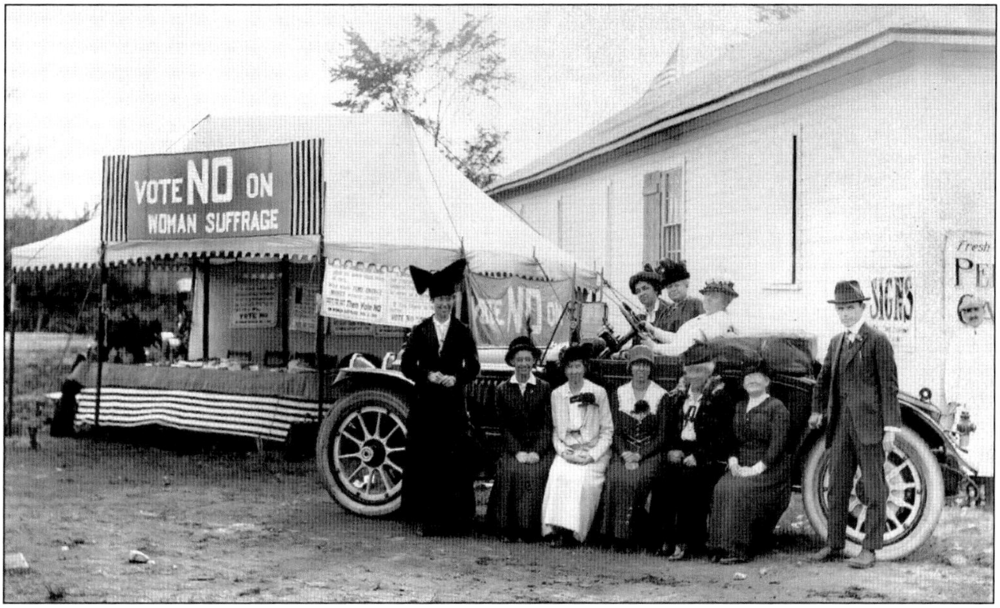

WOMEN'S SUFFRAGE. These Fitchburg women seem intent on supporting a "no" vote for women's suffrage at a time when the majority of women were fighting for the vote. From left to right are (first row) Elizabeth Russell, Margaret Reed, Bessie Blanchard, Katherine Hall, Alice Spring, Elizabeth Mather, and an unidentified man; (second row) Katherine Huonis, Mrs. Horace Gove, and Helen Wallace.

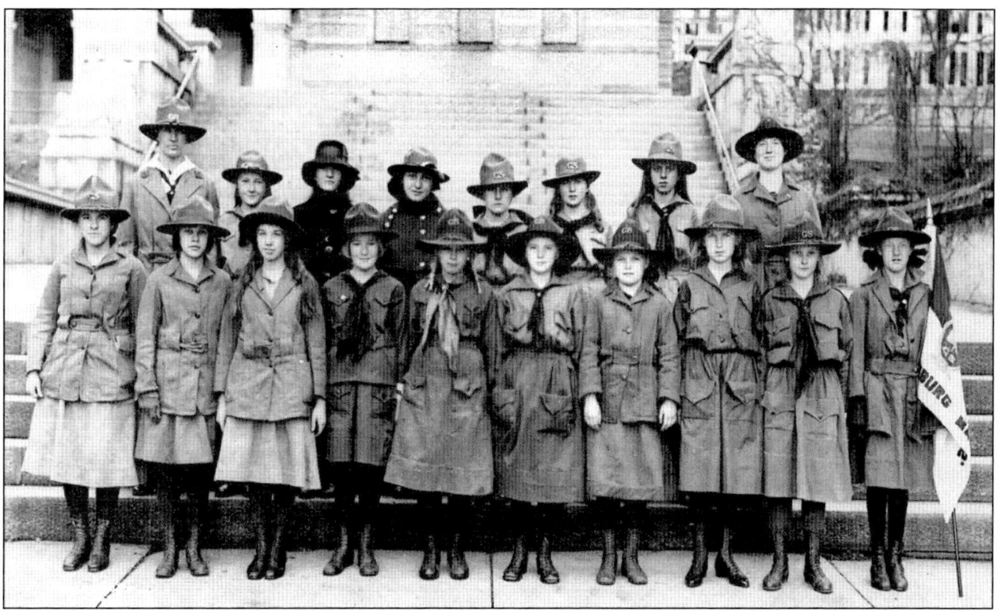

FITCHBURG'S FIRST GIRL SCOUT TROOP. In 1915, the members of the first Girl Scout troop in Fitchburg voted to name themselves the Forget-Me-Not troop. From left to right are (first row) Rachel Spencer, Marion Rice, Dorothy Bruce, Helen Coolidge, Lillian Soderholm, Irene Holm, Helen Soderholm, Margaret Gustafson, Margaret Swanson, and Corinne Jewel; (second row) captain H. E. Vickery, Katherine Lowe, Anna Nichols, Madeleine Buzzell, Christina Osgood, Una Jackson, Gwendolyn Hayes, and Marjorie Bruce.

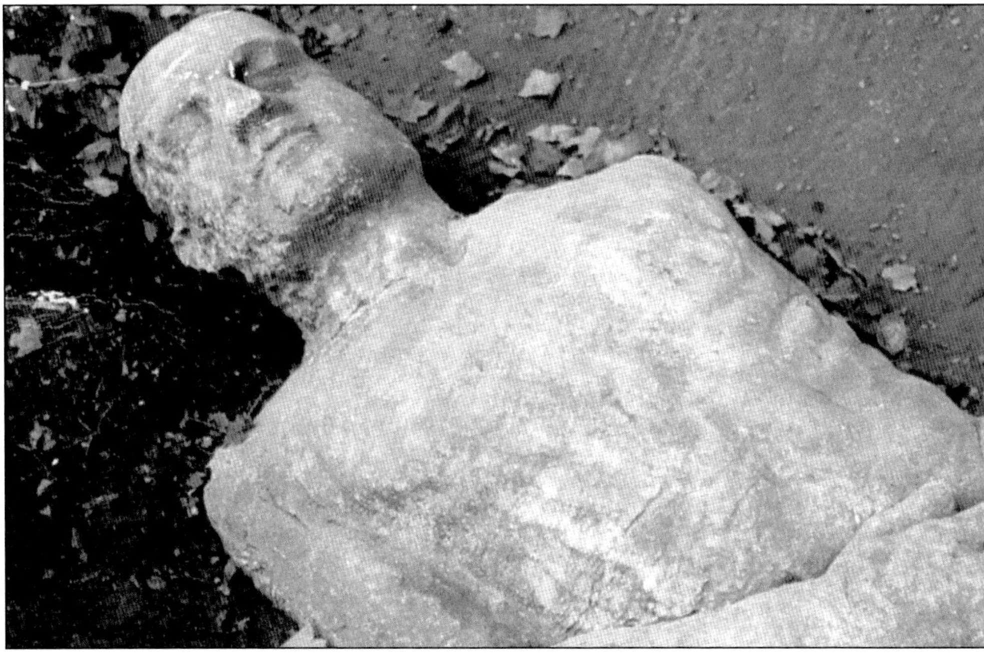

THE CARDIFF GIANT. Americans were stunned in 1869 when newspapers reported that a stone man had been dug up in Cardiff, New York. Controversy flared regarding his authenticity; P. T. Barnum declared it a fake, while some scholars proclaimed that it was ancient. A Fitchburg photographer gained possession of the giant in 1870, but shortly thereafter two sculptors admitted they had carved it. The Cardiff Giant was purchased in 1938 by the Farmer's Museum in Cooperstown, New York.

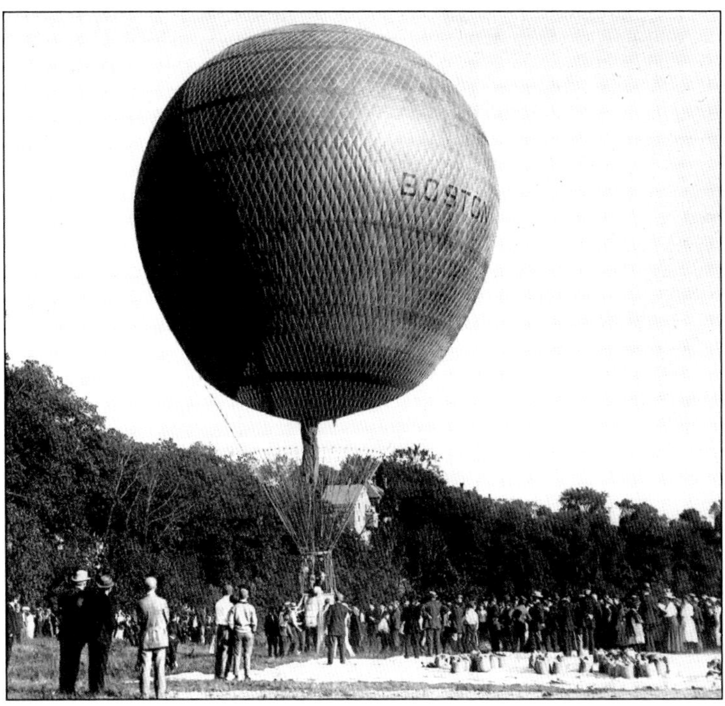

AERO PARK. On September 15, 1908, the *Boston* landed in Fitchburg for the dedication of the city's Aero Park. Charles J. Glidden of Boston and Prof. William H. Pickering, a noted Harvard astronomer, manned the basket of the balloon. Thousands of Fitchburg residents came to see the balloon and take part in the festivities.

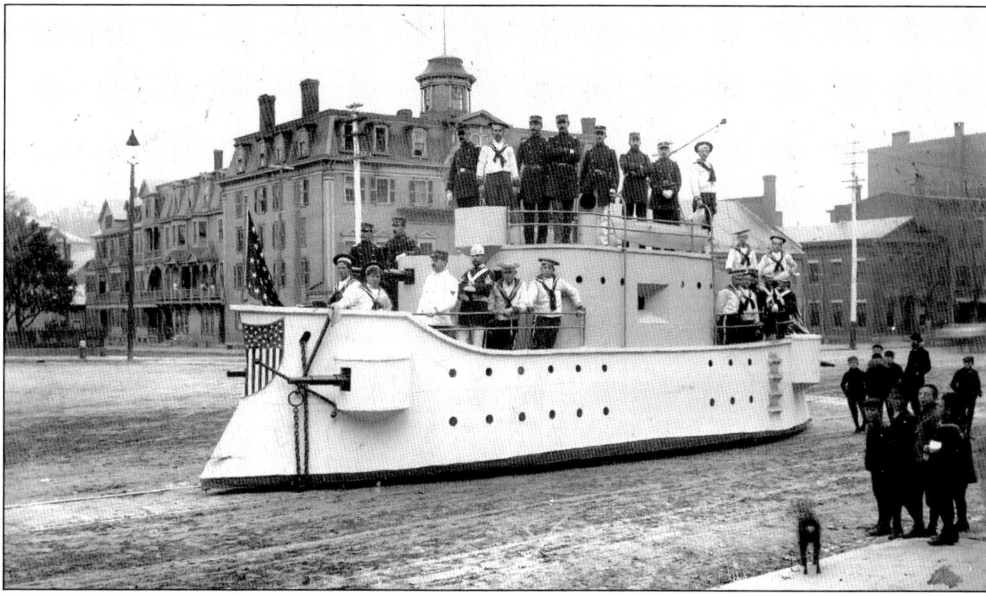

The McKinley Cruiser. During the 1896 presidential campaign, a group of enthusiastic Republicans organized to build a facsimile of a gunboat on a trolley. Named the McKinley Cruiser, it ran upon railway tracks during parades. After the election, the cruiser was anchored at the shoreline of Whalom Park and covered with multicolored lights for a nighttime display. It eventually fell into disrepair, and it burned on July 4, 1908.

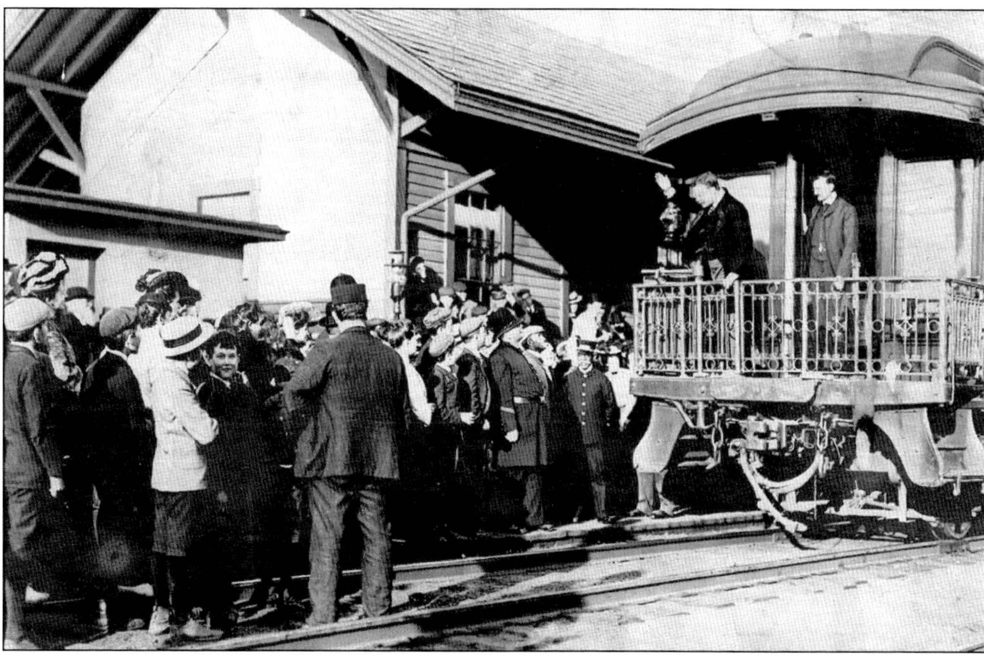

Roosevelt's Visit. The only president to visit Fitchburg while in office, Theodore Roosevelt made a brief train stop here on September 2, 1902. War veterans escorted him from the station to the Wallace Building, where he gave a speech. In some way, Roosevelt's visit was ironic, as he had succeeded to the presidency after the assassination of President McKinley in 1901 by an anarchist who used a revolver manufactured in Fitchburg by Iver Johnson.

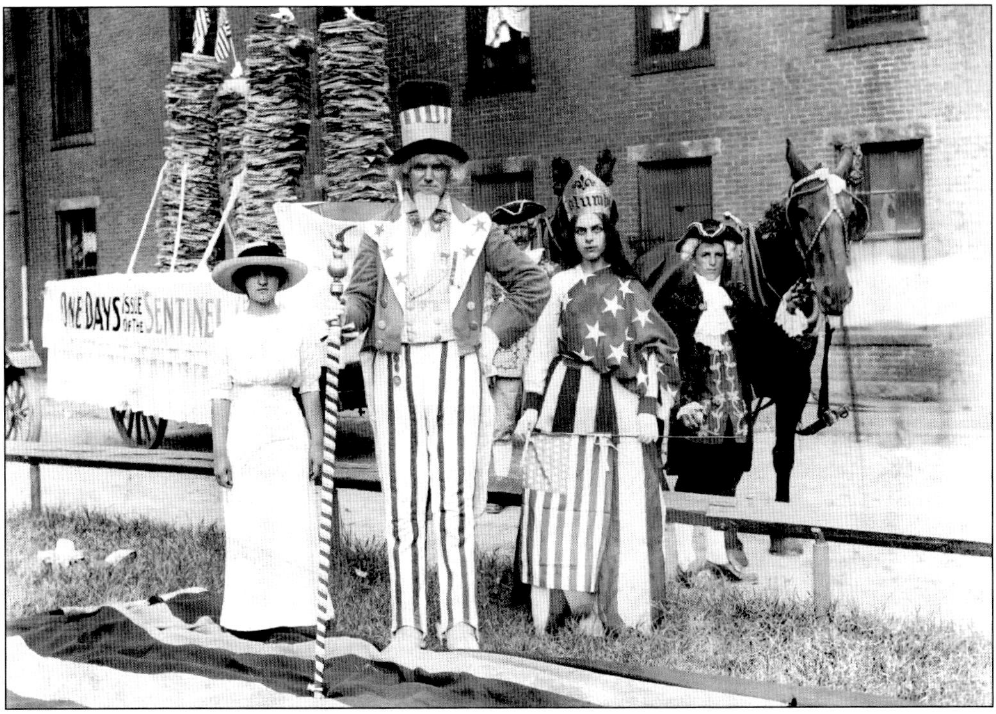

FITCHBURG'S 150TH ANNIVERSARY. In 1914, Fitchburg observed its 150th anniversary of separation from Lunenburg and its incorporation as a town. The Fourth of July parade that year celebrated not only the nation's independence but also the city's. As many as 5,000 people participated in the parade, while 70,000 watched as floats and a seemingly endless number of bands passed by.

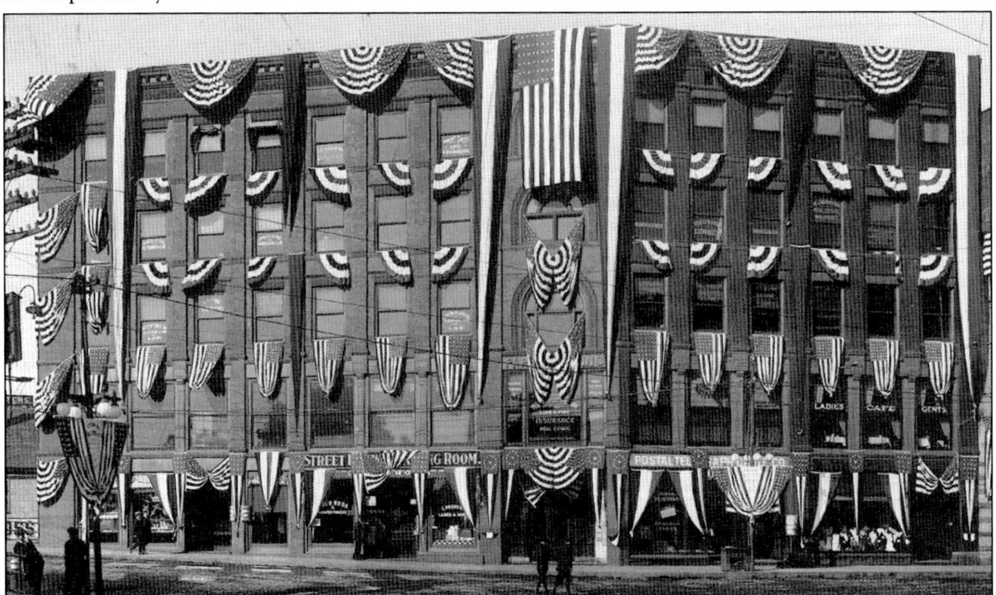

THE PARK BUILDING, DECORATED FOR THE FOURTH OF JULY. The Park Building, at Water and Main Streets, is decorated for Fitchburg's 150th anniversary celebration on July 4, 1914.